U.S. Fish & Wildlife Service

I0411474

Status Assessment and Conservation Plan for the Western Burrowing Owl in the United States

Biological Technical Publication

BTP-R6001-2003

© Michael Forsberg

U.S. Fish & Wildlife Service

Status Assessment and Conservation Plan for the Western Burrowing Owl in the United States

Biological Technical Publication

BTP-R6001-2003

David S. Klute[1,7]   William H. Howe[4]   Steven R. Sheffield[6,9]

Loren W. Ayers[2,8]   Stephanie L. Jones[1]   Tara S. Zimmerman[3]

Michael T. Green[3]   Jill A. Shaffer[5]

[1] U.S. Fish and Wildlife Service, Region 6, Nongame Migratory Bird Program, Denver, CO

[2] Wyoming Cooperative Fish and Wildlife Research Unit, University of Wyoming, Laramie, WY

[3] U.S. Fish and Wildlife Service, Region 1, Nongame Migratory Bird Program, Portland, OR

[4] U.S. Fish and Wildlife Service, Region 2, Nongame Migratory Bird Program, Albuquerque, NM

[5] U.S. Geological Survey, Northern Prairie Wildlife Research Center, Jamestown, ND

[6] U.S. Fish and Wildlife Service, Office of Migratory Bird Management, Arlington, VA

[7] Current Address: Colorado Division of Natural Resources

[8] Current Address: Wisconsin Department of Natural Resources

[9] Current Address: George Mason University

Author contact information:

David S. Klute, (Current address) Colorado Division of Wildlife, 6060 Broadway, Denver, CO 80216. Phone: (303) 291-7320, Fax: (303) 291-7456, e-mail: David.Klute@state.co.us.

Loren W. Ayers, (Current address) Bureau of Integrated Science Services, Wisconsin Department of Natural Resources, 101 S. Webster St., Madison, WI 53707-7921. Phone: (608) 261-6449, Fax: (608) 266-5226, e-mail: ayersl@mail01.dnr.state.wi.us.

Michael T. Green, U.S. Fish and Wildlife Service, Region 1, Nongame Migratory Bird Program, 911 Northeast 11th Avenue, Portland, OR 97232. Phone: (503) 231-6164, Fax: (503) 231-6164, e-mail: Michael_Green@fws.gov.

William H. Howe, U.S. Fish and Wildlife Service, Region 2, Nongame Migratory Bird Program, P.O. Box 1306, Albuquerque, NM 87103. Phone: (505) 248-6875, Fax: (505) 248-6674, e-mail: Bill_Howe@fws.gov.

Stephanie L. Jones, U.S. Fish and Wildlife Service, Region 6, Nongame Migratory Bird Program, P.O. Box 25486 DFC, Denver, CO 80225-0486. Phone: (303) 236-4409, Fax: (303) 236-8680, e-mail: Stephanie_Jones@fws.gov.

Jill A. Shaffer, U.S. Geological Survey, Northern Prairie Wildlife Research Center, 8711 37th St. SE, Jamestown, ND 58401. Phone: (701) 253-5547, Fax: (701) 253-5553, e-mail: jshaffer@usgs.gov.

Steven R. Sheffield, (Current address) Department of Biology, George Mason University, Fairfax, VA 22030, e-mail: srsheffield@att.net.

Tara S. Zimmerman, U.S. Fish and Wildlife Service, Region 1, Nongame Migratory Bird Program, 911 Northeast 11th Avenue, Portland, OR 97232. Phone: (503) 231-6164, Fax: (503) 231-6164, e-mail: Tara_Zimmerman@fws.gov.

For additional copies or information, contact:
Nongame Migratory Bird Program
U.S. Fish and Wildlife Service
P.O. Box 25486 DFC
Denver, CO 80225-0486

Recommended citation:
Klute, D. S., L. W. Ayers, M. T. Green, W. H. Howe, S. L. Jones, J. A. Shaffer, S. R. Sheffield, and T. S. Zimmerman. 2003. Status Assessment and Conservation Plan for the Western Burrowing Owl in the United States. U.S. Department of Interior, Fish and Wildlife Service, Biological Technical Publication FWS/BTP-R6001-2003, Washington, D.C.

Table of Contents

List of Figures

List of Tables

Executive Summary

The Western Burrowing Owl (*Athene cunicularia hypugaea*) is a grassland specialist distributed throughout w. North America, primarily in open areas with short vegetation and bare ground in desert, grassland, and shrub-steppe environments. Burrowing Owls are dependent on the presence of fossorial mammals (primarily prairie dogs and ground squirrels), whose burrows are used for nesting and roosting. Burrowing Owls are protected by the Migratory Bird Treaty Act in the United States and Mexico. They are listed as Endangered in Canada and Threatened in Mexico. They are considered by the U.S. Fish and Wildlife Service (USFWS) to be a Bird of Conservation Concern at the national level, in three USFWS regions, and in nine Bird Conservation Regions . At the state level, Burrowing Owls are listed as Endangered in Minnesota, Threatened in Colorado, and as a Species of Concern in California, Montana, Oklahoma, Oregon, Utah, Washington, and Wyoming.

Burrowing Owls historically bred from sc. and sw. Canada southward through the Great Plains and w. United States and south to c. Mexico. Although the historical breeding range is largely intact, range contractions have occurred primarily at peripheral regions, in s. Canada, the ne. Great Plains, and parts of California and the Pacific Northwest. Burrowing Owls winter in the sw. and sc. United States, throughout Mexico, and occasionally as far south as Panama.

Populations of Burrowing Owls have declined in several large regions, notably in the ne. Great Plains and Canada. However, estimates of population trends in many regions are generally inconclusive due to small samples sizes and high data variability. Population trends as determined from North American Breeding Bird Survey (BBS) data were inconsistent, with some regions exhibiting positive trends and other regions exhibiting negative trends. When taken as a whole, the BBS indicated an area of generally declining populations in the northern half of the Great Plains, and generally increasing populations in the interior U.S. and in some southwestern deserts. The Christmas Bird Count indicated a significant population decline in California (1966-1989). Local surveys have detected declining populations and/or range reductions in California, Iowa, Kansas, Minnesota, Nebraska, New Mexico, North Dakota, Oklahoma, Oregon, South Dakota, Texas, Washington, and throughout the range of the species in Canada.

Primary threats across the North American range of the Burrowing Owl are habitat loss due to land conversions for agricultural and urban development, and habitat degradation and loss due to reductions of burrowing mammal populations. The elimination of burrowing mammals through control programs and habitat loss has been identified as the primary factor responsible for declines of Burrowing Owls. Additional threats to Burrowing Owls include habitat fragmentation, predation, illegal shooting, pesticides and other contaminants. The types and significance of threats during migration and wintering are poorly understood.

The preservation of native grasslands and populations of burrowing mammals is ultimately critical for the conservation of Burrowing Owls. Efforts to maintain and increase populations of burrowing mammals through reduction of lethal control programs and landowner and land manager education should be undertaken. Burning, mowing, and grazing may be employed to maintain suitable habitat structure for nesting Burrowing Owls, although additional research is needed. Efforts to reintroduce or relocate Burrowing Owls should be critically reviewed to determine efficacy and best methods. Current large-scale monitoring efforts are generally inadequate. Effective programs to better determine actual population trends and demographics of Burrowing Owl populations should be developed and implemented.

Acknowledgments

Many individuals contributed significant time, literature, and expertise to this review including: R. Anthony, A. Axel, P. Arrowood, E. Atkinson, A. Bammann, J. Barclay, J. Belthoff, J. Brookshier, N. Brown, K. Brunson, D. Buckland, K. Burton, W. Busby, K. Butts, K. Clayton, L. Cole, C. Collins, C. Conway, T. Corman, E. Cummings, C. Cwiklinski, N. Dawson, K. De Smet, M. Desmond, J. Dinsmore, B. Domagalski, E. Dowd-Stukel, F. Esparza, C. Finley, T. Floyd, L. Fredrickson, D. Freed, J. Freilich, J. Friday, S. Grassel, R. Griebel, D. Harvey, M. Hetrick, B. Hodorff, G. Holroyd, S. Houston, M. Howery, S. Hutchings, L. Igl, D. Keinath, S. Kendall, N. Korfanta, J. Lincer, M. Lockwood, M. Martell, D. Mehlman, B. Millsap, P. Mineau, S. Moore, R. Murphy, J. Parrish, R. Peterson, D. Plumpton, D. Reinking, T. Rich, D. Rintoul, L. Romin, M. Rowe, C. Rustay, L. Sager, K. Scalise, J. Schmutz, C. Shackelford, G. Skiba, M.K. Skoruppa, J. Slater, K. Steenhof, C. Stowers, L. Trulio, T. Uhmann, T. VerCauteren, B. Vermillion, T. Wellicome, R. Williams, J. Winter, C. Wise, M. Woodin, J. Woollett, and J. Yamamoto.

Special thanks to G. Holroyd and T. Wellicome, with the Canadian Wildlife Service, for assistance in gathering literature, providing maps and graphs, and making contacts. Special thanks also to D. Rosenberg for providing additional information and thorough reviews. T. Uhmann and N. Brown provided bibliographies. M. J. Cowing and the Richard R. Olendorff Memorial Library at the Forest and Rangeland Ecosystem Science Center provided extensive literature. P. Sutherland provided assistance compiling the literature and editing the manuscript. Thanks also to D. Dark, K. Sims, and L. Semo for assistance with literature review, compiling, and editing. Thanks to A. Araya for providing valuable assistance.

We thank the following for providing reviews of an earlier draft: J. Barclay, B. Busby, J. Dillon, C. Finley, K. M. Giesen, D. B. Hall, L. Hanebury, G. Holroyd, N. Korfanta, D. W. Mehlman, E. J. Miller, R. K. Murphy, D. Rosenberg, J. S. Shackford, S. Sherrod, K. Steenhof, T. VerCauteren, and R. D. Williams.

Taxonomy

Two subspecies of Burrowing Owl (*Athene cunicularia*) occur in North America: the Western Burrowing Owl (*A. c. hypugaea*) and the Florida Burrowing Owl (*A. c. floridana*). Although this status assessment is focused on North American populations of the Western Burrowing Owl (henceforth Burrowing Owl), a state summary for the Florida Burrowing Owl is included in this document (Appendix A) to provide complete information on the species in the United States. The Florida state summary is an update of information included in Millsap (1996).

Class: Aves

Order: Strigiformes

Family: Strigidae

Genus: *Athene*

Species: *A. cunicularia*

Subspecies: *A. c. hypugaea, A. c. floridana*

Authority: (Molina, Subspp. Bonaparte)

Originally named *Strix cunicularia* by Molina in 1782, the Burrowing Owl received several taxonomic changes until placed in the genus *Speotyto* and now *Athene* (Clark et al. 1997, AOU 1998). *A. cunicularia* occurs as a breeding and/or wintering species throughout w. North America, Central America, and extensive portions of South America with disjunct populations in Florida and the Caribbean Islands. *A. c. hypugaea* occurs in North America to the eastern limits of the Great Plains and from s. British Columbia to Manitoba and into Central America as far south as Panama (Haug et al. 1993). This subspecies occurs primarily in prairies, grasslands, shrub-steppe, desert, and agricultural areas in North America (Haug et al. 1993). *A. c. floridana* occurs in Florida north to Madison and Duval counties (AOU 1998).

Legal Status

United States

From 1994-1996, the Western Burrowing Owl was designated by the U.S. Fish and Wildlife Service (USFWS) as a Category 2 species for consideration to be listed as a threatened or endangered species. In 1996 the Category 2 designation was discontinued. The Burrowing Owl currently is federally protected by the Migratory Bird Treaty Act (1918) in the United States and Mexico. The Western Burrowing Owl is listed by the USFWS as a National Bird of Conservation Concern (U.S. Fish and Wildlife Service 2002). It is also listed as a Bird of Conservation Concern in USFWS Regions 1 (Pacific Region, mainland only), 2 (Southwest Region), and 6 (Mountain-Prairie Region) as well as in Bird Conservation Regions (BCR) 9 (Great Basin), 11 (Prairie Potholes), 16 (S. Rockies/Colorado Plateau), 17 (Badlands and Prairies), 18 (Shortgrass Prairie), and U.S. Portions of BCR 32 (Coastal California), 33 (Sonoran and Mojave Deserts), 35 (Chihuahuan Desert) and 36 (Tamaulipan Brushlands) (U.S. Fish and Wildlife Service 2002). The Burrowing Owl is listed as Endangered, Threatened, or as a Species of Concern in 9 states and 4 Canadian provinces (Table 1). It is given a Global Heritage Status Rank of G4 (apparently secure globally though it may be quite rare in parts of its range) and is listed as a Convention on International Trade in Endangered Species (CITES), Appendix II species (NatureServe Explorer 2001).

Canada

In 1979, the Western Burrowing Owl was listed as "Threatened" based on Wedgwood (1979), reconfirmed in 1991 (Haug and Didiuk 1991), and changed to "Endangered" in 1995 (Wellicome and Haug 1995).

Mexico

In 1994, Burrowing Owls were listed as a federally Threatened (Amenazadas) species (Secretaria de Desarollo Social de Mexico 1994 *in* Sheffield 1997a).

Table 1. Legal status and natural heritage status of Burrowing Owls in the United States, Canada, and Mexico

Area	Legal status	Natural Heritage status[a]
United States	None	Apparently Secure
Arizona	None	Vulnerable
California	Species of Concern	Imperiled
Colorado	Threatened	Apparently Secure
Idaho	None	Vulnerable/Apparently Secure
Iowa	Accidental breeder	Unranked
Kansas	None	Vulnerable
Minnesota	Endangered	Critically Imperiled
Montana	Species of Concern	Vulnerable
Nebraska	None	Vulnerable
Nevada	None	Vulnerable
New Mexico	None	Apparently Secure
North Dakota	None	Unranked
Oklahoma	Species of Concern	Vulnerable
Oregon	Species of Concern	Imperiled
South Dakota	None	Vulnerable/Apparently Secure
Texas	None	Vulnerable
Utah	Species of Concern	Vulnerable
Washington	Species of Concern	Vulnerable
Wyoming	Species of Concern	Vulnerable
Canada	Endangered	Vulnerable
Alberta	Endangered	Vulnerable
British Columbia	Endangered	Critically Imperiled
Manitoba	Endangered	Critically Imperiled
Saskatchewan	Endangered	Imperiled
Mexico	Threatened	Unranked

[a]–Global status = Apparently Secure

Description

The Burrowing Owl is a small owl (19.5-25.0 cm, ~150 g), with long slender tarsi covered with short hair-like feathers that terminate in sparse bristles on the feet. The head is rounded, lacks ear tufts, and is chocolate in color with white streaking or spotting. There are buffy-white margins around the eyes and a white throat patch. Eyes are lemon-yellow and the beak is pale horn-colored. The wings are relatively long and rounded, the tail is short, and both are brown with buff-white barring. The undertail coverts are white. The dorsal area including head, back, and scapulars are heavily spotted with buffy-white. The belly of adults is buffy and heavily barred with brown on the sides. Juveniles are similar to adults but are unstreaked to lightly streaked, light to brownish buff below, and have more pale secondary coverts (Haug et al. 1993). The Burrowing Owl is the only North American strigiform not exhibiting reversed size dimorphism (Haug et al. 1993).

Distribution

Breeding

In Canada, the historical breeding range of the Burrowing Owl includes se. British Columbia, s. Alberta, s. Saskatchewan, and sw. Manitoba (Fig. 1, Haug et al. 1993, Wellicome and Holroyd 2001). In the United States the historical breeding range includes e. Washington and Oregon, s., c. and e. California, c. and e. Montana, s. Idaho, Utah, Nevada, Arizona, Wyoming, Colorado, New Mexico, North Dakota, South Dakota, Nebraska, w. and c. Kansas, w. and c. Oklahoma, w. Minnesota, nw. Iowa, and most of w. Texas (Fig. 1). The breeding range has contracted primarily on the eastern and northern edges (Wellicome and Holroyd 2001). Anecdotal observations suggest accidental breeding may have occurred in Wisconsin (R. Domalgalski, pers. commun.). Migrants or vagrants have been documented in Louisiana (B. Vermillion, pers. commun.), Missouri (Haug et al. 1993), Arkansas (James and Neal 1986), and Illinois (Illinois Natural History Information Network 2000). The breeding range extends south to c. Mexico (Fig. 1, Fig. 2) (Enriquez-Rocha 1997, Wellicome and Holroyd 2001).

Migration

Little information exists on migration routes and times. Burrowing Owls migrate north during March and April, arriving the first week of May in Saskatchewan (Haug et al. 1993). The majority of Burrowing Owls that breed in Canada and the n. United States are believed to migrate south during September and October.

Burrowing Owls banded in British Columbia, Washington, Oregon, and California migrated southward along the Pacific coast. Burrowing Owls banded in Alberta, Saskatchewan, Manitoba, Montana, and North Dakota migrated southward through Nebraska and Kansas into Texas. One Burrowing Owl from Manitoba was recovered in the Gulf of Mexico. Burrowing Owls banded in Wyoming, South Dakota, Nebraska, Colorado, Kansas, and Oklahoma have been recovered in Arkansas, Oklahoma, Texas, and Mexico. Recoveries indicate that some Burrowing Owls will winter in California and Baja California, Mexico. Burrowing Owls breeding in North and South Dakota are believed to winter in Texas.

Winter

The small number of banding recoveries (n = 27, 1927 through 1990) provides little information regarding wintering areas (Haug et al. 1993). Burrowing Owls winter regularly from Mexico (Fig. 2) to El Salvador and are casual to accidental to w. Panama (AOU 1998). They are recorded on the Christmas Bird Count (CBC) in Arizona, California, New Mexico, Oregon, Texas, and Mexico (Fig. 3; James and Ethier 1989). They will also winter north of these states, particularly in Oklahoma and Kansas, in very low abundance. They will also winter in low abundance in sc. Nevada (Hall et al. *In review*).

Little information exists on Burrowing Owls in Mexico and breeding and wintering areas have not been well described. Based on museum specimens, the Burrowing Owl is the third most common owl species in the country and sixty-three percent of museum specimens (n = 279) from Mexico were collected in the non-breeding season (Enriquez-Rocha 1997); however, it is unlikely that these collections reflect true relative abundance. These collections documented a wide distribution, occurring in 28 of the 32 Mexican states. Non-breeding data were from the Pacific region, some central states, and from the se. Gulf of Mexico (including the Yucatan Peninsula). Both breeding and nonbreeding records document Burrowing Owls in n. Mexico, Baja California, and some states from the Gulf of Mexico.

Fig. 1. Current and historical ranges of the Western Burrowing Owl in North America; modified from the Birds of North America species account (Haug et al. 1993), North American Breeding Bird Survey distribution map (Sauer et al. 2001), individual papers from the Proceedings of the Second International Burrowing Owl Symposium (Journal of Raptor Research 35(4) 2001), and personal communications with local experts. Historical range (pre-1970's) taken from Zarn (1974), Wedgwood (1978), and from personal communications with local experts. In states that lacked detailed distributional data, Burrowing Owls were presumed to be absent from areas of forest or rugged mountains. The historical range is unknown for Mexico (from Wellicome and Holroyd 2001).

Breeding Season

Nonbreeding Season

Both Seasons

No Records

Gulf of Mexico

Pacific Ocean

N

Fig. 2. Burrowing Owl distribution in Mexico during the breeding (16 April – 15 October) and non-breeding (16 October – 15 April) seasons as determined from 279 museum specimens and literature documentation (Enriquez-Rocha 1997).

Natural History

Breeding

Phenology—Burrowing Owls are generally found on the northern breeding grounds from mid-March through September (Haug et al. 1993). Courtship and pair formation occur in March and April in most areas (Grant 1965, Butts 1973) but may begin as early as late December in California (Thomsen 1971).

Incubation lasts 28-30 days and is performed by the female (Coulombe 1971, Thomsen 1971, Haug et al. 1993). The young begin feathering out at two weeks of age. The young run and forage by four weeks of age and are capable of sustained flight by six weeks. Burrowing Owl families often switch burrows every 10-15 days when the young are three to four weeks old and remain as a loose-knit group until early fall when the young may begin to disperse to nearby burrows (Haug et al. 1993, Dechant et al. 1999).

Diet—Burrowing Owls are opportunistic feeders, primarily taking arthropods, small mammals, birds, amphibians and reptiles (Haug et al. 1993). Seasonal variability in food habits occurs, with vertebrates occurring more commonly in the winter diet and arthropods occurring more frequently in the summer diet (Haug et al. 1993).

Foraging—Burrowing Owls forage in a variety of habitats, including cropland, pasture, prairie dog colonies, fallow fields, and sparsely vegetated areas (Butts and Lewis 1982, Thompson and Anderson 1988, Desmond 1991, Haug et al. 1993, Wellicome 1994). Vegetation >1 m tall may be too tall for Burrowing Owls to locate or catch prey (Haug and Oliphant 1987, 1990; Wellicome 1994).

Productivity—Burrowing Owls are capable of breeding at one year of age. However, some females may not breed the first year after hatching, or may breed away from the natal site the first year after hatching and then return to the natal site in their second year after hatching (Lutz and Plumpton 1999). Second broods have rarely been documented in the Burrowing Owl (Haug et al. 1993). Average clutch size over the range of the species was 6.5 eggs (range 4-12; Haug et al. 1993). In Canada, percent successful reproduction ranged from 45-97% and mean fledging rate ranged from 2.1 to 6.3 young/successful nest (Hjertaas et al. 1995). In British Columbia, 58% (n = 12) of nesting attempts were successful and produced 31 young with a mean brood size of 4.1 ± 1.3 young/successful nest and 2.6 young/attempt (Hjertaas et al. 1995). In Manitoba, average brood size was 5.1 young and overall productivity was 3.4 young/nesting pair (De Smet 1997). In New Mexico, Burrowing Owls produced 3.33 ± 1.49 nestlings and 2.55 ± 1.49 fledglings in human-altered habitats and 1.05 ± 1.23 nestlings and 0.68 ± 0.98 fledglings in natural habitats (Botelho and Arrowood 1996).

Territory—Burrowing Owls generally stay close to the nest burrow during daylight and forage farther from the nest between dusk and dawn (Haug 1985, Haug and Oliphant 1990). Nesting-territory size was 4.8-6.4 ha in Minnesota (n = 2) and 4-6 ha in North Dakota (n = estimated 5-9 pairs) (Grant 1965). Average diurnal ranges of Burrowing Owls in e. Wyoming encompassed 3.5 ha (number of foraging areas not given) (Thompson 1984). Foraging-areas are considerably larger than nesting-areas. In s. Saskatchewan, mean foraging territory size for males ranged from 14 to 481 ha (mean = 241 ha; n = 6) (Haug 1985, Haug and Oliphant 1990). In a heavily cultivated region of s. Saskatchewan, foraging territories for males averaged 35 ha (n = 4) (Sissons et al. 2001).

Aggregations—In nc. Colorado, mean inter-nest distances for Burrowing Owls nesting in black-tailed prairie dog colonies was 101 m (n = 8) (Plumpton 1992). Mean nearest-neighbor distance for Burrowing Owls nesting in 20 American badger excavations in w. Nebraska was 240 m, compared to mean nearest-neighbor distances of 105 m for 118 non-clustered nests in small prairie dog colonies and 125 m for 105 nest clusters in large prairie dog colonies (Desmond 1991, Desmond et al. 1995, Desmond and Savidge 1996). Available excavations may be limiting to Burrowing Owls nesting outside of prairie dog colonies

Within prairie dog colonies, Burrowing Owls have been observed to aggregate their nests into clusters. Mean densities of Burrowing Owls within clusters in larger colonies (≥ 35 ha) were 1.2-1.3 individuals/ha (n = 21). In smaller colonies (<35 ha) with random distributions, mean densities of Burrowing Owls ranged from 1.7 to 5.8 individuals/ha (n = 26). Clustered nest distributions may reduce depredation risks by allowing individuals to alert one another to potential predators (Butts 1973, Desmond 1991, Desmond et al. 1995, Desmond and Savidge 1996).

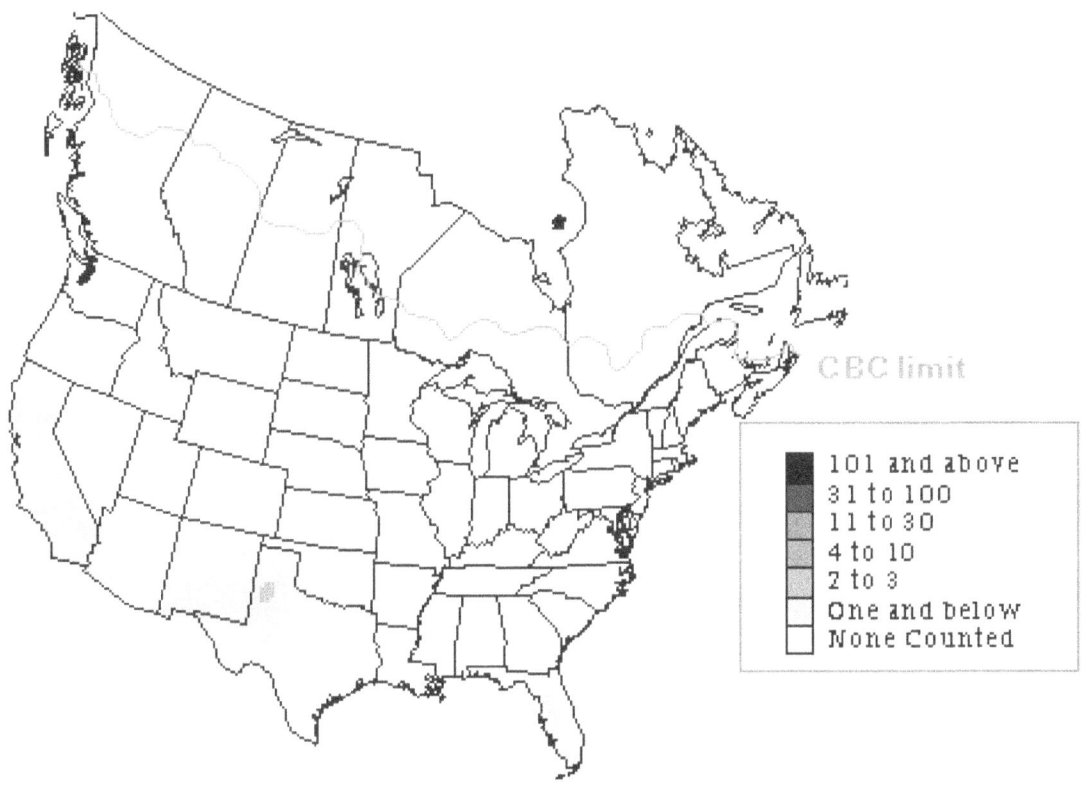

Fig. 3. Winter distribution of Burrowing Owls in the United States from Christmas Bird Count (CBC) data (1966-1989). Shading represents the species relative abundance (birds/100 party hours) averaged for each CBC circle and smoothed over the species distribution (Sauer et al. 1996).

In ne. Colorado, 27 prairie dog colonies with Burrowing Owls ranged in size from 1.9 to 167.6 ha (Hughes 1993). In w. Nebraska, fledging success rates were positively correlated with the size of prairie dog colonies (Desmond 1991).

Mortality and Predation—The annual mortality rate in Oklahoma was estimated at 62% (adults and young combined) (Butts 1973). At two sites in s. Saskatchewan, adult female survival (s) (s = 0.62, n = 12 and s = 1.00, n = 2) was higher than survival for adult males (s = 0.48, n = 11 and s = 0.38, n = 5) or juveniles (s = 0.45, n = 21 and s = 0.48, n = 25) (Clayton and Schmutz 1999).

Predators of Burrowing Owls include badger, domestic cat, weasel, skunk, domestic dog, coyote, Swainson's, Ferruginous, Red-tailed, and Cooper's hawks, Merlin, Prairie, and Peregrine falcons, Great Horned Owl, American Crow (Haug et al. 1993), snakes, bobcats and Northern Harrier (Leupin and Low 2001).

Site and Burrow Fidelity—Individual Burrowing Owls have moderate to high site fidelity to general breeding areas, prairie dog colonies, and even to particular nest burrows. Of 31 adults banded in Colorado in 1990, 39% returned in 1991, whereas only 5% of 369 Burrowing Owls banded as nestlings prior to 1994 returned in one or more years after hatch (Plumpton and Lutz 1993, Lutz and Plumpton 1999). Eight of the remaining 12 returning adults (66%) reused the same prairie dog town as the prior year (Plumpton and Lutz 1993). Adult males and females returned at similar rates (19% and 14%, respectively) (Lutz and Plumpton 1999). Adult males and females nested in formerly used sites at similar rates (75% and 63%, respectively). In Albuquerque, New Mexico, all returning males selected the same burrow they had previously inhabited unless the burrow had been destroyed (n = 9, Martin 1973). In Manitoba, 7% of failed nests (n = 57) were reused in consecutive years but 23% (n = 122) of successful nests were reused (De Smet 1997). Burrow fidelity has been reported in some areas; however, more frequently, Burrowing Owls reuse traditional nesting areas without necessarily using the same burrow (Haug et al. 1993, Dechant et al. 1999). Burrow and nest sites are re-used at a higher rate if the bird has reproduced successfully during the previous year (Haug et al. 1993).

Habitat

Breeding

Burrowing Owl nesting habitat consists of open areas with mammal burrows. They use a wide variety of arid and semi-arid environments, with well-drained, level to gently sloping areas characterized by sparse vegetation and bare ground (Haug et al. 1993, Dechant et al. 1999). Breeding habitats include native prairie, tame pasture, hayland, fallow fields, road and railway rights-of-way, and urban habitats (e.g., campuses, airports, and golf courses) (Dechant et al. 1999). Burrowing Owls do not occupy all apparently available habitat (i.e., prairie dog or ground squirrel colonies). Unused colonies have been documented in virtually all states within the current range of the Burrowing Owl.

Burrowing Owls require a mammal burrow or natural cavity surrounded by sparse vegetation. Burrow availability is often limiting in areas lacking colonial burrowing rodents (Desmond and Savidge 1996). Burrowing Owls frequently use burrows of black-tailed prairie dogs. They nest less commonly in the burrows of Douglas' ground squirrels, white-tailed prairie dogs, Gunnison's prairie dogs, yellow-bellied marmots, woodchucks, skunks, foxes, coyotes, and nine-banded armadillos (Dechant et al. 1999). Where mammal burrows are scarce, Burrowing Owls have been found nesting in natural rock and lava cavities (Gleason 1978, Gleason and Johnson 1985, Rich 1986).

Burrowing Owls may use "satellite" or non-nesting burrows, moving chicks at 10-14 days presumably to reduce risk of predation (Desmond and Savidge 1998) and possibly to avoid nest parasites (Dechant et al. 1999). Successful nests in Nebraska had more active burrows within 75 m of the nest burrow than unsuccessful nests (Desmond and Savidge 1999). Observations made at 15 burrow sites by James and Seabloom (1968) revealed that family units in sw. North Dakota used from one to three satellite burrows, although a few family units used from two to ten satellite burrows. In e. Wyoming, most (actual number not given) nesting areas contained between two and 11 available burrows (Thompson 1984). Three Burrowing Owl families in Iowa used from one to five satellite burrows (Scott 1940). In Oklahoma, black-tailed prairie dog colonies appeared to be the only habitat with a sufficient density of burrows to provide satellite burrows for Burrowing Owls (Butts and Lewis 1982).

Migration

No information is available on migration habitats. They are presumed to be similar to breeding habitats (Haug et al. 1993).

Winter

Little is known about wintering habitat requirements beyond what the species uses during the breeding season, but there seems to be increased use of agricultural fields with culverts in some areas (Haug et al. 1993, W. Howe, pers. commun.). In Louisiana, in winter, Burrowing Owls are typically found in dune vegetation or near woody debris on beaches, in pastures, and in agricultural fields (B. Vermillion, pers. commun.). In sc. Nevada, burrows used in winter were the same as those used during the breeding season (Hall et al. *In review*).

Populations

Population Estimates and Trends

Breeding Bird Survey—The Breeding Bird Survey (BBS) revealed a mixture of population trends throughout the Burrowing Owl breeding range in North America (Table 2, Fig. 4) (Sauer et al. 2002). BBS trends for Burrowing Owls are largely limited by small sample sizes and the species is not adequately sampled over a large part of their breeding range. Trends in nearly all regions are limited by important or potential deficiencies (Sauer et al. 2002). However, when taken as a whole, generally declining populations are present in the northern half of the Great Plains, and generally increasing populations are present in the northwest interior and in some southwestern deserts of the United States (Table 2, Fig. 4).

Christmas Bird Count—Burrowing Owl abundance is poorly monitored by the CBC. Most Burrowing Owls from the Great Plains winter in Mexico where CBC coverage is poor. On the Gulf Coast of Texas, wintering Burrowing Owls are difficult to detect and samples sizes are small. The effort to locate wintering Burrowing Owls has increased in recent years (G. Holroyd, pers. commun.). A significant decreasing trend was observed only in California; trends for other areas were non-significant (Table 3) (Sauer et al. 1996). James and Ethier (1989) detected stable populations in most wintering areas in New Mexico, Louisiana, and Mexico for 1955-85. There were no significant changes in Arizona, New Mexico, Texas, and Louisiana from 1954-86, or in Mexico between 1974 and 1985 (James and Ethier 1989)

Other Surveys, United States—Surveys in California in 1986-91 found population decreases of 23-52% in the number of breeding groups and 12-27% in the number of breeding pairs of owls (DeSante et al. 1997). Populations in w. Nebraska declined 58% (91 to 38 nesting pairs) between 1990-1996 (Desmond and Savidge 1998). Populations in New Mexico have exhibited mixed trends: stable or increasing populations were associated with the presence of suitable habitat and increased precipitation and food availability while decreasing populations were associated with loss of suitable habitat (Arrowood et al. 2001). In Wyoming, only 11% of 86 historical sites were occupied in 1998; however, the importance of this finding is uncertain due to the tendency for Burrowing Owl colonies to move (Korfanta et al. 2001). The Wyoming Game and Fish Department's Wildlife Observation System showed populations generally increasing between 1974-80 and then decreasing between 1981-97 (Korfanta et al. 2001). In North Dakota, Burrowing Owls have disappeared from the eastern third of the state and is uncommon to rare in the best habitats north and east of the Missouri River (Murphy et al. 2001). In sw. North Dakota the current population trend is not clear, but is probably closely tied to populations of prairie dogs (Murphy et al. 2001). Based on questionnaires, literature searches, personal contacts and field observations, Brown (2001) concluded that Burrowing Owls are widespread but uncommon in Arizona. In Oklahoma there are an estimated 800-1000 breeding Burrowing Owls, restricted primarily to the panhandle of the state (Sheffield and Howery 2001). In a survey of National Grasslands, Sidle et al. (2001) found higher occupancy of active prairie dog towns in the southern Great Plains (93%) than in the northern Great Plains (59%).

Table 2. North American Breeding Bird Survey trends, significance level (P), sample size (n) and 95% confidence intervals (CI) for the Burrowing Owl during three different survey periods (Sauer et al. 2002).

Area (data credibility)[a]	1966–2001					1966–1979			1980–2001		
	Trend[b]	P	n	95%	CI	Trend[b]	P	n	Trend[b]	P	n
State/Province											
Alberta (R)	-8.5	0.42	6	-27.2	10.1	51.8	0.26	3	3.9	0.93	3
Arizona (Y)	7.7	0.65	9	-23.8	39.20	—	—	—	-3.1	0.88	8
California (B)	5.9	0.01	32	1.9	9.8	-0.9	0.92	19	5.4	0.03	24
Colorado (Y)	-4.0	0.48	38	-14.9	6.9	-7.8	0.40	9	2.7	0.57	36
Idaho (R)	19.1	0.07	9	1.4	36.8	39.2	0.03	3	28.4	0.06	9
Kansas (Y)	-1.1	0.80	11	-9.1	7.0	10.8	0.34	8	11.7	0.69	8
Montana (R)	-12.6	0.11	10	-26.5	1.3	—	—	—	-14.8	0.19	9
Nebraska (Y)	6.5	0.57	13	-14.9	27.9	33.9	0.11	8	3.8	0.72	8
Nevada (Y)	10.9	0.30	9	-8.2	30.1	0.9	0.97	3	12.1	0.14	6
New Mexico (Y)	0.7	0.85	37	-7.0	8.4	-3.9	0.03	6	2.2	0.77	35
North Dakota (R)	-3.2	0.44	13	-10.9	4.6	19.6	0.15	7	-15.8	0.00	9
Oklahoma (R)	-11.5	0.00	10	-14.1	-8.8	14.2	0.37	6	-4.5	0.34	8
Oregon (Y)	3.8	0.63	11	-11.0	18.5	-14.2	0.66	5	15.5	0.20	8
Saskatchewan (R)	-26.0	0.04	2	-29.3	-22.7	—	—	—	—	—	—
South Dakota (Y)	-7.2	0.16	19	-16.9	2.5	5.2	0.52	14	-11.4	0.08	10
Texas (Y)	-1.9	0.39	28	-6.3	2.4	8.4	0.27	14	-5.2	0.26	24
Utah (Y)	0.9	0.89	14	-11.3	13.0	—	—	—	-6.6	0.14	14
Washington (Y)	-7.8	0.60	7	-35.2	19.7	—	—	—	-19.4	0.20	6
Wyoming (Y)	-23.7	0.04	11	-42.3	-5.2	10.5	0.76	2	5.9	0.53	9
Physiographic strata											
South Texas Brushlands	-3.9	0.46	2	-10.9	3.0	—	—	—	—	—	—
High Plains Border (Y)	5.7	0.45	17	-8.5	19.8	3.1	0.84	11	20.0	0.55	11
High Plains (Y)	-4.0	0.43	50	-14.0	6.0	-1.9	0.85	17	2.4	0.61	46
Drift Prairie (Y)	-26.0	0.01	8	-37.7	-14.3	-13.5	0.40	7	—	—	—

Table 2. Continued

Area (data credibility)[a]	1966–2001					1966–1979			1980–2001		
	Trend[b]	P	n	95%	CI	Trend[b]	P	n	Trend[b]	P	n
Glaciated Missouri Plateau (R)	-11.0	0.04	15	-20.0	-2.0	23.0	0.12	6	-12.8	0.16	10
Great Plain Roughlands (R)	-2.6	0.40	30	-8.6	3.4	16.9	0.03	12	-10.4	0.04	22
Rolling Red Plains (Y)	-0.9	0.77	7	-7.0	5.1	-2.7	0.81	3	1.1	0.75	7
Staked Plains (B)	-2.3	0.39	21	-7.6	2.9	10.3	0.27	10	-4.3	0.38	19
Chihuahuan Desert (Y)	1.8	0.80	22	-12.2	15.8	43.4	0.33	7	-1.1	0.90	20
Great Basin Deserts (Y)	7.3	0.55	8	-15.3	29.9	—	—	—	-1.9	0.83	8
Mexican Highlands (Y)	7.1	0.42	2	-3.6	17.8	—	—	—	-8.1	0.55	2
Sonoran Desert (Y)	6.6	0.03	10	1.6	11.5	-2.6	0.84	5	5.7	0.11	8
Mojave Desert (Y)	-1.4	0.84	6	-14.4	11.6	20.6	0.36	4	-20.2	0.33	4
Wyoming Basin (Y)	-31.0	0.07	4	-53.6	-8.4	10.5	0.76	2	29.0	0.60	2
Intermountain Grassland (Y)	2.8	0.57	27	-6.7	12.3	—	—	—	6.8	0.03	23
Basin and Range (Y)	9.9	0.30	13	-7.8	27.6	0.7	0.96	3	5.8	0.43	10
Columbia Plateau (R)	12.8	0.04	28	1.1	24.4	33.0	0.00	9	21.6	0.01	24
Central Valley (Y)	2.6	0.41	15	-3.3	8.5	-9.6	0.65	9	1.4	0.76	12
USFWS Regions											
Region 1 (Y)	7.1	0.00	68	3.5	10.7	5.7	0.41	31	7.2	0.00	53
Region 2 (Y)	-1.2	0.45	84	-4.4	2.0	-0.5	0.72	29	-1.8	0.63	75
Region 6 (Y)	-4.4	0.29	129	-12.6	3.7	-0.7	0.92	48	-0.2	0.95	103
Country											
Canada (R)	-12.1	0.01	8	-18.4	-5.9	23.8	0.36	4	-18.7	0.02	4
United States (Y)	-1.5	0.57	291	-6.5	3.6	0.0	0.99	113	1.6	0.63	237
Survey-wide (Y)	-1.5	0.57	299	-6.5	3.6	0.2	0.96	117	1.5	0.41	241

[a]—Data credibility measure. (R) = RED: Data with an important deficiency. (Y) = Yellow: Data with a potential deficiency. (B) = BLUE: Data with at least 14 samples in the long term, of moderate precision, and of moderate abundance on routes.

[b]—Mean percent change per year

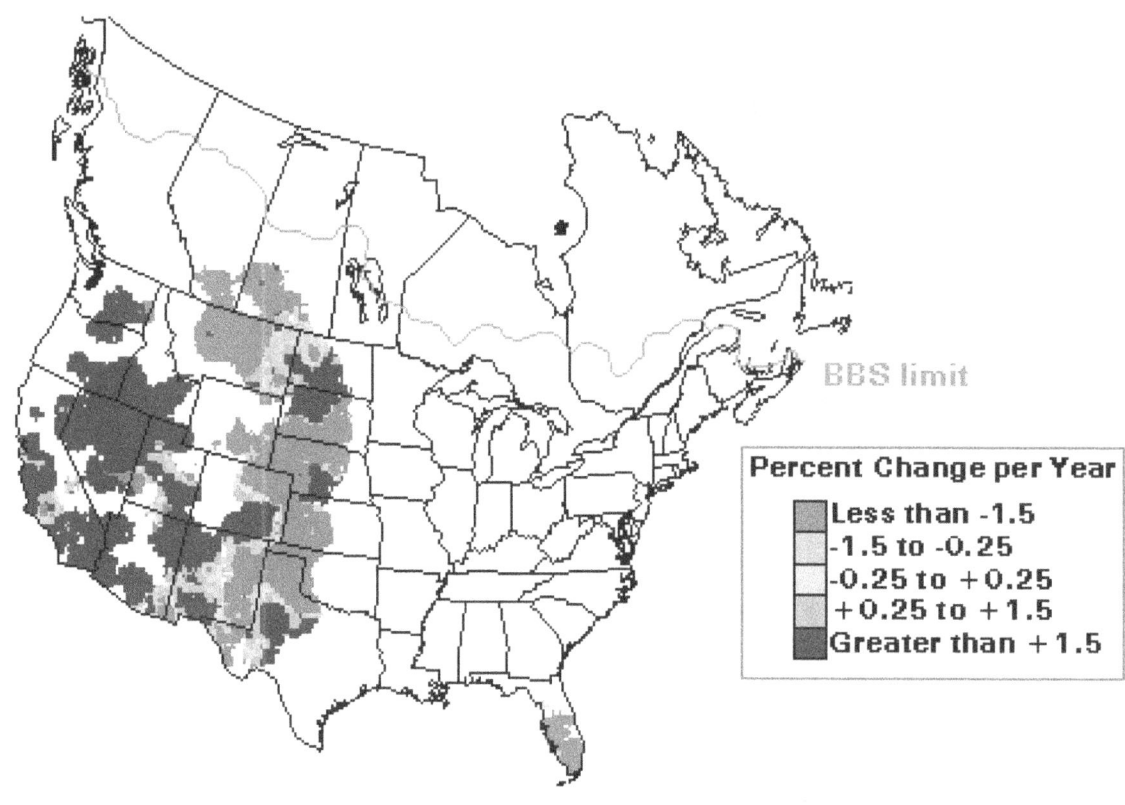

Fig. 4. Breeding Bird Survey trends for Burrowing Owls in the United States and Canada (1966-96, Sauer et al. 2002). These trends do not necessarily reflect statistical significance (see Table 2).

Table 3. Christmas Bird Count trends, sample sizes (n), 95% confidence intervals (CI), significance levels (P), and relative abundance (RA) for the Burrowing Owl in areas with sufficient data for analysis, 1959-1988 (Sauer et al. 1996).

State	Trend[a]	n	95%	CI	P	RA[b]
Arizona	0.2	16	−1.7	2.1	>0.10	0.10
California	−1.2	97	−2.3	−0.1	≤ 0.05	0.29
Texas	1.2	52	−1.3	3.8	>0.10	0.23
Survey-wide	0.2	240	−1.5	1.9	>0.10	0.13

[a]–Mean percent change per year.

[b]–Mean number of birds per 100 party hours.

Field-based, quantitative population estimates do not exist for most states (Table 4). However, James and Espie (1997) submitted surveys to state biologists in 1992 to determine approximate total breeding populations of Burrowing Owls, based on expert opinion and not necessarily based on field investigations of true population levels. Additional population estimates have been made for California, Colorado, Kansas, Montana, and Oklahoma (Table 4).

Other Surveys, Canada—Burrowing Owls declined in Canada from the mid-1970s through at least the early 1990s (Kirk et al. 1994/95) with up to 50% declines in some areas (Dundas and Jensen 1994/95). No complete censuses have been conducted in Canada, but a variety of studies show widespread range contraction and declining density (Hjertaas et al. 1995). Burrowing Owls declined in Alberta, Saskatchewan, and Manitoba at over 20% per year over the past decade (Wellicome and Holroyd 2001). Skeel et al. (2001) documented a 95% decline in Burrowing Owls reported by landowners in Saskatchewan for an average annual decline of 21.5% from 1998-2000. They are effectively extirpated from Manitoba with one pair nesting every second year since 1999 (K. De Smet, pers. commun.). Shyry et al. (2001) reported a significant decrease in the density of Burrowing Owl nests near Hannah, Alberta between 1991 and 2000. The density of nests near Brooks, Alberta did not significantly change from 1991 to 2000.

Based on a survey of biologists, the total breeding population for Canada was estimated as approximately 2,000-20,000 pairs, with the major populations occurring in Alberta and Saskatchewan (Table 4) (James and Espie 1997). In Alberta, the population estimate dropped from 1,500 to 800 birds (47% decline) from 1978-1990 (Wellicome 1997).

Other Surveys, Mexico—Burrowing Owls breed in much of Mexico but the population is unknown. In nw. Chihuahua they occurred on 62% (n = 34) of surveyed prairie dog colonies for a total of 87 owls. Numbers ranged from 0-16 owls/prairie dog colony and 0.00-7.69 owls/ha (VerCauteren et al. *In review*). Two BBS routes in the same area of nw. Chihuahua average 19 and 32 Burrowing Owls per route between 1998 and 2001. As many as 26 adults were visible from a single point on one occasion (W. Howe, pers. commun.).

Densities

In Nebraska, total numbers of Burrowing Owls increased, but density decreased with increasing size of prairie dog towns (Desmond and Savidge 1996). In large (>35 ha) prairie dog towns, distribution was found to be less dense but clumped, and clumping was not related to burrow availability (Desmond et al. 1995). Burrowing Owl density in black-tailed prairie dog colonies was negatively correlated with the density of inactive burrows (Desmond 1991). The density of Burrowing Owls in prairie dog colonies in ne. Colorado was positively related to the percentage of active burrows (Hughes 1993). At least 50% of the burrows were active in 26 of 27 occupied colonies. For prairie dog colonies with over 90% active burrows, mean density was 2.85 owls/ha, and for those with 70-80% active burrows, mean density was 0.57 owls/ha.

Changes in Breeding Season Distribution

United States—The Burrowing Owl has been nearly extirpated from all former breeding range in w. Minnesota, most areas east of the Missouri River in North Dakota, e. Nebraska and Oklahoma, e. and c. Kansas, in large portions of the San Francisco Bay area in California, and in the Rogue Valley in sw. Oregon (DeSante et al. 1997, Martell et al. 2001, Murphy et al. 2001, Sheffield and Howery 2001, Wellicome and Holroyd 2001).

In California, the Burrowing Owl has been extirpated as a breeding species during the last 10-15 years from approximately 8% of its former range (J. Barclay, pers. commun.). They were apparently extirpated as breeding birds during the past decade from Sonoma, Marin, Santa Cruz, and Napa counties, and only one breeding pair apparently still existed in San Mateo County in 1991. The population around the north end of San Francisco, San Pablo, and Suisun Bays was also reduced to a very small remnant. Breeding in central California has been reduced to only three isolated populations: a moderate but declining population of about 720 pairs in the Central Valley; about 143 pairs in the lowlands around the southern arm of San Francisco Bay between Alameda and Redwood City; and a very small, isolated population of about 10 pairs in the Livermore area (DeSante et al. 1997).

In a comparison with historical distributions, Murphy et al. (2001) found that Burrowing Owls were greatly reduced or completely extirpated from nw. and c. North Dakota. Declines in Burrowing Owls may be related to loss of grassland habitat and burrowing rodents in the state (Murphy et al. 2001).

Table 4. Burrowing Owl population estimates for states, provinces, and countries. James and Espie (1997) surveyed state/provincial biologists in 1992 to determine approximate total breeding populations. Other populations estimates are presented only for statewide/province-wide estimates; additional local population estimates can be found in Appendix A: State Summaries of Burrowing Owl Status.

Area	James and Espie (1997)[a]	Other statewide/province-wide estimates (source)
United States	20,000–200,000	
Arizona	100–1,000	None
California	1,000–10,000	9,266 pairs (1991–1993; DeSante et al., unpubl.)
Colorado	1,000–10,000	15,796–20,408 individuals (Hanni 2001)[b]
Idaho	1,000–10,000	None
Iowa	<10	None
Kansas	100–1,000	1,000–10,000 pairs (W. Busby, pers. commun.)
Minnesota	<10	None
Montana	100–1,000	644 + 114 pairs (Atkinson 2000)[c] 300 pairs (Holroyd and Wellicome 1997)
Nebraska	100–1,000	None
Nevada	1,000–10,000	None
New Mexico	1,000–10,000	None
North Dakota	100–1,000	None
Oklahoma	100–1,000	800–1,000 individuals (Sheffield and Howery 2001)
Oregon	1,000–10,000	None
South Dakota	100–1,000	None
Texas	>10,000	None
Utah	1,000–10,000	None
Washington	100–1,000	None
Wyoming	1,000–10,000	None
Canada	2,000–20,000	
Alberta	1,000–10,000	800 birds (in 1990; Wellicome 1997)
British Columbia	<10	<10 pairs (Leupin and Low 2001)
Manitoba	10–100	10–20 pairs (K. De Smet, pers. commun.)
Saskatchewan	1,000–10,000	None
Mexico	Unknown	

[a]–numbers of breeding pairs

[b]–estimates are only for e. Colorado, which represents the majority of breeding habitat in the state.

[c]–estimate is based on surveys of known prairie dog colonies.

In w. Minnesota, Burrowing Owls were considered common in the 1920's; however, significant declines had occurred by the 1960's (Martell et al. 2001). During 1965-1985 only 10 breeding records were recorded. A reintroduction program was attempted from 1986-1990; however no successful nesting has been recorded since 1992.

Canada—The Burrowing Owl has been extirpated from the northern portions of the range in Saskatchewan and Alberta, and all former range in Manitoba and British Columbia (Wellicome 1997, Shyry et al. 2001, Wellicome and Holroyd 2001). Extirpation from all of Canada may occur within a few decades (Wellicome and Haug 1995).

Mexico—Unknown.

Re-occupancy Rates

Of 292 nest burrows that had been occupied in some previous year (1976-83), 39.4% were re-occupied in Idaho in some subsequent year (up to seven years later) (Rich 1984). Burrows in rock outcrops were re-used 48.9% of the time (n = 113) compared to 31.4% (n = 159) for nests in soil mounds. Outcrop sites also were used more often in consecutive years; 23 were used for two years, and 12 were used for three consecutive years. Fifteen mound nests were used for two years, five were used for three years, and one was used four consecutive years. Greater reuse of outcrop sites could be related to their stability as no burrows in outcrops were destroyed. However, nests in old badger burrows were destroyed by plowing, cattle trampling, drifting sand, dredging, and other unknown causes (Rich 1984).

In Colorado, 90% of 18 prairie dog towns and 25% of four nesting burrows were reused between 1990 and 1991 (Plumpton and Lutz 1993). In sc. Idaho in 1994-95, 50% (n = 30) of individual burrows were reused in a subsequent year (Belthoff and King 1997). Of 10 burrows that fledged young in 1994, 70% were reused at least once. Conversely, burrows tended to remain unoccupied in years following nest failures; six nests remained unused in 1995 and 1996 after failing in 1994 (Belthoff and King 1997). In sw. Idaho, low nest reoccupancy was documented (11% from 1991 to 1994, and 42% from 1993 to 1994) (Lehman et al. 1998).

Korfanta et al. (2001) estimated 17% reoccupancy (range: 8-28%) of historic breeding sites in e. Wyoming. The average age of sites reoccupied by Burrowing Owls in 1998 (12.4 years; n = 10) was not significantly different from the average age of all historic observations (13.1 years, n = 86) (Korfanta et al. 2001). In 1999 and 2000, the Rocky Mountain Bird Observatory (RMBO) conducted extensive roadside surveys of potential Burrowing Owl habitat in se. Wyoming. In 1999, they located 71 colonies of Burrowing Owls, totaling 180 individuals (Hutchings et al. 1999). In 2000, they located 107 sites with Burrowing Owls for a total of 575 owls; site reoccupancy was 66% between 1999 and 2000 (T. VerCauteren, pers. commun.).

Monitoring Activities

Range-wide Surveys

There are no ongoing or standardized large-scale monitoring programs that target Burrowing Owls in the United States or Canada other than the BBS and CBC. These surveys do not adequately sample this species throughout its range (Sauer et al. 2002). There are no range-wide monitoring programs in Mexico.

Local Surveys

In Wyoming, Burrowing Owls are voluntarily reported by state and federal biologists, researchers, Audubon Society members, and the general public to the Wyoming Game and Fish Departments (WGFD) Wildlife Observation System (WOS) (Korfanta et al. 2001).

The New Mexico Burrowing Owl Working Group (NMBOWG) has initiated a volunteer monitoring system to collect data on Burrowing Owl populations in the state (C. Finley, pers. commun.).

In e. Colorado, w. Nebraska, w. Kansas, and e. Wyoming, RMBO conducts monitoring of prairie birds, including Burrowing Owls. The objectives are to investigate trends in population and distribution, and to determine local densities of birds (T. VerCauteren, pers. commun.).

Manitoba monitors Burrowing Owl populations through its Threatened Grassland Birds Project (Dundas and Jensen 1994/1995). Monitoring in Saskatchewan and Alberta is conducted through Operation Burrowing Owl (Dundas and Jensen 1994/1995).

Proposed Protocols and Surveys

In California, the California Burrowing Owl Consortium has developed Survey Protocol and Mitigation Guidelines to survey Burrowing Owl populations and to evaluate impacts from development projects. The following web site has the survey protocol and mitigation guidelines (http://www2.ucsc.edu/scpbrg/section1.htm).

In Wyoming, the Arizona Coop. Fish & Wildlife Research Unit conducted standardized population surveys for nesting Burrowing Owls on public lands. The objectives of this project were to determine the factors that influence burrow occupancy, nesting productivity, burrow fidelity, natal recruitment, conduct an annual survival in Wyoming, and to provide a paired comparison between tape and passive surveys in number of birds detected (C. Conway, pers. commun.).

Threats

Habitat: Breeding

Habitat Loss and Fragmentation—Primary threats across the North American range of the Burrowing Owl are habitat loss and fragmentation primarily due to intensive agricultural and urban development, and habitat degradation due to declines in populations of colonial burrowing mammals (Grant 1965, Konrad and Gilmer 1984, Ratcliff 1986, Haug et al. 1993, Dundas and Jensen 1994/95, Rodriguez-Estrella et al. 1998, Sheffield 1997a, Dechant et al. 1999). The dramatic reduction of prairie habitat in the United States has been linked to reduction of Burrowing Owl populations (Sheffield 1997a).

Fragmentation and isolation may be threats to small and localized populations. Fragmentation of nesting habitat may reduce the opportunity for unpaired owls to find mates (Sheffield 1997a). Fragmentation of grassland habitat in Canada has increased the populations of predators that prey on Burrowing Owls (Wellicome and Haug 1995). In contrast, in w. Nebraska landscapes dominated by croplands, Burrowing Owls had higher fledging success (mean of 3.23 fledglings/pair) than owls nesting in rangeland landscapes (mean of 1.49 fledglings/pair) (Desmond 1991). Larger home ranges have been observed in fragmented landscapes (Warnock and James 1997). Higher post-fledging mortality from vehicle collisions occurred in an agricultural landscape with >90% of land area under cultivation compared to an unfragmented rangeland with <20% cultivation (Clayton and Schmutz 1997).

Burrows—Elimination of burrowing rodents through control programs has been identified as the primary factor in the recent and historical decline of Burrowing Owl populations (Butts and Lewis 1982; Pezzolesi 1994; Desmond and Savidge 1996, 1998, 1999; Toombs 1997; Dechant et al. 1999; Desmond et al. 2000; Murphy et al. 2001). Some black-tailed prairie dog colonies have become so isolated through fragmentation that re-population through natural dispersal and colonization is difficult (Benedict et al. 1996). Declines of Burrowing Owl populations in North Dakota north and east of the Missouri River may be related to declines in Richardson's ground squirrel populations (Murphy et al 2001). In w. Nebraska, a 63% decline in Burrowing Owl numbers over a seven year period in 17 black-tailed prairie dog colonies was associated with declines in black-tailed prairie dog densities due to population control activities (Desmond et al. 2000). Burrow habitat in abandoned prairie dog towns becomes unsuitable for Burrowing Owls within one to three years (Butts 1973).

Grazing—Burrowing Owls prefer grasslands moderately or heavily grazed by cattle or prairie dogs (James and Seabloom 1968, Butts 1973, Wedgwood 1976, MacCracken et al. 1985, Bock et al. 1993). The response of Burrowing Owls to cattle grazing is related to the effects of prairie dog grazing and must be evaluated in conjunction with the presence of previously excavated burrows. In sc. Saskatchewan, heavily grazed, poor soils were used frequently by Burrowing Owls, and moderate to heavy grazing on good soils reduced lush vegetative growth and provided suitable habitat (Wedgwood 1976). Burrowing Owls in Saskatchewan and Alberta nested in pastures with shorter vegetation than occurred in randomly chosen pastures, and preferred native or tame pastures over cultivated land (Clayton 1997). In the Oklahoma Panhandle, Butts (1973) suggested that grazing of taller grasses may attract ground squirrels and prairie dogs, thus increasing burrow availability. In North Dakota, Burrowing Owls nested in moderately or heavily grazed mixed-grass pastures, but not in hayed or lightly grazed mixed-grass (Kantrud 1981). Declines in Burrowing Owl populations in North Dakota north and east of the Missouri River may be due to a reduction over the past 20 years in the amount of sheep grazing that occurs in the region (Murphy et al. 2001). In the Platte River Valley of Nebraska, preferred nest sites were in heavily grazed or mowed native grasslands (Faanes and Lingle 1995). Optimal breeding habitat in portions of Colorado, Montana, Nebraska, North Dakota, South Dakota, and Wyoming occurred in heavily grazed areas with aridic ustoll soils and grazed areas with typic boroll soils (Kantrud and Kologiski 1982).

Burning—Little information exists on the response of Burrowing Owls to burning. In nc. Oregon, they were observed nesting in badger excavations in areas that recently had been burned, suggesting that fire may create suitable habitat by reducing vegetation around potential nest sites (Green and Anthony 1989). In nw. North Dakota, post-European settlement fire suppression may be responsible for the development of a taller, denser, and woodier plant community than previously existed (Murphy 1993), and these vegetational shifts may have been responsible for the local extirpation of Burrowing Owls.

Mowing—In nc. Colorado, mowing has been used to control growth of grasses and woody vegetation in areas where black-tailed prairie dogs have been eliminated. Abandoned black-tailed prairie dog colonies that were not mowed were not used by owls (Plumpton 1992). Mowing also may enhance the attractiveness of nest sites for Burrowing Owls returning from the wintering grounds (Plumpton and Lutz 1993). Mowing throughout the breeding season apparently does not adversely affect nesting Burrowing Owls (Dechant et al. 1999).

Habitat: Winter

Threats to Burrowing Owl wintering habitats are largely the same as those to Burrowing Owl breeding habitats; however, documentation and research addressing these threats is much more limited for wintering habitats. VerCauteren et al. (*In review*) reported poisoning of prairie dogs, urban development, and agriculture as the primary threats to prairie dogs and Burrowing Owl habitat in winter. Approximately 50% of the prairie dog colonies resurveyed by VerCauteren et al. (*In review*) were extant, although many of the remaining towns were greatly fragmented.

Overutilization for Commercial, Recreational, Scientific, or Educational Purposes

Not known to be a threat. Burrowing Owls have been trapped and sold in Mexico (G. Holroyd, pers. commun.), although the extent of this practice is unknown.

Predation and Disease

Predation—Cultivation and fragmentation of grassland habitat in Canada have allowed populations of predators that prey on Burrowing Owls to increase (Wellicome and Haug 1995). Burrowing Owls are usually tolerant of human activity but vulnerable to predation by dogs and cats. In Minnesota, high predation rates played a role in the failure of four years of reintroduction efforts (Martell et al. 2001). On Santa Barbara Island, California, a small population of Burrowing Owls (approx. 20) were extirpated by Barn Owls in 1984 and again in 1987 following crashes in the deer mouse population (Drost and McCluskey 1992).

Disease—Not known to be a direct threat (see *Indirect Effects of Disease*, below).

Inadequacy of Existing Regulatory Mechanisms

Burrowing Owls are protected by the Migratory Bird Treaty Act (1918) in the United States and Mexico, which makes it illegal to take, possess, buy, sell, purchase, or barter any migratory bird listed in 50 C.F.R., Part 10. In the United States, the Burrowing Owl was listed as an ESA Category 2 Candidate species until February 1996, when the Category 2 designation was discontinued. Burrowing Owls are listed as Endangered in Canada and as Threatened in Mexico.

Other Natural or Manmade Factors

Disturbance at Nest and Roost Sites—Not known to be a threat.

Ingestion of Plastics, Lead, Etc.—Not known to be a threat.

Collisions with Stationary/Moving Structures—Little information. No Burrowing Owl mortality due to collisions with communication towers was documented (Shire et al. 2000). Burrowing Owls may be susceptible to collisions with vehicles because Burrowing Owls often fly low to the ground. Collisions with vehicles have been cited as a significant source of mortality by several researchers (Haug et al. 1993). Military aircraft have been involved with strikes to Burrowing Owls in e. New Mexico (W. Howe, pers. commun.). Gillihan (2000) documented a Burrowing Owl killed by a collision with a barbed wire fence.

Shooting, Trapping, and Hunting—Illegal shooting may be responsible for substantial mortality in some areas, accounting for 10 of 15 deaths in Oklahoma (Butts 1973). Other studies, however, have not mentioned shooting as a source of mortality (Coulombe 1971, Thomsen 1971, Martin 1973).

Population Size and Isolation—Johnson (1997) reported that a population of Burrowing Owls in California showed a higher genetic similarity than did a collection of geographically separated Burrowing Owl populations. This suggested that some potentially detrimental inbreeding was occurring in the population (Johnson 1997). However, Korfanta (2001) found that populations of Burrowing Owls were genetically indistinguishable, suggesting a high degree of population connectivity and dispersal among populations.

Introduced Species—Not known to be a threat.

Indirect Effects of Disease—Burrowing Owl populations can be negatively impacted, and even eliminated, by epizootics of sylvatic plague that affect prairie dog colonies and thus reduce available habitat for Burrowing Owls (Dechant et al. 1999).

Pesticides and Other Contaminants/Toxics

Based on a survey of biologists, eleven states and provinces reported pesticides as a potential factor in declines (James and Espie 1997). Use of insecticides and rodenticides in Burrowing Owl habitat can be especially detrimental. Pesticides not only reduce the food supply and the number of burrowing mammals, but these chemicals also may be toxic to Burrowing Owls (Ratcliff 1986, James and Fox 1987, James et al. 1990, Baril 1993, PMRA 1995, Hjertaas 1997a, Sheffield 1997b). Burrowing Owls have been reported to ingest poisoned rodents and to forage on the ground for insects in areas with poison grains also on the ground (Butts 1973, James et al. 1990). In s. Saskatchewan, owls in pastures treated with strychnine-coated grain weighed less than those in control pastures, suggesting a sublethal effect or a reduction in small-rodent prey (James et al. 1990). A breeding population in the Oklahoma Panhandle declined by 71% within one year after sodium fluoroacetate (1080) was applied to the prairie dog colony with nesting owls (Butts 1973). Burrows occasionally are fumigated and sealed in the course of rodent-control programs (Butts 1973). Anti-coagulant rodenticides (e.g., brodifacoum and other second generation [or super-warfarin] compounds) and other types of rodenticides (e.g., strychnine) have been shown to cause mortality in many different owl species, with the ingestion of as few as one poisoned prey item (Sheffield 1997b). Burrowing Owls located in proximity to strychnine-coated grain used to control Richardson's ground squirrels were found to have significantly decreased adult body mass and slightly decreased breeding success as compared to control owls (James et al. 1990). Burrowing Owls are known to scavenge dead rodents and other prey items on occasion, making them highly susceptible to secondary poisoning by insecticides and rodenticides (Sheffield 1997b).

There have been few studies examining exposure and effects of insecticides on Burrowing Owls; however, available evidence indicates that anti-cholinesterase insecticides can negatively impact Burrowing Owl populations (Sheffield 1997a, b). In Saskatchewan, reproductive output of Burrowing Owls was not diminished significantly by one or more exposures to carbaryl within 50 or 400 m of the nest burrow; however, spraying of carbofuran within 50 m of the nest burrow caused a 54% reduction in the number of young per nest (James and Fox 1987). When both carbaryl and carbofuran were sprayed within 400 m of the nest, productivity of pairs decreased about 35% more than when carbaryl alone was applied. Direct overspray of carbofuran to the nest burrow resulted in an 83% reduction in brood size and an 82% reduction in nesting success (James and Fox 1987, Fox et al. 1989). Carbofuran application within 50 m of the nest burrow, without direct overspray, resulted in a 17% reduction in brood size and a 27% reduction in nesting success compared with burrows exposed to carbaryl or chloropyrifos. Use of granular formulations of carbofuran is restricted in the United States and Canada (PMRA 1995; L. Cole and P. Mineau, pers. commun.), as is most of its liquid formulations in Canada (PMRA 1995). Liquid carbofuran is still registered for several uses in the United States, and of particular danger to the Burrowing Owls are uses of this chemical in corn and alfalfa fields (Dechant et al. 1999).

Burrowing owl populations in California were sampled for contaminants in the spring of 1996 in the San Joaquin Valley (Lemoore Naval Air Station [NAS]), the Imperial Valley (Sonny Bono Salton Sea National Wildlife Refuge [Salton Sea NWR]), and Carrizo Plain Natural Area (Gervais et al. 2000). Sites were representative of the general agricultural practices in the region; the Carrizo Plain site was a large native grassland. Eggs, blood, feather, and footwash samples were collected from Lemoore NAS and Carrizo Plain, and eggs were collected from Salton Sea NWR. Eggshells from 45 owl nests collected prior to 1937 were obtained from the Western Foundation of Vertebrate Zoology and measured. Eggshell thickness declined 20.58% from Burrowing Owl eggs collected prior to 1937 compared to those collected in 1996. In addition, the eggs from Lemoore NAS were significantly thinner than those from the Salton Sea NWR or Carrizo Plain and contained high concentrations of DDE, ranging from 1.5 to 33 ppm wet weight. Carrizo Plain and Salton Sea NWR eggs contained up to 0.38 and 3.4 ppm DDE, respectively. Feathers from owls nesting at Lemoore NAS also contained levels of DDE, suggesting recent and local exposure. Two Lemoore eggs also contained PCB. Selenium concentrations in eggs were at low concentrations typical of uncontaminated eggs. Footwash samples indicated exposure to the organophosphorus pesticide chlorpyrifos at Lemoore NAS, although no exposure was reported within 1 km of the Burrowing Owl burrows in the months prior to sampling (Gervais et al. 2000). Despite the fact that DDT was banned in 1972, its degradation product DDE clearly remains a threat to wildlife within the San Joaquin Valley. Contaminant loads in these owls also may make them more susceptible to other unrelated stresses, such as weather or exposure to other toxicants (e.g., dicofol), that have similar estrogenic effects as well as thinning effects on eggshells (Gervais et al. 2000).

Recommendation on Current Conservation Status

Data for Western Burrowing Owls in most of the U.S. are insufficient to estimate trends in abundance. Limited data suggest that they are decreasing in some areas, but may be stable or increasing in others. Overall, BBS data (which are reasonably reliable when sample size is adequate) suggest a long-term decline (-1.5%/yr for the U.S.), but this estimate is not statistically significant; the 95% confidence interval for the trend estimate is between –6.5%/yr and +3.6%/yr. Western Burrowing Owls have experienced significant population declines at the northern, western, and eastern fringes of their range, including some local extirpations; however, they continue to occupy the majority of their historical range. Primary threats are habitat loss due to anthropogenic activities, reductions in abundances of burrowing mammals, and contaminants.

Currently, the Western Burrowing Owl is listed by the USFWS as a Bird of Conservation Concern-2002 in most of the BCR's in which it occurs, in every USFWS Region where it occurs, and on the National list (U.S. Fish & Wildlife Service 2002). This designation is intended to stimulate collaborative, proactive conservation actions among public and private land managers and others. Recommended conservation measures include efforts to monitor their demographics and trends more precisely, and to understand the factors affecting their populations during migration and winter. Conservation efforts should focus on protection of suitable habitats in desert, grassland, and shrub-steppe environments. Additional conservation efforts should focus on determining the status of Burrowing Owls in Mexico and on reversing the declines and local extirpations in the Great Plains and Canada. The conservation of burrowing mammals is essential to improve the status of Burrowing Owls, and the listing of the black-tailed prairie dog as a Candidate species should assist in the conservation of both species.

The Migratory Bird Management program of the USFWS recommends retaining the Western Burrowing Owl on the BCC lists on which it currently appears. The listing of the Burrowing Owl as a Bird of Conservation Concern highlights its potential vulnerability and need for increased monitoring and conservation attention by multiple Federal and State agencies and private organizations. The success of these efforts will be reviewed as the Birds of Conservation Concern list is revised.

Management and Conservation

Habitat

Habitat Features—Large, contiguous areas of treeless, native grasslands should be maintained (Warnock 1997, Warnock and James 1997, Clayton and Schmutz 1999). However, because Burrowing Owls forage over tall grass and nest and roost in short grass, a mosaic of grassland habitats are important and a patchwork of reserves with sustainable land uses in nesting and buffer areas is recommended (Clayton and Schmutz 1999). Standardized mitigation protocols to minimize impacts from developments and disturbances should be developed (Holroyd et al. 2001). Government programs and policies that impact Burrowing Owl habitat should be reviewed to ensure that land-use changes have positive effects on Burrowing Owl populations and habitats. Furthermore, management plans for public lands should include issues relative to the conservation of Burrowing Owls, fossorial mammals, and their associated habitats (Holroyd et al. 2001).

The following management recommendations are from the Columbia Basin in Oregon (Green and Anthony 1997): (1) Provide elevated perches near potential nest burrows in grassland areas if the average vegetation height is 5-15 cm; (2) Provide fresh cattle dung near nesting areas if dung is not available and mammalian predators, especially badgers, occur in the area. Burrowing Owls use shredded manure to line their nests and burrow entrances, possibly to mask nest odors as a predator-avoidance strategy (Haug et al. 1993, Dechant et al. 1999). In nc. Oregon, 72% of 32 successful nests were lined with manure, whereas only 13% (n = 15) of depredated nests were lined with manure; (3) Place artificial nest boxes no closer together than 110 m; (4) Construct boxes with width and length dimensions of at least 36 cm and place soil around the inside wall; or construct boxes with only three walls, with a funnel-shaped tunnel entrance; and (5) Select sites for establishing or increasing nest sites that have approximately 55% (40-70%) bare ground and average shrub coverage of <15%.

Fire—Fire may create suitable habitat by reducing vegetation around potential nest sites (Green and Anthony 1989). Post-settlement fire suppression may be responsible for the development of a taller, denser, and woodier plant community than previously existed in North Dakota (Murphy 1993).

Mowing—To encourage Burrowing Owl use in areas where black-tailed prairie dogs and other grazers have been eliminated, mowing may be used to control growth of grasses and woody vegetation. Abandoned black-tailed prairie dog colonies that were not mowed were not used by owls (Plumpton 1992). Mowing also may enhance the attractiveness of nest sites for Burrowing Owls returning from the wintering grounds (Plumpton and Lutz 1993). Mowing throughout the breeding season in mid- to late summer apparently does not adversely affect nesting Burrowing Owls (T. Wellicome, pers. commun.). Mowing can maintain abandoned prairie dog colonies at an early successional stage, with short (<8 cm) vegetation (Plumpton 1992, Plumpton and Lutz 1993). Mowing abandoned colonies may be effective in the short term; however, burrows may require maintenance by prairie dogs to remain suitable for Burrowing Owls (MacCracken et al. 1985, Desmond and Savidge 1999).

Grazing—Livestock grazing may be used to maintain abandoned prairie dog colonies where native burrowing mammals have been eliminated. Heavy grazing on saline, gravelly, stony, or sandy areas and moderate to intense grazing on fertile soils could create suitable habitat that otherwise would support tall vegetation (Wedgwood 1976). However, the effect of grazing on Burrowing Owl habitat and populations is unknown.

Burrowing Mammals

Conservation of those species of burrowing mammals that form Burrowing Owl nest sites is essential for maintaining populations of Burrowing Owls. Some populations of black-tailed prairie dogs are in danger of local extirpation, and their colonies may have become so isolated that re-population through natural dispersal and colonization is unlikely (Benedict et al. 1996). Fragmentation and isolation of habitat patches are potentially important factors in the decline of black-tailed prairie dog populations (Dechant et al. 1999). Burrows may require maintenance by prairie dogs in order to ensure their long-term suitability for owls and it may be necessary to release prairie dogs into inactive colonies (MacCracken et al. 1985, Desmond et al. 2000). Holroyd et al. (2001) suggested the expansion of prairie dog colonies on public lands, and the development of economic incentives to make it profitable to maintain prairie dog populations on private lands.

Regulation of poisoning and shooting of prairie dogs, particularly on public lands, may be necessary (Benedict et al. 1996, Toombs 1997). If lethal control of burrowing mammals is necessary, restricting the timing of control activities to avoid the period when Burrowing Owls choose nest sites or are nesting is recommended (Butts 1973). Traps, poisoned meat, or poisoned grain should not be used for rodent control, but rather burrows unoccupied by owls should be fumigated (Butts 1973, Thomson 1988). However, fumigation may have negative impacts on other burrow dependent species. The area of prairie dog colonies should be increased, possibly by reintroducing prairie dogs where they have been eliminated or by releasing additional prairie dogs into active colonies to promote colony expansion (Pezzolesi 1994, Toombs 1997). It is particularly important to protect colonies ≥ 35 ha in area, which provide adequate space for nesting Burrowing Owls (Desmond et al. 1995, Dechant et al. 1999).

Reintroduction and Relocation

Reintroduction—Reintroduction programs have been attempted in British Columbia, Manitoba, Minnesota, and Oklahoma with no success. In British Columbia, an ongoing captive breeding program reared and released over 140 Burrowing Owls between 1992 and 1998. Released birds have raised broods, overwintered at release sites, and migrated south in winter, but few have returned to the release site in spring (Leupin and Low 2001, Munro et al. 1984). In Manitoba, reintroductions between 1986 and 1996 used a variety of methods, including the aid of aviaries and artificial burrows, but resulted in low reproduction and poor return rates and reintroductions were discontinued (De Smet 1997). In Minnesota, 105 juveniles were released in a reintroduction program over four years, but no successful breeding occurred and the program was discontinued (Haug et al. 1993, Martell et al. 2001). Holroyd et al. (2001) recommended a review of Burrowing Owl reintroduction techniques and development of new techniques due to failure of previously used methods.

Relocations and Artificial Burrows—Relocations are those in which Burrowing Owls are evicted from their occupied burrows and artificial burrows are constructed as near to the eviction burrows as possible to provide acceptable unoccupied burrows for their use. Ninety percent (n = 6) of artificial burrows in California were immediately occupied and these burrows supported successfully breeding birds for three consecutive years (Trulio 1995). Artificial burrows were used when they were approximately 50-100 m from the burrow (Thomsen 1971, Haug and Oliphant 1990). Artificial burrows more than 100 m from the eviction burrow may greatly reduce the chances that new burrows will be used.

The rates of survival and reproduction of Burrowing Owls relocated to artificial burrows as well as the long-term use of artificial burrows and the ability of these burrows to maintain populations are unknown. The design and installation of artificial nest burrows should be summarized and the conservation value of this practice determined (Holroyd et al. 2001). Follow-up research needs to be conducted to determine the breeding success of relocated Burrowing Owls (Holroyd et al. 2001).

Pesticide Use

If insect control is necessary, insecticides with the lowest toxicity to nontarget organisms should be used (James and Fox 1987, Fox et al. 1989). Municipal governments and agricultural representatives should be encouraged to reduce or restrict the use of pesticides, and to use pesticides of low toxicity to nontarget species (Thomson 1988). Pesticides should not be sprayed within 400-600 m of Burrowing Owl nest burrows during the breeding season (Haug 1985, Haug and Oliphant 1990, James and Fox 1987). The possible negative effects of pesticides on Burrowing Owl populations should be considered on breeding and wintering grounds (Holroyd et al. 2001).

Monitoring

A standardized, range-wide survey for Burrowing Owls should be developed and implemented. Potential survey protocols should be tested to ensure the quantitative validity of the methodology (Holroyd et al. 2001). Most current monitoring programs have problems due to limited coverage or sample size (see Monitoring Activities, above). A standardized range-wide roadside survey using call playback has been recommended. This method was 80% effective at detecting Burrowing Owls using a 15 minute period (five minutes listening, five minutes call playback, five minutes listening periods), in early morning and in the early breeding season (Duxbury and Holroyd 1998). The use of recorded calls can significantly increase Burrowing Owl detections, particularly males (Haug and Didiuk 1993). Both historical sites and areas previously unoccupied by owls should be monitored. Because of low nest reoccupancy rates for Burrowing Owls, long-term monitoring of abundance should not be based solely on surveys of historical breeding sites (Lehman et al. 1998).

Migration

Little information is available. Research projects conducted by Saskatchewan Environment and Resource Management and the Canadian Wildlife Service have attempted to relocate radio-transmittered Burrowing Owl on their wintering grounds. Burrowing Owls marked during the breeding season in Canada (Saskatchewan and Alberta) have been relocated in s. Texas and c. Mexico (Veracruz and Michoacan states). Tagged Burrowing Owls were capable of migrating 200 km per night, taking at least 2-3 weeks to move from breeding to wintering grounds. It is estimated that Burrowing Owls take 6-8 weeks to move from wintering to breeding grounds (http://www.serm.gov.sk.ca/ecosystem/speciesatrisk/ burrowingowl.htm, http://members.aol.com/ joemoell/owl2.html, G. Holroyd, pers. commun.).

Wintering Areas

Very little information is available. Although the general wintering range of Burrowing Owls is known, very little is known about habitats used during the winter (Holroyd et al. 2001). Conservation of Burrowing Owls may depend on acquiring knowledge about the wintering areas and about movement patterns, timing, and ecology during migration and winter. Very few studies have been carried out in Mexico, Central America, or South America. The rapid population decline in Canadian provinces, despite apparent availability of suitable habitat, suggests unknown factors in winter and migration may be affecting survival or return rates (Schmutz 1997).

Education

Private landowners and the general public should be educated about the status of Burrowing Owls, the benefits of protecting habitat for the species and for burrowing mammals, and the negative effects of insecticides (Butts 1973, James and Fox 1987, Thomson 1988, Hjertaas 1993, Dechant et al. 1999, Holroyd et al. 2001). Stewardship of Burrowing Owls and their habitat should be encouraged on public land in the United States, Canada, and Mexico (Holroyd et al. 2001). An educational program should be developed for schools and outdoor education programs, and the media should be included in these activities (Thomson 1988, Holroyd et al. 2001). A project to improve the public image of prairie dogs should be undertaken (Benedict et al. 1996, Holroyd et al. 2001). Operation Burrowing Owl (a private stewardship program in Canada) has been extremely successful at obtaining landowner cooperation in conservation efforts, and has provided valuable population trend data for Burrowing Owls in Canada (Hjertaas 1997b). RMBO and Hawks Aloft, Inc. have also developed successful education and public participation programs.

Current Activities and Programs

United States—In California, the Burrowing Owl Consortium, an *ad hoc* group of biologists and advocates, meets two times a year. The Consortium members inform each other and the public of important issues related to the species, and subcommittees of the Consortium undertake projects designed to help the species (L. Trulio, pers. commun.). The California Burrowing Owl Consortium prepared the *Burrowing Owl Survey Protocol and Mitigation Guidelines* in 1993 to provide more consistent treatment of impacts to Burrowing Owls during development projects. This document was submitted to the California Department of Fish and Game and became the basis of their 1995 *Staff Report on Burrowing Owl Mitigation* (California Department of Fish and Game, unpubl. report).

RMBO manages "Prairie Partners", a program that requests voluntary cooperation from private landowners to conserve shortgrass prairie birds and their habitat through effective stewardship (Hutchings et al. 1999). In 1999, "Prairie Partners" documented 468 Burrowing Owl locations (79.3% on public land). Information is provided to landowners about shortgrass prairie conservation and Burrowing Owl natural history. The program also provides information about landowner attitudes toward Burrowing Owls and prairie dogs.

RMBO also published "Sharing Your Land with Shortgrass Prairie Birds" (Gillihan et al. 2001) which includes a section on Burrowing Owl identification, natural history, and habitat requirements and a booklet focusing on grasslands and grassland birds for elementary and secondary classroom use (Hutchings et al. 1999). These materials are being distributed to landowners, managers, and schools.

The New Mexico Burrowing Owl Working Group (NMBOWG) was formed in response to population declines at some sites in New Mexico (Hawks Aloft, Inc. 2002). The NMBOWG is an volunteer, collaborative effort of non-profit organizations, government agencies, private enterprises and individuals. The working group attempts to encourage communication, support research, and facilitate improved Burrowing Owl sighting accuracy and reporting. The NMBOWG currently supports on-going research projects at four sites: Holloman and Kirtland Air Force Bases, New Mexico State University, and the Turner Ranch. The NMBOWG has initiated a volunteer monitoring system to collect data on Burrowing Owl populations in the state (C. Finley, pers. commun., Hawks Aloft, Inc. 2002).

Canada—Operation Burrowing Owl is a program designed to address declines of Burrowing Owls in Saskatchewan and Alberta. Activities include increasing public awareness, placing nest boxes, encouraging voluntary land protection, and providing monetary incentives to landowners to protect nesting habitat and avoid pesticide use around nest sites (Hjertaas 1997*b*). As of 1993, several hundred landowners were enrolled in the project and were protecting over 20,000 ha of breeding habitat, which supported several hundred breeding pairs (Dundas and Jensen 1994/95).

Through the Critical Wildlife Habitat Program, Threatened Grassland Birds Project in Manitoba, nearly 3,500 ha of critical habitat have been leased or voluntarily protected for Burrowing Owls and other grassland species, and over 300 artificial nest burrows have been installed (Dundas and Jensen 1994/95).

The Canadian Burrowing Owl Recovery Team was formed in 1989 to coordinate and promote research and conservation activities to prevent the decline of this species in Canada. This team meets annually to review information and to develop and implement recovery plans. The British Columbia recovery team has attempted to reintroduce Burrowing Owls into that province for over a decade. In Alberta, a provincial recovery team was formed in 2001 to develop and implement a provincial action plan. Several organizations conduct public education programs to increase awareness of Burrowing Owl conservation issues. The Saskatchewan Burrowing Owl Interpretive Centre in Moose Jaw was specifically established to promote awareness of Burrowing Owl conservation both to visitors and through extensive school extension programs. The Alberta Fish and Game Association through their Operation Grassland Community delivers similar programs in the province. The Canadian Species at Risk Habitat Stewardship Program funds non-government partners to deliver habitat stewardship projects in all four western provinces which benefit Burrowing Owls, their habitats and other prairie wildlife. (G. Holroyd, pers. commun.).

Research Needs

Coordinated, range-wide research on population demographics needs to be conducted to determine causes of populations declines (Holroyd and Wellicome 1997, Holroyd et al. 2001). Metapopulation dynamics, influence of landscape patterns, and the effects of fragmentation and isolation on populations are not well understood. Basic distribution data and factors affecting survival during migration and on wintering grounds are poorly known and may be important in determining causes of population declines (Holroyd et al. 2001). A standardized survey to monitor population trends in Canada, the U.S., and Mexico is recommended as many population estimates are simply based on "best guesses" and current large-scale monitoring programs are largely inadequate (Holroyd et al. 2001).

Management strategies currently in use need to be evaluated for their effectiveness and the resulting information made easily available to managers. Further investigations also are needed on land use impacts, prescribed fire, grazing, mowing, habitat enhancements (e.g., artificial burrows and perches), relocation and reintroduction, and impact of predators on nest success (Millsap et al. 1997, Sheffield 1997a, Holroyd et al. 2001). Rates of habitat conversion and degradation (e.g., agricultural conversion or decline in burrowing mammal colonies) are rarely reported and more work is needed to determine rate and extent of habitat loss (James and Espie 1997). Modeling of Burrowing Owl habitat selection has been suggested to better understand the role of anthropogenic factors in population declines (Holroyd et al. 2001).

Although some research exists on carbofuran, studies of many other pesticides are also needed (James and Espie 1997, Holroyd et al. 2001). Indirect and sublethal effects of pesticides are largely unknown. The extent of mortality and vulnerability to shooting, particularly during prairie dog and ground squirrel control, is generally unknown.

Some education programs have already been successfully developed and implemented. However, additional research is needed to determine landowner and land manager attitudes to Burrowing Owls and burrowing mammals and to determine best methods for improving attitudes and conservation efforts on private and public lands.

Literature Cited

An extensive bibliography of articles pertaining to the Burrowing Owl was compiled by L. Ayers. The bibliography is available on the internet at the following address: http://uwadmnweb.uwyo.edu/fish_wild/buow/citations.html

American Ornithologists' Union. 1998. Check-list of North American Birds. Seventh Edition. American Ornithologists' Union, Washington, DC.

Arrowood, P. C., C. A. Finley, and B. C. Thompson. 2001. Analyses of Burrowing Owl populations in New Mexico. Journal of Raptor Research 35:362-370.

Baril, A. 1993. Pesticides and wildlife in the prairies: current regulatory issues. Pages 44-48 *in* G. L. Holroyd, H. L. Dickson, M. Regnier, and H. C. Smith, editors. Proceedings of the third endangered species and prairie conservation workshop. Natural History Occasional Paper 19. Provincial Museum of Alberta, Edmonton, Alberta, Canada.

Belthoff, J. R. and B. A. King. 1997. Between-year movements and nest burrow use by Burrowing Owls in southwestern Idaho. Technical Bulletin No. 97-3, Idaho Bureau of Land Management.

Benedict, R. A., P. W. Freeman, and H. H. Genoways. 1996. Prairie legacies—mammals. Pages 149-167 *in* F. B. Samson and F. L. Knopf, editors. Prairie conservation: preserving North America's most endangered ecosystem. Island Press, Covelo, California.

Bock, C. E., V. A. Saab, T. D. Rich, and D. S. Dobkin. 1993. Effects of livestock grazing on Neotropical migratory landbirds in western North America. Pages 296-309 *in* D. M. Finch and P. W. Stangel, editors. Status and management of Neotropical migratory birds. U.S.D.A. Forest Service, General Technical Report RM-229.

Botelho, E. S., and P. C. Arrowood. 1996. Nesting success of western Burrowing Owls in natural and human-altered environments. Pages 61-68 *in* D. Bird, D. Varland, and J. Negro, editors. Raptors in human landscapes: Adaptation to Built and Cultivated Environments. Academic Press, Inc.

Brown, N. L. 2001. The howdy owls of Arizona: a review of the status of *Athene cunicularia*. Journal of Raptor Research 35:344-350.

Butts, K. O. 1973. Life history and habitat requirements of Burrowing Owls in western Oklahoma. M.S. Thesis. Oklahoma State University, Stillwater, Oklahoma.

Butts, K. O., and J. C. Lewis. 1982. The importance of prairie dog towns to Burrowing Owls in Oklahoma. Proceedings of the Oklahoma Academy of Science 62:46-52.

Clark, R. J., J. L. Lincer, and J. S. Clark. 1997. Appendix A: a bibliography on the Burrowing Owl (*Speotyto cunicularia*). Pages 145-170 *in* J. Lincer and K. Steenhof, editors. The Burrowing Owl, its biology and management including the proceedings of the First International Burrowing Owl Symposium. Raptor Research Report Number 9.

Clayton, K. M. 1997. Post-fledging ecology of Burrowing Owls in Alberta and Saskatchewan: dispersal, survival, habitat use, and diet. M.S. Thesis. University of Saskatchewan, Saskatoon, Saskatchewan, Canada.

Clayton, K. M., and J. F. Schmutz. 1997. Burrowing Owl (*Speotyto cunicularia*) survival in prairie Canada. Pages 107-110 *in* J. R. Duncan, D. H. Johnson, and T. H. Nicholls, editors. Biology and conservation of owls of the Northern Hemisphere. U.S.D.A. Forest Service, General Technical Report NC-190. North Central Forest Experiment Station, St. Paul, Minnesota.

Clayton, K. M., and J. K. Schmutz. 1999. Is the decline of Burrowing Owls *Speotyto cunicularia* in prairie Canada linked to changes in Great Plains ecosystems? Bird Conservation International 9:163-185.

Coulombe, H. N. 1971. Behavior and population ecology of the Burrowing Owl, *Speotyto cunicularia*, in the Imperial Valley of California. Condor 73:162-176.

De Smet, K. D. 1997. Burrowing Owl (*Speotyto cunicularia*) monitoring and management activities in Manitoba, 1987-1996. Pages 123-130 *in* J. R. Duncan, D. H. Johnson, and T. H. Nicholls, editors. Biology and conservation of owls of the Northern Hemisphere: Second International Symposium. U.S.D.A., Forest Service General Technical Report NC-190, North Central Forest Experiment Station, St. Paul, Minnesota.

Dechant, J. A., M. L. Sondreal, D. H. Johnson, L. D. Igl, C. M. Goldade, P. A. Rabie, and B. R. Euliss. 1999. Effects of management practices on grassland birds: Burrowing Owl. Northern Prairie Wildlife Research Center, Jamestown, North Dakota. Northern Prairie Wildlife Research Center Home Page. http://www.npwrc.usgs.gov/resource/literatr/grasbird/buow/buow.htm

DeSante, D.F. and E. Ruhlen. 1995. A census of Burrowing Owls in California, 1991-1993. Institute for Bird Populations, Point Reyes Station, California.

DeSante, D. F., E. D. Ruhlen, S. L. Adamany, K. M. Butron, and S. Amin. 1997. A census of Burrowing Owls in central California in 1991. Pages 38-48 *in* J. Lincer and K. Steenhof, editors. The Burrowing Owl, its biology and management including the proceedings of the First International Burrowing Owl Symposium. Raptor Research Report Number 9.

Desmond, M. J. 1991. Ecological aspects of Burrowing Owl nesting strategies in the Nebraska panhandle. M.S. Thesis. University of Nebraska, Lincoln, Nebraska.

Desmond, M. J., and J. A. Savidge. 1996. Factors influencing Burrowing Owl (*Speotyto cunicularia*) nest densities and numbers in western Nebraska. American Midland Naturalist 136:143-148.

Desmond, M. J., and J. A. Savidge. 1998. Burrowing Owl conservation in the Great Plains. Page 9 *in* Abstracts of the Second International Burrowing Owl Symposium, Ogden, Utah.

Desmond, M. J., and J. A. Savidge. 1999. Satellite burrow use by Burrowing Owl chicks and its influence on nest fate. *In* P. D. Vickery and J. R. Herkert, editors. Ecology and conservation of grassland birds in the western hemisphere. Studies in Avian Biology 19.

Desmond, M. J., J. A. Savidge, and K. M. Eskridge. 2000. Correlations between Burrowing Owl and black-tailed prairie dog declines: a 7-year analysis. Journal of Wildlife Management 64:1067-1075.

Desmond, M. J., J. A. Savidge, and T. F. Seibert. 1995. Spatial patterns of Burrowing Owl (*Speotyto cunicularia*) nests within black-tailed prairie dog (*Cynomys ludovicianus*) towns. Canadian Journal of Zoology 73:1375-1379.

Drost, C. A., and R. C. McCluskey. 1992. Extirpation of alternative prey during a small rodent crash. Oecologia 92:301-304.

Dundas, H., and J. Jensen. 1994/95. Burrowing Owl status and conservation. Bird Trends 4:21-22.

Duxbury, J. M., and G. L. Holroyd. 1998. Testing a possible standardized, road-side survey technique for Burrowing Owls. Abstract and notes. Second International Burrowing Owl Symposium, Ogden, Utah.

Enriquez-Rocha, P. L. 1997. Seasonal Records of the Burrowing Owl in Mexico. 1997. Pages 49-51 *in* J. Lincer and K. Steenhof, editors. The Burrowing Owl, its biology and management including the Proceedings of the First International Burrowing Owl Symposium. Raptor Research Report Number 9.

Faanes, C. A., and G. R. Lingle. 1995. Breeding birds of the Platte River Valley of Nebraska. Northern Prairie Wildlife Research Center home page, Jamestown, North Dakota. http://www.npwrc.usgs.gov/resource/distr/birds/platte/platte.htm (Version 16JUL97).

Fox, G. A., P. Mineau, B. Collins, and P. C. James. 1989. The impact of the insecticide carbofuran (Furadan 480F) on the Burrowing Owl in Canada. Technical Report Series No. 72. Canadian Wildlife Service, Ottawa, Canada.

Gervais J. A., D. K. Rosenberg, D. M. Fry, L. J. Trulio, and K. K. Sturm. 2000. Burrowing owls and agricultural pesticides: evaluation of residues and risks for three populations in California, USA. Environmental Toxicology and Chemistry 19:337-343.

Gillihan, S. W. 2000. Barbed wire fence fatal to Burrowing Owl. Journal of the Colorado Field Ornithologists 34:220-221.

Gillihan, S. W., D. J. Hanni, S. W. Hutchings, T. Toombs, and T. VerCauteren. 2001. Sharing your land with shortgrass prairie birds. Unpublished Report. Rocky Mountain Bird Observatory, Brighton, Colorado.

Gleason, R. S. 1978. Aspects of the breeding biology of Burrowing Owls in southeastern Idaho. M.S. Thesis. University of Idaho, Moscow, Idaho.

Gleason, R. S., and D. R. Johnson. 1985. Factors influencing nesting success of Burrowing Owls in southeastern Idaho. Great Basin Naturalist 45:81-84.

Grant, R. A. 1965. The Burrowing Owl in Minnesota. Loon 37:2-17.

Green, G. A., and R. G. Anthony. 1989. Nesting success and habitat relationships of Burrowing Owls in the Columbia Basin, Oregon. Condor 91:347-354.

Green, G. A., and R. G. Anthony. 1997. Ecological considerations for management of breeding Burrowing Owls in the Columbia Basin. Pages 117-121 *in* J. Lincer and K. Steenhof, editors. The Burrowing Owl, its biology and management including the Proceedings of the First International Symposium. Raptor Research Report Number 9.

Hall, D. B., P. D. Greger, and A. V. Housewright. *In review.* Burrowing owl ecology on the Nevada Test Sites. DOE/NV/11718–701. U.D. Department of Energy, National Nuclear Security Administration Nevada Operations Office, Las Vegas, Nevada.

Hanni, D. J. 2001. Comparison of four methodologies used to monitor shortgrass prairie birds in eastern Colorado. Unpublished Report. Rocky Mountain Bird Observatory, Brighton, Colorado.

Haug, E. A. 1985. Observations on the breeding ecology of Burrowing Owls in Saskatchewan. M.S. Thesis. University of Saskatchewan, Saskatoon, Saskatchewan.

Haug, E. A., and A. B. Didiuk. 1991. Updated status report on the Burrowing Owl, *Athene cunicularia hypugaea*, in Canada. Committee on the Status of Endangered Wildlife in Canada.

Haug, E. A., and A. B. Didiuk. 1993. Use of recorded calls to detect Burrowing Owls. Journal of Field Ornithology 64:188-194.

Haug, E. A., and L. W. Oliphant. 1990. Movements, activity patterns, and habitat use of Burrowing Owls in Saskatchewan. Journal of Wildlife Management 54:27-35.

Haug, E. A., B. A. Millsap, and M. S. Martell. 1993. Burrowing Owl (*Speotyto cunicularia*). *In* A. Poole and F. Gill, editors. The birds of North America, No. 61. The Academy of Natural Sciences, Philadelphia, Pennsylvania; The American Ornithologists' Union, Washington, DC.

Hawks Aloft, Inc. 2002. New Mexico Burrowing Owl Working Group web page. http://www.hawksaloft.org/burrowingowl.html.

Hjertaas, D. 1993. The Burrowing Owl recovery program. Pages 350-352 *in* G. L. Holroyd, H. L. Dickson, M. Regnier, and H. C. Smith, editors. Proceedings of the Third Endangered Species and Prairie Conservation Workshop. Natural History Occasional Paper 19. Provincial Museum of Alberta, Edmonton, Alberta.

Hjertaas, D. G. 1997*a*. Recovery plan for the Burrowing Owl in Canada. Pages 107-111 *in* J. Lincer and K. Steenhof, editors. The Burrowing Owl, its biology and management including the Proceedings of the First International Burrowing Owl Symposium. Raptor Research Report Number 9.

Hjertaas, D. G. 1997*b*. Operation Burrowing Owl in Saskatchewan. Pages 112-116 *in* J. L. Lincer and K. Steenhof, editors. The Burrowing Owl, its biology and management including the Proceedings of the First International Burrowing Owl Symposium. Raptor Research Report Number 9.

Hjertaas, D., S. Brechtel, K. De Smet, O. Dyer, E. Haug, G. Holroyd, P. James, and J. Schmutz. 1995. National recovery plan for the Burrowing Owl. Report No. 13. Recovery of Nationally Endangered Wildlife Committee. Ottawa, Canada.

Holroyd., G. L., and T. I. Wellicome. 1997. Report on the Burrowing Owl (*Speotyto cunicularia*) conservation workshop. Pages 612-615 *in* J. R. Duncan, D. H. Johnson, and T. H. Nicholls, editors. Biology and conservation of owls of the Northern Hemisphere. U.S.D.A. Forest Service, General Technical Report NC-190. North Central Forest Experiment Station, St. Paul, Minnesota.

Holroyd, G. L., R. Rodriguez-Estrella, and S. R. Sheffield. 2001. Conservation of the Burrowing Owl in western North American: issues, challenges, and recommendations. Journal of Raptor Research 35:399-407.

Hughes, A. J. 1993. Breeding density and habitat preference of the Burrowing Owl in northeastern Colorado. M.S. Thesis. Colorado State University, Fort Collins, Colorado.

Hutchings, S., M. Carter, E. Atkinson, T. VerCauteren, C. Finley, S. Gillihan, and J. Nocedal. 1999. Prairie Partners: promoting stewardship of shortgrass prairie. Unpublished Report, Colorado Bird Observatory, Brighton, Colorado.

Illinois Natural History Information Network. 2000. Illinois birds: Burrowing Owl (*Athene cunicularia*). Illinois Natural History Survey webpage. Http://www.inhs.uiuc.edu/chf/pub/ifwis/birds/index.html (version August, 2000).

James, D. A., and J. C. Neal. 1986. Arkansas Birds: their distribution and abundance. University of Arkansas Press, Fayetteville, Arkansas.

James, P. C., and R. H. M. Espie. 1997. Current status of the Burrowing Owl in North America: an agency survey. Pages 3-5 *in* J. Lincer and K. Steenhof, editors. The Burrowing Owl, its biology and management including the Proceedings of the First International Burrowing Owl Symposium. Raptor Research Report Number 9.

James, P. C. and T. J. Ethier. 1989. Trends in the winter distribution and abundance of Burrowing Owls in North America. American Birds 43:1224-1225.

James, P. C., and G. A. Fox. 1987. Effects of some insecticides on productivity of Burrowing Owls. Blue Jay 45:65-71.

James, P. C., G A. Fox, and T. J. Ethier. 1990. Is the operational use of strychnine to control ground squirrels detrimental to Burrowing Owls? Journal of Raptor Research 24:120-123.

James, T. R., and R. W. Seabloom. 1968. Notes on the burrow ecology and food habits of the Burrowing Owl in southwestern North Dakota. Blue Jay 26:83-84.

Johnson, B. S. 1997. Demography and population dynamics of the Burrowing Owl. Pages 28-33 *in* J. Lincer and K. Steenhof, editors. The Burrowing Owl, its biology and management including the Proceedings of the First International Burrowing Owl Symposium. Raptor Research Report Number 9.

Kantrud, H. A. 1981. Grazing intensity effects on the breeding avifauna of North Dakota native grasslands. Canadian Field-Naturalist 95:404-417.

Kantrud, H. A., and R. L. Kologiski. 1982. Effects of soils and grazing on breeding birds of uncultivated upland grasslands of the northern Great Plains. U.S. Fish and Wildlife Service, Wildlife Research Report 15.

Kirk, D. A., D. Hussell, and E. Dunn. 1994/95. Raptor population status and trends in Canada. Bird Trends 4:2-9.

Konrad, P. M., and D. S. Gilmer. 1984. Observations on the nesting ecology of Burrowing Owls in central North Dakota. Prairie Naturalist 16:129-130.

Korfanta, N. M. 2001. Population genetics of migratory and resident Burrowing Owls (*Athene cunicularia*) elucidated by microsatellite DNA markers. M.S. Thesis. University of Wyoming, Laramie, WY.

Korfanta, N. M., L. W. Ayers, S. H. Anderson, and D. B. McDonald. 2001. A preliminary assessment of Burrowing Owl status in Wyoming. Journal of Raptor Research 35 :337-343.

Lehman, R. N., L. B. Carpenter, K. Steenhof, and M. N. Kochert. 1998. Assessing relative abundance and reproductive success of shrubsteppe raptors. Journal of Field Ornithology 69:244-256.

Leupin, E. E. and D. J. Low. 2001. Burrowing Owl reintroduction efforts in the Thompson-Nicola region of British Columbia. Journal of Raptor Research 35:392-398.

Lutz, R. S., and D. L. Plumpton. 1999. Philopatry and nest site reuse by Burrowing Owls: implications for productivity. Journal of Raptor Research 33:149-153.

MacCracken, J. G., D. W. Uresk, and R. M. Hansen. 1985. Vegetation and soils of Burrowing Owl nest sites in Conata Basin, South Dakota. Condor 87:152-154.

Martell, M., H. B. Tordoff, and P. T. Redig. 1994. The introduction of three native raptors into the Midwestern United States. Raptor Conservation Today: 465-470.

Martell, M. S., J. Schladweiler, and F. Cuthbert. 2001. Status and attempted reintroduction of Burrowing Owls in Minnesota, USA. Journal of Raptor Research 35:331-336.

Martin, D. J. 1973. Selected aspects of Burrowing Owl ecology and behavior. Condor 75:446-456.

Millsap, B. A. 1996. Florida Burrowing Owl. Pages 579-587 *in* J. A. Rodgers, Jr., H. W. Kale II, and H. T. Smith, editors. Rare and Endangered Biota of Florida, Vol V. Birds. University Press of Florida, Gainesville, Florida.

Millsap, B. A, M. I. Bellocq, and M. Mullenix. 1997. Overview of the literature on the Burrowing Owl. Pages 6-10 *in* J. Lincer and K. Steenhof, editors. The Burrowing Owl, its biology and management including the Proceedings of the First International Burrowing Owl Symposium. Raptor Research Report Number 9.

Munro, W. T., R. C. Lincoln, and R. W. Ritcey. 1984. Reestablishing Burrowing Owls—experiences in British Columbia. Proceedings of the Western Association of Fish and Wildlife Agencies 64:165-170.

Murphy, R. K. 1993. History, nesting biology, and predation ecology of raptors in the Missouri Coteau of northwestern North Dakota. Ph.D. dissertation. Montana State University, Bozeman, Montana.

Murphy, R. K., D. W. Hasselblad, C. D. Grondahl, J. G. Sidle, R. E. Martin, and D. W. Freed. 2001. Status of the Burrowing Owl in North Dakota. Journal of Raptor Research 35:322–330.

NatureServe Explorer: An Online Encyclopedia of Life. 2001. Version 1.6. Arlington, Virginia. Http://www.natureserve.org/explorer.

Pezzolesi, L. S. W. 1994. The western Burrowing Owl: increasing prairie dog abundance, foraging theory, and nest site fidelity. M.S. Thesis. Texas Tech University, Lubbock, Texas.

Plumpton, D. L. 1992. Aspects of nest site selection and habitat use by Burrowing Owls at the Rocky Mountain Arsenal, Colorado. M.S. Thesis. Texas Technical University, Lubbock, Texas.

Plumpton, D. L., and R. S. Lutz. 1993. Nesting habitat use by Burrowing Owls in Colorado. Journal of Raptor Research 27:175-179.

Pest Management Regulatory Agency (PMRA). 1995. Carbofuran. Decision Document E95-05. Pest Management Regulatory Agency, Health Canada, Ottawa, Ontario, Canada.

Ratcliff, B. D. 1986. The Manitoba Burrowing Owl survey, 1982-1984. Blue Jay 44:31-37.

Restani, M., L. R. Rau, and D. L. Flath. 2001. Nesting ecology of Burrowing Owls occupying prairie dog towns in southeastern Montana. Journal of Raptor Research 35:296-303.

Rich, T. 1984. Monitoring Burrowing Owl populations: implications of burrow re-use. Wildlife Society Bulletin 12:178-180.

Rich, T. 1986. Habitat and nest-site selection by Burrowing Owls in the sagebrush steppe of Idaho. Journal of Wildlife Management 50:548-555.

Rodriguez-Estrella, R., F. Chavez Ramirez, and G. L. Holroyd. 1998. Current knowledge of the Burrowing Owl in Mexico: what is needed for a conservation plan? Abstract and notes. Second International Burrowing Owl Symposium, Ogden, Utah.

Sauer, J. R., J. E. Hines, and J. Fallon. 2001. The North American Breeding Bird Survey Results and Analysis 1966-2000. Version 2001.2. U.S. Geological Survey, Patuxent Wildlife Research Center, Laurel, Maryland. http://www.mbr-pwrc.usgs.gov/bbs.

Sauer, J. R., J. E. Hines, and J. Fallon. 2002. The North American Breeding Bird Survey Results and Analysis 1966-2001. Version 2002.1. U.S. Geological Survey, Patuxent Wildlife Research Center, Laurel, Maryland. http://www.mbr-pwrc.usgs.gov/bbs/bbs2001.html.

Sauer, J. R., S. Schwartz, and B. Hoover. 1996. The Christmas Bird Count Home Page. Version 95.1 U.S. Geological Survey, Patuxent Wildlife Research Center, Laurel, Maryland. http://www.mbr.nbs.gov/bbs/cbc.html.

Schmutz, J. K. 1997. Selected microhabitat variables near nests of Burrowing Owls compared to unoccupied sites in Alberta. Pages 80-83 in J. Lincer and K. Steenhof, editors. The Burrowing Owl, its biology and management including the Proceedings of the First International Burrowing Owl Symposium. Raptor Research Report Number 9.

Scott, T. G. 1940. The Western Burrowing Owl in Clay County, Iowa, in 1938. American Midland Naturalist 24:585-593.

Sheffield, S. R. 1997a. Current status, distribution, and conservation of the Burrowing Owl (Speotyto cunicularia) in Midwestern North America. Pages 399-407 in J. R. Duncan, D. H. Johnson, and T. H. Nicholls, editors. Biology and conservation of owls of the Northern Hemisphere. U.S.D.A. Forest Service, General Technical Report NC-190. North Central Forest Experiment Station, St. Paul, Minnesota.

Sheffield, S. R. 1997b. Owls as biomonitors of environmental health hazards. Pages 383-398 in Biology and conservation of owls of the North Hemisphere. USDA Forest Service, General Technical Report NC-190.

Sheffield, S. R. and M. Howery. 2001. Current status, distribution, and conservation of the Burrowing Owl in Oklahoma. Journal of Raptor Research 35:351-356.

Shire, G. G., K. Brown, and G. Winegard. 2000. Communication towers: A deadly hazard to birds. American Bird Conservancy, Washington, DC.

Shyry, D. T., T. I. Wellicome, J. K. Schmutz, G. L. Erickson, D. L. Scobie, R. F. Russell, and R. G. Martin. 2001. Burrowing Owl population-trend surveys in southern Alberta: 1991-2000. Journal of Raptor Research 35:310-315.

Sidle, J. G., M. Ball, T. Byer, J. J. Chynoweth, G. Foli, R. Hodorff, G. Moravek, R. Peterson, and D. N. Svingen. 2001. Occurrence of Burrowing Owls in black-tailed prairie dog colonies on Great Plains National Grasslands. Journal of Raptor Research 35:316-321.

Sissons, R., K. Scalise, and T. I. Wellicome. 2001. Nocturnal foraging habitat use of the Burrowing Owl in a heavily cultivated region of southern Saskatchewan. Journal of Raptor Research 35:304–309.

Skeel, M. A., J. Keith, and C. S. Palaschuk. 2001. A population decline recorded by Operation Burrowing Owl in Saskatchewan. Journal of Raptor Research 35:371-377.

Thompson, C. D. 1984. Selected aspects of Burrowing Owl ecology in central Wyoming. M.S. Thesis. University of Wyoming, Laramie, Wyoming.

Thompson, C. D. and S. H. Anderson. 1988. Foraging behavior and food habits of Burrowing Owl in Wyoming. Prairie Naturalist 20:23-28.

Thomsen, L. 1971. Behavior and ecology of Burrowing Owls on the Oakland Municipal Airport. Condor 73:177-192.

Thomson, K. A. 1988. Management of Burrowing Owls in Manitoba, population distribution and plan for recovery. M.S. Thesis. Natural Resource Institute, University of Manitoba, Winnipeg, Manitoba.

Toombs, T. P. 1997. Burrowing Owl nest-site selection in relation to soil texture and prairie dog colony attributes. M.S. Thesis. Colorado State University, Fort Collins, Colorado.

Trulio, L. A. 1995. Passive relocation: a method to preserve Burrowing Owls on disturbed sites. Journal of Field Ornithology 66:99-106.

U.S. Fish & Wildlife Service. 2002. Birds of Conservation Concern. U.S. Department of the Interior, Fish and Wildlife Service, Administrative Report, Arlington, Virginia. http://migratorybirds.fws.gov/reports/bcc2002.pdf.

VerCauteren, T. L., S. W. Gillihan, and S. W. Hutchings. 2001. Distribution of Burrowing Owls on public and private lands in Colorado. Journal of Raptor Research 35:357-361.

VerCauteren, T. L., D. J. Hanni, and S. Hutchings. *In review*. Occurrence of Burrowing Owls on black-tailed prairie dog colonies in northern Mexico during the winter. Journal of Raptor Research.

Warnock, R. G. 1997. Spatial, temporal and turnover dynamics of Burrowing Owl (*Speotyto cunicularia*) distribution in the extensively fragmented grasslands of Saskatchewan. M.S. Thesis, University of Regina, Regina, Saskatchewan.

Warnock, R. G., and P. C. James. 1997. Habitat fragmentation and Burrowing Owls (*Speotyto cunicularia*) in Saskatchewan. *In* J. R. Duncan, D. H. Johnson, and T. H. Nicholls, editors. Biology and conservation of owls of the Northern Hemisphere: Second International Symposium. U.S.D.A., Forest Service General Technical Report NC-190, North Central Forest Experiment Station, St. Paul, Minnesota.

Wedgwood, J. A. 1976. Burrowing Owl in south-central Saskatchewan. Blue Jay 34:26-44.

Wedgwood, J. A., 1978. The status of the Burrowing Owl in Canada. Committee on the Status of Endangered Wildlife in Canada, Ottawa, Ontario.

Wedgwood, J. A. 1979. Status report on the Burrowing Owl, *Athene cunicularia*. Committee on the Status of Endangered Wildlife in Canada.

Wellicome, T. I. 1994. Taverner award recipient's report: Is reproduction in Burrowing Owls limited by food supply? Picoides 7:9-10.

Wellicome, T. I. 1997. Status of the Burrowing Owl (*Speotyto cunicularia hypugaea*) in Alberta. Wildlife Status Report No. 11. Alberta Environmental Protection, Wildlife Management Division, Edmonton, Alberta.

Wellicome, T. I., and E. A. Haug. 1995. Second update of status report on the Burrowing Owl (*Speotyto cunicularia*) in Canada. Committee on the Status of Endangered Wildlife in Canada, Canadian Wildlife Service, Environment Canada, Ottawa, Ontario.

Wellicome, T. I., and G. L. Holroyd. 2001. The Second International Burrowing Owl Symposium: background and context. Journal of Raptor Research 35:269-273.

Zarn, M. 1974. Habitat management series for unique or endangered species. U.S. Department of Interior, Bureau of Land Management, Technical Note T/N-250 (no. 11), Denver, Colorado.

Appendix A: State Summaries of Burrowing Owl Status

Arizona

Summary: Combining historical and recent records, Burrowing Owls have been documented (breeding and/or wintering) in 14 of 15 counties (all except Greenlee County, Fig. A-1) (Brown 2001). A family group was observed in the San Rafael Valley, Santa Cruz County in 2002 (J. Ruth, pers. commun.). Although not present in the early 1900's along the lower Colorado River, Burrowing Owls are now common there, suggesting that agriculture may have benefitted the species in that region (Rosenberg et al. 1991, Brown 2001). However, the vegetation maintenance regime of farming and water districts may cause these populations to remain unstable due to unreliable and temporary habitats (Brown 2001). Main concentrations in the Tucson area are located at Davis-Monthan Air Force Base (DMAFB) and along the west branch of the Santa Cruz River (Estabrook and Mannan 1998).

Statewide Burrowing Owls populations appear to be relatively stable to slightly decreasing (T. Corman, pers. commun.); however, no quantitative information has been gathered on Burrowing Owls since Phillips et al. (1964; Brown 2001). Some local populations are decreasing, especially in urban and agricultural areas, and some populations have been extirpated (Brown 2001).

Status determination in the sw. United States in 1979 and 1988 was precluded by insufficient information (Johnson et al. 1979, Johnson-Duncan et al. 1988). A preliminary review of Burrowing Owls in Arizona was conducted in 1998, through extensive literature reviews, questionnaires, requests for observations, and personal observations (Brown 2001). A formal status could not be given due to the lack of quantitative information on this species in Arizona. Through survey responses, state biologists estimated 100 to 1,000 pairs in 1992 (James and Espie 1997).

BBS: No significant trends were detected over any survey periods (Sauer et al. 2002).

CBC: No significant trend was detected over the survey period (Sauer et al. 1996).

Atlas: Based on preliminary information collected by the Arizona Breeding Bird Atlas (Arizona Breeding Bird Atlas, Unpubl. data, 1993-2001, C. Wise, pers. commun.), the overall breeding range in Arizona has not changed substantially in the 1990's. Burrowing Owls were reported in 78 (4%) of 1825 BBA blocks (Fig A-1, T. Corman, pers. commun).

Research/Monitoring: The Urban Raptor Nest Watch Program of the Arizona Game and Fish Department (c. Arizona) recorded six nests for the Phoenix Metro Area in 1994, three in 1995, and five or six in 1996 (F. Esparza, pers. commun.). Estabrook and Mannan's (1998) urban study found 77 active breeding burrows in the Tucson area in 1997; 28 of these were on DMAFB and the majority of the others were on the west branch of the Santa Cruz River. The number of active burrows appeared to remain stable year-round on DMAFB and fairly stable in the Santa Cruz River flood plain; the vegetation maintenance regime along the flood plain often destroys active burrows (Estabrook and Mannan 1998).

Conservation Activities: Artificial burrows have been placed in some urban areas of the greater Phoenix area (T. Corman, pers. commun.). Artificial burrows have also been constructed at Cibola National Wildlife Refuge along the Lower Colorado River.

Major Populations: A major population occurs at the Davis-Monthan Air Force Base and west branch Santa Cruz River flood plain near Tucson. Unconfirmed high numbers of Burrowing Owls have been reported along the irrigation canals around the Yuma area. Burrowing Owls have been reported from a variety of other areas throughout Arizona; however, no quantitative information has been documented other than in the Tucson region (Estabrook and Mannan 1998).

State Status: None

Natural Heritage Rank: G4/S3 (rare and uncommon in the state)

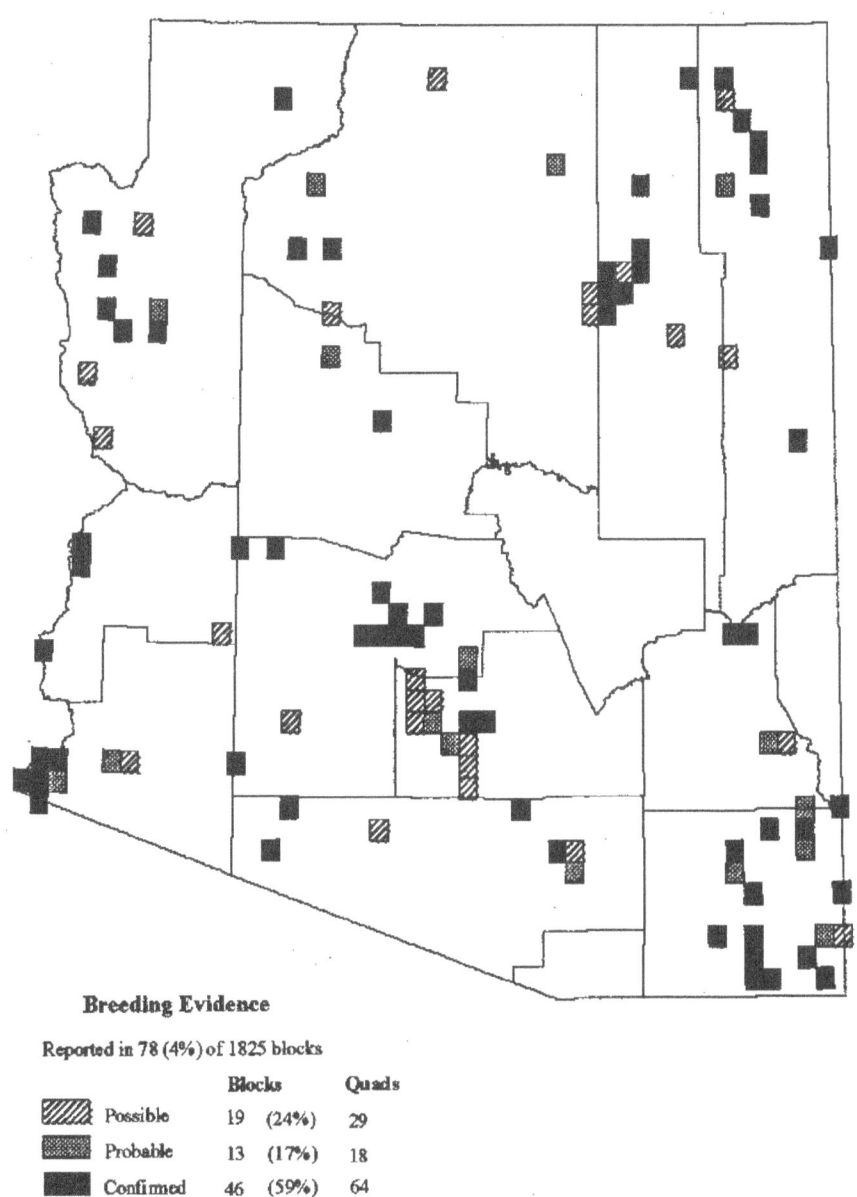

Breeding Evidence

Reported in 78 (4%) of 1825 blocks

		Blocks		Quads
//	Possible	19	(24%)	29
	Probable	13	(17%)	18
	Confirmed	46	(59%)	64

Fig. A-1. Distribution of the Burrowing Owl in Arizona from the Arizona Breeding Bird Atlas project (Arizona Breeding Bird Atlas, Unpubl. data (1993-2001), C. Wise, pers. commun.)

Habitat Condition: Arizona BBA activities located Burrowing Owls in the following habitat types: semi-desert grassland, plains grassland, cropland, Great Basin desert-scrub, lower Colorado River biome of the Sonoran Desert-scrub, barren ground, Great Basin grassland, Arizona upland biome of Sonoran Desert-scrub, Mojave Desert-scrub, rural, and residential (Brown 2001). From survey data, Brown (2001) indicated they also use parks (golf courses, cemeteries), cultivated woodlands (orchards, tree farms) and airports (including Air Force bases).

Burrowing Owls inhabit grass, forb, and open shrub stages of pinyon pine and ponderosa pine habitats (Carothers et al. 1973, Karlaus and Eckert 1974, Zenier et al. 1990). Other areas in Arizona where the owls might be found include washes, irrigation canals, near water tanks or corrals on rangelands, and in vacant lots, and other disturbed sites in urban and rural areas (Rosenberg et al. 1991, Witzeman 1997, deVos 1998, Brown 2001). Occasionally they are found in sandy, sparsely vegetated riparian woodlands in the Lower Colorado River Valley (Rosenberg et al. 1991).

Burrowing Owls are predominately associated with prairie dog towns and round-tailed ground squirrel populations (deVos 1998, Latta et al. 1999, Brown 2001). Both of these burrowing mammals usually inhabit open environments and provide burrows and short vegetation (Hoffmeister 1986, deVos 1998).

Shrub encroachment by mesquite in se. Arizona has eliminated extensive tracts of grassland habitat for the Burrowing Owl (Brandt 1951). In n. Arizona, Burrowing Owls formerly inhabited Anita and Pasture Washes in the Grand Canyon region, but the habitat is now unsuitable due to shrub encroachment (Brown 2001). Such habitat change has been due to grazing practices and prairie dog control programs (Brandt 1951, Brown 2001).

Threats: The Arizona Partners in Flight Bird Conservation Plan (Latta et. al 1999) lists the following threats: 1) Reduction of prairie dogs and ground squirrels through control programs and plague events indirectly limit habitats available to Burrowing Owls; 2) Urban and agricultural development directly reduces available habitat; 3) Urbanization also increases the risk of contraction of Trichomoniasis from doves (Estabrook and Mannan 1998); and 4) increased mortality from vehicles, humans, and domestic and feral animals.

Literature Cited:

Arizona Breeding Bird Atlas. Unpubl. Data. 1993-1999. Arizona Game and Fish Department, Nongame Branch, Phoenix, Arizona.

Brandt, H. 1951. Arizona and its bird life. The Bird Research Foundation, Cleveland, OH.

Brown, N. L. 2001. The Howdy Owls of Arizona: A review of the status of *Athene cunicularia*. Journal of Raptor Research 35:344-350.

Carothers, S. W., J. R. Haldeman, and R. P. Balda. 1973. Breeding birds of the San Francisco Mountain Area and the White Mountains. Tech. Series. No. 12. Northern Arizona Soc. of Science and Art, Inc. Flagstaff, Arizona.

deVos, J. C., Jr. 1998. Burrowing Owl (*Athene cunicularia*). Pp 166-169 *in* R. L. Glinski, editor. The Raptors of Arizona. University of Arizona Press, Tucson, AZ and Arizona Game and Fish Department., Phoenix, Arizona.

Estabrook, T. S., and R. W. Mannan. 1998. Urban habitat selection by Burrowing Owls; Final Report. Heritage Grant U96006; Arizona Game and Fish Department, Phoenix, Arizona.

Hoffmeister, D. F. 1986. Mammals of Arizona. Univ. of Arizona Press, Tucson, Arizona and Arizona Game and Fish Department, Phoenix, Arizona.

James, P. C., and R. H. M. Espie. 1997. Current status of the Burrowing Owl in North America: an agency survey. Pages 3-5 *in* J. Lincer and K. Steenhof, editors. The Burrowing Owl, its biology and management including the Proceedings of the First International Burrowing Owl Symposium. Raptor Research Report Number 9.

Johnson, R. R., L. T. Haight, and J. M. Simpson. 1979. Owl populations and species status in the southwestern United States. *in* P. P. Schaeffer, and S. M. Ehlers, editors. Proceedings of the National Audubon Society's Symposium on the Owls of the West: their Ecology and Conservation, Tiburon, California.

Johnson-Duncan, E. E., D. K. Duncan, and R. R. Johnson. 1988. Small nesting raptors as indicators of change in the southwest desert. Pp 232-236 *in* Glinksi, Pendelton, Moss, LeFranc, Millsap, and Hoffman, editors. Proceedings of the Southwest Raptor National Wildlife Federation Scientific and Technical Series No. 11. Washington, DC.

Karlaus, K. E., and A. W. Eckert. 1974. The owls of North America. Doubleday, Garden City, New York.

Latta, M. J., C. J. Beardmore, and T. E. Corman. 1999. Arizona Partners in Flight Bird Conservation Plan. Version 1.0. Nongame and Endangered Wildlife Program Technical Report 142. Arizona Game and Fish Department, Phoenix, Arizona.

Phillips, A. R, J. T. Marshall, and G. Monson. 1964. The Birds of Arizona. University of Arizona Press, Tucson, Arizona.

Rosenberg, K. V., R. D. Ohmart, W. C. Hunter, and B. W. Anderson. 1991. Birds of the Lower Colorado River Valley. University of Arizona Press, Tucson, Arizona.

Sauer, J. R., J. E. Hines, and J. Fallon. 2002. The North American Breeding Bird Survey, Results and Analysis 1966–2001. Version 2002.1. U.S. Geological Survey, Patuxent Wildlife Research Center, Laurel, Maryland. http://www.mbr-pwrc. usgs.gov/bbs/bbs2001.html.

Sauer, J. R., S. Schwartz, and B. Hoover. 1996. The Christmas Bird Count Home Page. Version 95.1. Patuxent Wildlife Research Center, Laurel, Maryland.

Zeiner, D. C., W. F. Laudenslayer, Jr., K. Mayer, and M. White, editors. 1990. California's Wildlife, Volume 11: Birds. The Resources Agency, Sacramento, California.

Witzeman, J. L., S. R. Demaree, and E.L. Radke. 1997. Birds of Phoenix and Maricopa county, Arizona. Maricopa Audubon Society.

Additional Author For Arizona State Summary:

Nikolle L. Brown, 7779 N. Leonard, Clovis, California 93611

California

Summary: California supports one of the largest year-round (resident) and winter (migrant) populations of Burrowing Owls within the United States. The distribution of Burrowing Owls has changed considerably since introduction of industrial agriculture and increased urbanization, reflecting both losses and gains in local populations. Surveys conducted during 1991-93 reported >9,000 breeding pairs. Most Burrowing Owls occurred within the Central (24%) and Imperial Valleys (71%), primarily in agricultural areas. Burrowing Owls have disappeared or declined in several southern California and San Francisco Bay counties and in coastal areas. Without increased regulatory protection of habitat, Burrowing Owls will likely be extirpated in some areas. However, the large and widespread current population and the Burrowing Owl's high reproductive performance in disturbed environments suggests that the California population is not under immediate or foreseeable threat. Changes in agricultural practices, particularly regarding water conveyance, and urbanization have the potential to quickly affect California's Burrowing Owl population. Evaluation of the ability of large publicly managed lands to support Burrowing Owl populations is important to assess the Burrowing Owl's viability in California.

BBS: Significant increases in relative abundance in California over the 1966-2001 survey period (Trend = 5.5, P <0.01, n = 32) and the 1980-2001 subinterval (Trend = 5.0, P <0.05, n = 24). Data credibility is good indicating adequate sample size, moderate precision, and moderate abundance on routes (Sauer et al. 2002).

CBC: Significant decreasing trends in Burrowing Owl relative abundance were detected from 1959-88 (Trend = –1.2, P <0.05, n = 97) (Sauer et al. 1996).

Atlas: Several counties have atlases, but no single state atlas is available.

Research/Monitoring: Historical accounts indicated that the Burrowing Owl was widely distributed and relatively common in California grasslands (Canfield 1869, Dawson 1923, Grinnell and Miller 1944). Numbers during winters were reported to have declined between 1954-1986 (James and Ethier 1989). Additional declines were reported from the San Francisco Bay area, where development has reduced the amount of Burrowing Owl habitat (DeSante et al. unpubl. ms, Trulio 1997). Johnson (1997) reported a rapid decline in numbers of nesting Burrowing Owls on a 370-acre study site on the University of California Davis campus (Yolo Co.).

The Institute for Bird Populations conducted a volunteer-based survey in 1991-1993 within most of the range of Burrowing Owls in California (DeSante et al. 1997, DeSante et al. unpubl. ms.). They estimated over 9,000 breeding pairs of Burrowing Owls in California (Fig. A-1). Most Burrowing Owls found during the survey were in agricultural areas although it was likely that higher numbers exist in large grasslands than revealed through the surveys (DeSante et al. *In press*). Based on comparisons of survey results and observations made during the early 1980s, DeSante et al. (unpubl. ms.) reported that Burrowing Owls were extirpated during the last 10-15 years from several areas in California, including Napa, Marin, San Francisco, Santa Cruz, and Ventura counties, and coastal San Luis Obispo county and Coachella Valley. Few individuals were observed in Sonoma, Santa Barbara, Orange, coastal Monterey, and San Mateo counties. Most of these areas maintained few Burrowing Owls prior to reported declines; occasional observations of Burrowing Owls nesting in some of these counties have been reported recently (D. DeSante, pers. commun.). The most apparent decline of Burrowing Owls was reported from the Bay area, where DeSante et al. (1997) estimated an approximately 50% decline in Burrowing Owl numbers from the 1980s to the early 1990s.

A multi-site demographic study was initiated in 1997 and coordinated through The Institute for Bird Populations, Oregon State University, and San Jose State University. The study included four sites by 1998, representing the primary habitats in which most of California's Burrowing Owl populations exist. This included South San Francisco Bay ("Bay Area") representing urban environments, Naval Air Station Lemoore ("Lemoore") representing small grassland patches surrounded by agriculture, Carrizo Plain National Monument ("Carrizo"), representing large grasslands, and the Imperial Valley, representing intensive agriculture with nests restricted to field borders. Preliminary results from this study (Rosenberg et al., unpubl. data) demonstrate variability in density and demographic performance among sites (Table A-1).

The number of pairs/ha within the entire study area was similar among sites except for Imperial Valley, which had densities approx. 8 times that of all other sites (Table A-1). By contrast, the number of pairs/ha of potential nest habitat, varied dramatically. Survival rates of Burrowing Owls captured as adults were similar among sites, with Imperial Valley having the highest rates (Table A-1), although there was high temporal variation that was site-specific (Rosenberg et al., unpubl. data). Mortality was high at Carrizo, with predation by other raptors identified as the single largest cause (Rosier et al., unpubl. ms). Reproductive rates, estimated as the number of 21-28 day-old young (Gorman et al., unpubl. ms.), varied among sites (Table A-1), but temporal variation within sites was greater. Temporal variation was apparently related to the abundance of vertebrate prey (Haley 2002, Gervais 2002, Ronan 2002). Reproductive rates were highest in the two agricultural sites, Lemoore and Imperial Valley. Nest failure was largely responsible for differences among the four sites.

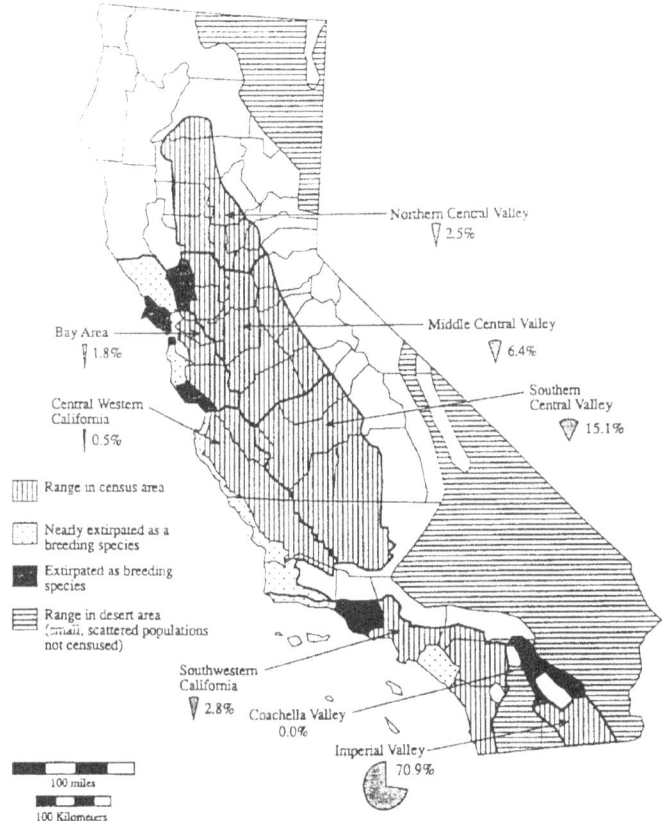

Fig. A-2. Distribution of Burrowing Owl Populations in California, 1991-1993 (9,266 breeding pairs, estimate) (DeSante et al. unpubl. ms.).

For Burrowing Owls, estimates of juvenile survival rates have rarely been reported (but see Gervais 2002), due in part to the difficulty of separating survival from emigration. If one assumes that survival is lower for juveniles than adults (i.e., <0.5, Table A-1), then stability is most likely to occur only when reproductive rates are >2 young/nest (Table A-2). This reproductive rate was achieved or exceeded at each site in some years.

Densities, survival rates, and reproductive rates of Burrowing Owls were high in a wide range of modified habitat conditions. These demographic characteristics were highest in agricultural areas (Lemoore and Imperial Valley) and similar between the urban area of southern San Francisco Bay and the grasslands of Carrizo. If we assume that Carrizo's population growth rate over the long-term is close to stable, then the modified environments of agriculture and urban landscapes (given the conditions at the time of the study) seem likely to provide habitat for stable populations of Burrowing Owls based on the preliminary results from the demographic study. The documented long-term decline in the San Francisco Bay Area is due to nest habitat loss. Further work determining densities of Burrowing Owls in large grasslands, survival rates of juvenile Burrowing Owls, and dispersal patterns

of both juveniles and adults will be required for a better understanding of the long-term viability of Burrowing Owls in California. These analyses are now underway for the California demographic studies reported here.

Conservation Activities: The Burrowing Owl Consortium, an ad hoc group of Burrowing Owl biologists and advocates in the San Francisco Bay prepared the *"Burrowing Owl Survey Protocol and Mitigation Guidelines"* in 1993 (California Burrowing Owl Consortium 1997), the basis of California Department of Fish and Game's (1995) *"Staff Report on Burrowing Owl Mitigation."* Repeated conflicts between Burrowing Owls and development projects have lead some municipalities and larger-scale planning boards to consider preparing Burrowing Owl habitat conservation programs for their respective jurisdictions.

In an effort to better inform the public, a brochure and two videos on the Burrowing Owl in California were prepared by The Institute for Bird Populations and Oregon State University. These have been distributed at no charge to federal and state natural resource agencies, visitor centers at locations with Burrowing Owls, and to elementary and high schools.

Table A-1. Comparison of mean density, survival, and reproductive rates of Burrowing Owls at four sites in California.

Site	Years of Study	Area (km^2)	Pairs observed	Crude Density[a]	Ecological Density[b]	Survival[c]	No. Young[d]
Bay Area	98-01	60 (estimate)	64	1.1	5.2	0.55	1.6/3.1
Lemoore	97-00	76.1	67	0.9	15.2	0.44	2.8/3.8
Carrizo	97-00	183.5	38.9	1.0	1.0	0.23/0.61	1.9/4.0
Imperial Valley	98-01	11.8	99	8.3	145.6	0.60	2.1/2.9

[a] Number of estimated pairs/km^2.

[b] Number of estimated pairs/km^2 of potential nest habitat. A width of 20 m was used along canals and drains to estimate the area of nest habitat within the Imperial Valley.

[c] Apparent annual survival rates are based on the single best average estimate with years and sex pooled. At Carrizo, survival rate was estimated as an annual interval from mark-recapture data (0.23) and from radio-telemetry data (0.61) over a 3 month interval during the breeding season. The mark-recapture estimate from Carrizo is negatively biased due to high breeding dispersal (Rosier et al., unpubl. ms.). Apparent survival is an estimate of survival under the assumption that emigration from the study area does not exist.

[d] Number of young reported are, first, the average number for all nests assessed, and, second, the number at successful nests. Estimates are based on counts during 5, 30-min observation (Gorman et al, unpubl. ms.; Rosenberg and Haley *In press*).

Table A-2. Estimates of juvenile survival rates necessary for population stability under different adult reproductive and survival rates.

Adult Survival	Reproductive Rate	Necessary Juvenile Survival
0.5	1.5	0.67
0.5	2.0	0.50
0.5	2.5	0.40
0.6	1.5	0.54
0.6	2.0	0.40
0.6	2.5	0.32

Major Populations: Genetic analyses of Burrowing Owls from three of the demographic study sites (Lemoore, Carrizo, Imperial Valley) failed to identify population differentiation (Korfanta 2001). This was likely due to the continuous habitat relative to the long-distance dispersal of juveniles and some adults (Rosier et al., unpubl. ms). Owls are most abundant within the Central and Imperial Valleys (Fig. A-1). Based on the survey of DeSante et al. (unpubl. ms), most (91%) Burrowing Owls occur on private lands. However, the difficulty of detecting Burrowing Owls nesting within large grasslands (Ronan 2002, Rosenberg et al., unpubl. data) coupled with the densities estimated for Carrizo (Table A-1) suggests that large publicly managed grasslands within public lands may have large numbers of Burrowing Owls.

State Status: Species of Special Concern—declining population levels, limited ranges, and/or continuing threats have made them vulnerable to extinction.

Natural Heritage Rank: G4/S2—imperiled in the state because of rarity or because of some factor(s) making it very vulnerable to extirpation from the state.

Habitat Use and Condition: Burrowing Owl nesting habitat is similar to the characteristics of land preferred for agricultural, residential, and commercial development. Because California's human population growth will continue, grassland and desert habitat can be expected to be further reduced. The primary regions of grasslands and deserts supporting Burrowing Owl populations are those managed by public agencies such as Bureau of Land Mangament and Department of Defense, although quantitative estimates of potential habitat have not yet been computed. Presumably, large areas of undeveloped deserts have sparse but stable (over the long-term) Burrowing Owl populations. Areas undergoing rapid urbanization, such as the San Francisco Bay area and many parts of southern California, have lost and will continue to lose habitats that once supported Burrowing Owl populations. The Central Valley and Imperial Valley have lost most of their native vegetation to large-scale agriculture, but Burrowing Owls are abundant (DeSante et al. *In press*; Rosenberg and Haley *In press*).

In California, Burrowing Owls have shown incredible tolerance for human encroachment and degradation of native habitats. In urban areas, they are often found nesting within landfills, golf courses, airports, and vacant lots within highly developed areas (Haug et al. 1993, Trulio 1997). The primary criterion for Burrowing Owl occurrence is a nest burrow. Because of this, habitat quality is spatially variable and highly dynamic. In modified ecosystems, habitat quality is often dependent on individual landholders and sensitive to a wide variety of land uses, such as farming practices.

Threats: Valley-bottoms in or near population centers are highly valued for residential and commercial development. Rapid development within the San Francisco Bay Area and other municipalities is responsible for declines in Burrowing Owl numbers in these areas. Further loss of Burrowing Owls on private lands within urban areas is expected under current land-use regulations. Because of the large numbers of Burrowing Owls that reside within the agricultural matrix of the Central and Imperial Valleys, change in methods of farming practices, particularly water conveyance, is likely to impact Burrowing Owl numbers (Rosenberg and Haley *In press*). Because Burrowing Owls in agricultural systems spend a large proportion of their time foraging in fields (Rosenberg and Haley *In press*), pesticide use will remain a threat to these populations. Some populations maintain substantial body burdens of persistent pesticides that may inhibit reproduction (Gervais et al. 2000), although these levels appear to fluctuate through time, making their impact difficult to predict (Gervais 2002). Throughout California, ground-squirrel control programs may affect Burrowing Owl numbers and persistence in local areas because most nest burrows are constructed by these species.

Burrowing Owls and their nests are protected by California Fish and Game Code and the U. S. Migratory Bird Treaty Act. Avoiding violation of these regulations usually requires that disturbance at occupied nest territories be reduced or eliminated during the nesting season. The California Environmental Quality Act offers some protection by stipulating that significant impacts to the species be mitigated. Although outright killing of the birds and active nests is addressed by California Fish and Game Code and the Migratory Bird Treaty Act, the loss of habitat is not. Existing regulatory mechanisms have not been effective at preventing or discouraging intentional destruction of Burrowing Owl habitat, including nest sites.

Vehicle collisions have been cited as a potentially significant source of mortality (Haug et al. 1993; Clayton and Schmutz 1997, Rosenberg et al., unpubl. data). The risk of vehicle collisions is likely greater in developed areas with dense human populations or along areas where Burrowing Owls nest predominately near roads.

Literature Cited:

California Burrowing Owl Consortium. 1997. Burrowing Owl survey protocol and mitigation guidelines. Appendix B, pp 171-177 *in* Lincer, J. L. and K. Steenhof, editors. The Burrowing Owl, its biology and management including the Proceedings of the First International Burrowing Owl Symposium. Raptor Research Report Number 9.

California Department of Fish and Game. 1995. Staff report on Burrowing Owl mitigation. Unpublished report.

Canfield, C. S. 1869. Habits of the Burrowing Owl in California. American Naturalist 2:583-586.

Clayton K. M., and J. K. Schmutz. 1997. Burrowing (*Speotyto cunicularia*) owl survival in prairie Canada. Pages 107-110 *in* J. R. Duncan, D. H. Johnson, and T. H. Nicholls, editors. Biology and conservation of owls of the northern hemisphere: 2nd International Symposium, Winnipeg, Manitoba, Canada. General Technical Report NC-190, USDA, Forest Service, North Central Forest Experiment Station, St. Paul, Minnesota.

Dawson, W. L. 1923. Birds of California, Volume 2. South Moulton Company, San Francisco, California.

DeSante, D.F., E.D. Ruhlen, S.L. Adamany, K.M. Burton and S. Amin. Pp.38-48 *in* Lincer, J.L. and K. Steenhof, Eds. 1997. The Burrowing Owl, It's Biology and Management: Proceedings of the First International Burrowing Owl Symposium. Raptor Research Report No. 9.

DeSante, D. F., E. D. Ruhlen, and D. K. Rosenberg. *In press*. Density and abundance of burrowing owls in the agricultural matrix of the Imperial Valley, California. Studies in Avian Biology.

Gervais, J. A. 2002. Evaluating space use and pesticide exposure risk for Burrowing Owl in an agricultural environment. Ph.D. Dissertation, Oregon State Univ., Corvallis, Oregon.

Gervais, J. A., D. K. Rosenberg, D. M. Fry, L. Trulio and K. K. Sturm. 2000. Burrowing Owls and agricultural pesticides: evaluation of residues and risks for three populations in California, USA. Environmental Toxicology and Chemistry 19:337-343.

Grinnell, J. and A.H. Miller. 1944. The Distribution of the Birds of California. Cooper Ornithological Club. Berkeley, California.

Haley, K. A. 2002. The role of food limitation and predation on reproductive success of burrowing owls in southern California. M.S. Thesis, Oregon State Univ., Corvallis, Oregon.

Haug, E. A., B.A. Millsap and M.S. Martell. 1993. Burrowing Owl (*Speotyto cunicularia*). *in* A. Poole and F. Gill, editors. The Birds of North America, No. 61. The Academy of Natural Sciences, Philadelphia, PA and The American Ornithologists' Union, Washington, DC.

James, P. C. and T .J. Ethier. 1989. Trends in the winter distribution and abundance of Burrowing Owls in North America. American Birds 43:1224-1225.

Johnson, B. S. 1997. Demography and population dynamics of the Burrowing Owl. Pages 28-33 *in* J. L. Lincer and K. Steenhof, editors. The Burrowing Owl, its biology and management including the Proceedings of the First International Burrowing Owl Symposium. Raptor Research Report Number 9.

Korfanta, N. M. 2001. Population genetics of migratory and resident Burrowing Owls (*Athene cunicularia*) elucidated by microsatellite DNA markers. M.S. Thesis. University of Wyoming, Laramie, Wyoming.

Ronan, N. A. 2002. Habitat selection, reproductive success, and site fidelity of burrowing owls in a grassland ecosystem. M.S. Thesis, Oregon State University, Corvallis, Oregon.

Rosenberg, Daniel K., and K. L. Haley. *In press*. The ecology of Burrowing Owls in the agroecosystem of the Imperial Valley, California. Studies in Avian Biology.

Sauer, J. R., J. E. Hines, and J. Fallon. 2002. The North American Breeding Bird Survey, Results and Analysis 1966–2001. Version 2002.1. U.S. Geological Survey, Patuxent Wildlife Research Center, Laurel, Maryland. http://www.mbr-pwrc.usgs.gov/bbs/bbs2001.html.

Sauer, J. R., S. Schwartz, and B. Hoover. 1996. The Christmas Bird Count Home Page. Version 95.1. Patuxent Wildlife Research Center, Laurel, Maryland.

Trulio, L. 1997. Burrowing Owl demography and habitat use at two urban sites in Santa Clara County, California. Pages 84-89 *in* J. L. Lincer and K. Steenhof, editors. The Burrowing Owl, its biology and management including the Proceedings of the First International Burrowing Owl Symposium. Raptor Research Report Number 9.

Sources of Unpublished Manuscripts and Data

DeSante, D. F., E. D. Ruhlen, and D. K. Rosenberg. The distribution and abundance of Burrowing Owls in California: evidence for a declining population. The Institute for Bird Populations, Contribution No. 58.

Gorman, L., D. K. Rosenberg, N. A. Ronan, K. L. Haley, J. A. Gervais, and V. Franke. In prep. Evaluation of methods for estimation of burrowing owl reproductive rates.

Rosenberg, D., L. Trulio, D. Chromczak, J. Gervais, K. Haley, and N. Ronan. Unpubl. data. Ecology of burrowing owls in California. (Data collected at four sites in California, 1996-2000.)

Rosier, J., N. Ronan, and D. Rosenberg. In revision. Breeding season survival and dispersal of Burrowing Owls in an extensive California Grassland. (Data collected at Carrizo Plain National Monument.)

Additional Contributors for California State Summary:

John H. Barclay[1]
Jennifer A. Gervais[2]
Katherine L. Haley[2]
Noelle A. Ronan[2]
Daniel K. Rosenberg[3]

[1] Albion Environmental, Inc., 1414 Soquel Ave., No. 205, Santa Cruz, CA 95062

[2] Department of Fisheries and Wildlife, 104 Nash Hall, Oregon State University, Corvallis, OR 97331.

[3] Department of Forest, Range, and Wildlife Sciences, 5230 Old Main Hill, Utah State University, Logan, UT 84322-5230.

Colorado

Summary: Burrowing Owls are a breeding species across the plains of e. Colorado, with scattered occurrences in the Grand Valley (wc. Colorado), the San Luis Valley (sc. Colorado), and South Park (c. Colorado; Jones 1998). During mild winters, rarely an individual will winter in Colorado. Based on survey results of state biologists, James and Espie (1997) estimated 1,000-10,000 pairs of Burrowing Owls in Colorado in 1992. Rocky Mountain Bird Observatory estimated the total Burrowing Owl population of e. Colorado to be 20,408 individuals based on driving line transects and 15,796 individuals based on road-based point counts (Hanni 2001). Some Colorado counties no longer have Burrowing Owls where they did occur within recent years (Andrews and Righter 1992, J. Slater, pers. commun.).

BBS: No significant trends were detected over any survey period (Sauer et al. 2002).

CBC: N/A

Atlas: According to the 1998 Colorado Breeding Bird Atlas, breeding was confirmed for the species in 18 latilong blocks and four of the ten west slope latilong blocks in which Burrowing Owls have occurred historically (Fig. A-3, Jones 1998). They were found in 40% of the priority blocks in the eastern plains and the number of blocks with Burrowing Owls gradually decreased from east to west and south to north. The distribution of blocks with Burrowing Owls approximated that found in 1999 surveys by the Rocky Mountain Bird Observatory (RMBO, formerly Colorado Bird Observatory) (Hutchings et al. 1999). Jones (1998) documented breeding in the Grand Valley from Grand Junction to the Utah border, but not in nw. Colorado or South and Middle Parks. Burrowing Owls were recorded in only three blocks in sw. Colorado and four in the San Luis Valley (Jones 1998). Level of breeding evidence for priority blocks with Burrowing Owls was 152 confirmed (59%), 54 probable (21%) and 53 possible (20%).

Research/Monitoring Biddle (1996) stated that burrows which are vacated by prairie dogs soon become unsuitable to Burrowing Owls as they fall into disrepair, but also suggested additional associations between prairie dogs and Burrowing Owls may decrease the suitability of sites for breeding in the absence of prairie dogs. From anecdotal evidence, she found that towns recently vacated by prairie dogs, yet with available burrows, did not contain breeding Burrowing Owls. She noted one town in Logan County, Colorado, had no prairie dogs or Burrowing Owls in 1994, and breeding Burrowing Owls were present in 1995 after prairie dogs recolonized the site. Ongoing research is continuing at the Rocky Mountain Arsenal National Wildlife Refuge investigating relationships between prairie dog populations affected by epizootic plagues and Burrowing Owl populations (M. Hetrick, pers. commun.).

Lutz and Plumpton (1999) banded 60% of the known population on the Rocky Mountain Arsenal as either adults or as nestlings from 1990-94. Most (n = 513; 92%) were never reencountered after the year they were banded. Of adults banded in 1990, 39% returned in 1991 while only 5% of chicks banded in 1990 returned (Plumpton and Lutz 1993). Overall, 42 banded Burrowing Owls (8%) returned to the area in one year and used the area for two-four years (Lutz and Plumpton 1999). Adult males and females returned at similar rates (19% and 14%, respectively). Adult males and females nested in formerly used sites at similar rates (75% and 63%, respectively). They found no difference in productivity between philopatric adults and presumed new adults; however, past brood size was greater for females that returned to former nest sites (mean = 4.9 ± 0.69 young) than for females that changed nest sites in subsequent years (mean = 2.2 ± 0.79 young; Lutz and Plumpton 1999). Females banded as nestlings returned as adults after a year absence from the study area. Males banded as nestlings returned in the year following hatch, with one exception. Fledging rate ranged from 0-9 young per nest (mean = 3.62 ± 0.19 young/nest, n = 167). The majority of returning adults (66%) reused the same prairie dog town as the prior year and 90% of prairie dog towns and 20% of nesting burrows were reused (Plumpton and Lutz 1993).

Plumpton (1992) found nesting Burrowing Owls occupied burrows with a shorter distance to the nearest road, and shorter grass and forb height than generally available, while using black-tailed prairie dog towns with greater burrow density and percentage of bare ground than available. VerCauteren et al. (*In review*) found Burrowing Owl density was inversely related to the area of prairie dog towns, but total number of Burrowing Owls was positively related to town size. In concordance with Plumpton (1992), VerCauteren et al. (*In review*) found the number of Burrowing Owls in e. Colorado was significantly correlated with number of prairie dogs and number of burrows. Biddle (1996) found the number of shortgrass patches within 1000 m of prairie dog towns could be used to predict the presence of Burrowing Owls in Logan County, Colorado, with the probability increasing as the number of patches increased. Plumpton (1992) found that periodic mowing could maintain vegetation structure for Burrowing Owls when prairie dogs were eliminated by epizootics or chemical extirpation.

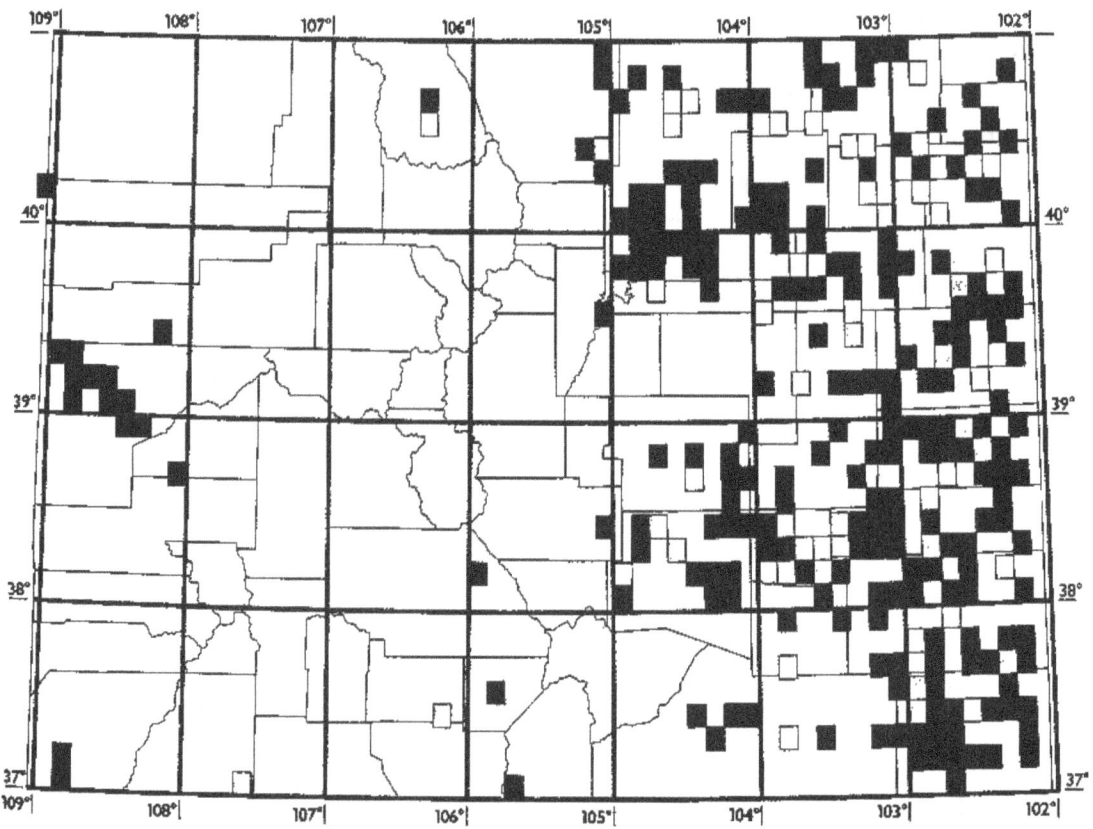

Fig. A-3. Distribution of Burrowing Owls in Colorado from the Colorado Breeding Bird Atlas project (Jones 1998).

Conservation Activities: Management efforts directed toward retention of active prairie dog towns (Plumpton 1992, Biddle 1996) and cropped vegetation (<8 cm) by either sciurids or mowing would be beneficial to nesting Burrowing Owls. The Colorado Division of Wildlife is planning to implement black-tailed prairie dog conservation efforts (J. Slater, pers. commun.).

The RMBO manages "Prairie Partners", a program that asks for voluntary cooperation from private landowners to conserve shortgrass prairie birds and their habitat through effective stewardship (Hutchings et al. 1999). In 1999, "Prairie Partners" documented 468 Burrowing Owl locations (79.3% on public land). Information is provided to landowners on shortgrass prairie conservation and Burrowing Owl natural history. The program also provided information about landowner attitudes toward Burrowing Owls and prairie dogs.

RMBO published "Sharing Your Land with Shortgrass Prairie Birds" (Gillihan et al. 2001) which includes a section on Burrowing Owl identification, natural history, and habitat requirements and a booklet focusing on grasslands and grassland birds for elementary and secondary classroom use (Hutchings et al. 1999). These materials are being distributed to landowners, managers, and schools.

Major Populations: Major populations are found at Rocky Mountain Arsenal in sc. Adams County and the following counties in Colorado according to VerCauteren et al. (2001): Baca, Bent, Cheyenne, Crowley, Kit Carson, Kiowa, Prowers, Pueblo, and Weld.

State Status: Threatened

Natural Heritage Rank: G4/S4B (S4—widespread, abundance, and apparently secure in state, with many occurrences during the breeding season, but of long-term concern).

Habitat Use and Condition: Habitat on the eastern plains is generally in good condition, but along the Front Range it is being rapidly converted to urban development. With the exception of Comanche and Pawnee National Grasslands (on the eastern plains), and a few other state and federal lands, Burrowing Owl habitat is found mostly on private lands (88% of eastern Colorado is in private ownership) (J. Slater, pers. commun.). Habitat loss is responsible for complete or near extirpation of Burrowing Owls in some areas; however, some areas have suitable habitat with no Burrowing Owls, thereby indicating other factors may be influencing Burrowing Owl populations in Colorado (Andrews and Righter 1992).

Threats: Rapid urban/suburban/exurban development along the Front Range of Colorado (Pueblo to Fort Collins) is reducing Burrowing Owl habitat by reduction of black-tailed prairie dogs and their habitat. Furthermore, direct eradication of prairie dogs is eliminating available burrows and short vegetation preferred by Burrowing Owls. Sylvatic plague events in prairie dogs are causing at least temporary reductions in habitat (J. Slater, pers. commun.). Increased use of desert areas in the Grand and Uncompahgre Valleys in w. Colorado has increase disturbance at many historical sites (R. Levad, pers. commun.).

The Burrowing Owl is a Colorado Threatened Species with an increased fine for killing them, but there are no legal implications for habitat destruction. The Colorado Division of Wildlife recommends Burrowing Owl surveys before any land development occurs and recommends avoidance measures, but there is no legal requirement to follow these recommendations (J. Slater, pers. commun.).

Research in Colorado indicated that radiotelemetry transmitter packages have a significant impact on Burrowing Owl behavior. Telemetered adults spent significantly less time resting and alert, and more time out-of-sight of nest burrows (Plumpton 1992). Telemetered Burrowing Owls also had significantly lower productivity than non-telemetered Burrowing Owls (D. Plumpton, unpubl. data).

Literature Cited:

Andrews, R., and R. Righter. 1992. Colorado Birds: A reference to their distribution and habitat. Denver Museum of Natural History, Denver, Colorado.

Biddle, P. B. 1996. Do landuse patterns influence Burrowing Owl nest site selection in northeastern Colorado? M.S. Thesis. Colorado State University, Fort Collins, Colorado.

Gillihan, S. W., D. J. Hanni, S. W. Hutchings, T. Toombs, and T. VerCauteren. 2001. Sharing your land with shortgrass prairie birds. Rocky Mountain Bird Observatory, Brighton, Colorado.

Hanni, D. J. 2001. Comparison of four methodologies used to monitor shortgrass prairie birds in eastern Colorado. Rocky Mountain Bird Observatory, Brighton, Colorado.

Hutchings, S., M. Carter, E. Atkinson, T. VerCauteren, C. Finley, S. Gillihan, and J. Nocedal. 1999. Prairie Partners: Promoting stewardship of shortgrass prairie. Unpubl. Rep., Colorado Bird Observatory, Brighton, Colorado.

James, P. C., and R. H. M. Espie. 1997. Current status of the Burrowing Owl in North America: an agency survey. Pages 3-5 *in* J. Lincer and K. Steenhof, editors. The Burrowing Owl, its biology and management including the Proceedings of the First International Burrowing Owl Symposium. Raptor Research Report Number 9.

Jones, S. R. 1998. Burrowing Owl. Pages 220-221 *in* H. E. Kingery, editor. Colorado Breeding Bird Atlas. Colorado Breeding Birds Atlas Partnership and Colorado Division of Wildlife.

Lutz, R. S., and D. L. Plumpton. 1999. Philopatry and nest site reuse by Burrowing Owls: implications for productivity. Journal of Raptor Research 33:149-153.

Plumpton, D. L. 1992. Aspects of nest site selection and habitat use by Burrowing Owls at the Rocky Mountain Arsenal, Colorado. M.S. Thesis. Texas Technical University, Lubbock, Texas.

Plumpton, D. L., and R. S. Lutz. 1993. Nesting habitat use by Burrowing Owls in Colorado. Journal of Raptor Research 27:175-179.

Sauer, J. R., J. E. Hines, and J. Fallon. 2002. The North American Breeding Bird Survey, Results and Analysis 1966-2001. Version 2002.1 U.S. Geological Survey, Patuxent Wildlife Research Center, Laurel, Maryland. http://www.mbr-pwrc.usgs.gov/bbs/bbs2001.html.

VerCauteren, T. L., S. W. Gillihan, and S. W. Hutchings. 2001. Distribution of Burrowing Owls on public and private lands in Colorado. Journal of Raptor Research 35:357-361.

Although a separate subspecies from the Western Burrowing Owl (A. c. hypugaea), a state summary for the Florida Burrowing Owl (A. c. floridana) is included in this document to provide complete information on the species in the United States. This state summary is an update of information included in Millsap (1996).

Florida

Summary: Burrowing Owls are a mostly resident species primarily from c. Florida southward, though many northerly breeding birds apparently retreat to s. Florida during winter. Some breeding occurs regularly as far north as Duval County (as of 1975) and as far west as Okaloosa County (Eglin Air Force Base, as of 1993) in the western part of the Florida Panhandle. During 1995, a pair of Burrowing Owls summered but did not successfully breed in Decatur County, Georgia, near the Florida border, representing the furthest north breeding season occurrence, presumably of the Florida subspecies.

The Florida and Bahamas breeding populations have been named a separate subspecies (*A. c. floridana*) from populations in w. North America and populations elsewhere in the West Indies and South America (Ridgway 1914, Clark 1997). However, questions have been raised regarding the validity of morphological criteria used to determine subspecies within Burrowing Owls (Millsap 1996), as well as the identification of some Florida specimens collected during winter as representative of *A. c. hypugaea*, which have been found throughout the state (Stevenson and Anderson 1994). One female examined by Millsap from the breeding population in Okaloosa County exhibited characteristics of populations from western North America (Stevenson and Anderson 1994). Millsap (1996) recommends reevaluation of Burrowing Owl subspecies based on modern systematic methods, and some preliminary work in this regard is underway (Denton et al. *In review*).

The earliest treatments of Burrowing Owls in Florida indicated that most were located in the central Peninsular counties where dry prairies were most prevalent (Osceola, Okeechobee and DeSoto counties) and in the Gulf coastal lowlands, with the Tampa Bay area near the center (Rhodes 1892, Howell 1932, Bent 1938, Millsap 1996). Burrowing Owls have declined precipitously in these "natural" habitats with the loss of Florida prairies since the late 1800's (Bent 1938, Nicholson 1954, Owre 1978, Abrahamsom and Hartnett 1990, Cox et al. 1994, Stevenson and Anderson 1994, Millsap 1996). However, the species appears to have expanded since the 1940's through to at least the 1970's by taking advantage of human altered situations (airports, some agricultural situations with dirt canal banks and road berms, and early stages of development).

BBS: No significant trends detected for Florida (Sauer et al. 2002). However, for the few routes where Burrowing Owls were consistently detected (10 out of 81 statewide; 7 out of 34 in Peninsular Florida and 2 out of 10 in Subtropical Florida), the tendency was for fewer detections over time, but this may not be reflective of true population trends. High numbers of Burrowing Owls in Florida are concentrated in developing areas which are not generally well represented on BBS routes.

CBC: Insufficient data is available for determining clear trends from Christmas Bird Count (CBC) data. Over a three-year period (1993-1996, as a sample), Burrowing Owls were detected in two years on 11 Counts and in one year on eight Counts, out of a statewide total of 53 each year. The vast majority of CBCs each year detected fewer than 15 Burrowing Owls (8 of 11, 9 of 11, and 6 of 8, respectively). Many well-known breeding sites consistently fail to detect any Burrowing Owls during winter indicating either seasonal movements or an inherent decrease of detectability from breeding to non-breeding seasons. This species becomes mostly nocturnal during winter (Stevenson and Anderson 1994).

Atlas: The Florida Breeding Bird Atlas is unpublished, but data collected from 1987 – 1991 provide relative recent distributional data statewide. Atlas data show the Florida Burrowing Owl occurring over a relatively wide area of the state, from Madison and Duval counties south to the middle Keys. Within this broad range, the species can best be considered local and spotty in distribution and dependent on the availability of suitable habitat. During the BBA period, Burrowing Owls were conspicuously absent from the extensive wetlands of the Everglades and Big Cypress areas of South Florida, from the Panhandle, and from much of the northeastern Atlantic Coast (since then they have been observed nesting on Eglin AFB in the Panhandle).

Research/Monitoring There is no statewide monitoring program for Florida Burrowing Owls. Several local monitoring efforts have been undertaken in suburban and ruderal areas where Burrowing Owls have recently become established. Through these local monitoring efforts, we know that populations in many such areas collapse soon after densely packed housing or other development dominates the landscape (Courser 1976, Consiglio and Reynolds 1987, Millsap 1996).

A long-term research project has been underway in Cape Coral in sw. Florida to better document the reasons Burrowing Owl populations become established in some developing areas and then collapse at some threshold of development. This research has been undertaken with the goal of establishing management recommendations for communities interested in the conservation of this species (Millsap and Bear 1997, 2000, Millsap 2002). Burrowing Owls prefer "neighborhoods" when over

25% of the area is in developed lots but start to collapse when development exceeds 60%, possibly irretrievably so when over 70% of the area is in developed lots. Millsap (2002), presents data that adult males, adult females, and juveniles respond differently to landscape features in terms of survival and emigration. This complex situation requires more study, but it appears that some desirable level of development through zoning may allow for reasonably large and stable Burrowing Owl populations to persist within urban-suburban landscapes.

Conservation Activities: Active education programs appear to be working in Cape Coral to reduce harassment, and resulting nest failure, of Burrowing Owls. Most documented harassment is linked to school-aged children. The implementation of a formal "mandatory" Burrowing Owl education program in Cape Coral public schools has coincided with increasing local nesting success (Millsap and Bear 2000; similar results in Broward County have been reported, Consiglio and Reynolds 1987). Millsap and Bear (2000) also suggested buffer zones be established by the City of Cape Coral or developers, which can be useful in shielding owls from disturbance where construction is underway during the nesting season. They suggested a minimum of a 10-m buffer may be effective, but larger buffers are likely better. Finally, they suggested the most important conservation actions municipalities may undertake is to develop conservation agreements with the managers of public facilities such as schools, athletic fields, churches, parks, libraries, and office building complexes that provide open grounds necessary for Burrowing Owl habitat.

Although Burrowing Owl populations using urban-suburban environments have received much recent attention, it is still necessary to conserve populations persisting in natural habitats, especially Florida's dry prairies. Cox et al. (1994) used a combination of Breeding Bird Atlas (Kale et al. 1992) information and overlay of existing dry prairie acreage to address the site protection needs for this and other dry prairie associated species. They concluded that the greatest opportunities to conserve natural habitat for Burrowing Owl specifically on already identified conservation areas included the Kissimmee Prairie region, with Avon Park Air Force Range, Audubon Kissimmee Prairie Preserve, Arbuckle State Forest, and Three Lakes State Wildlife Management Area. This region supports key sites maintaining a large viable population of Burrowing Owls within historically important habitats. Outside existing conservation lands, there are patches of native dry prairie that could also be important for linking all the region's potentially isolated subpopulations together if these sites receive long-term protection from conversion. The priority sites include patches between Avon Park Air Force Range and Lake Kissimmee and between Avon Park Air Force Range and Three Lakes State

Wildlife Management Area. With these connections in place, this entire region could constitute one large Florida Burrowing Owl population (Cox et al. 1994).

Two other concentration areas exist, worthy of conservation attention (Cox et al. 1994). The Miami Ridge presently supports sizeable population of Burrowing Owls in se. Florida, but these largely agricultural lands are quickly progressing towards urban-suburban development. Experiences in other similarly developing areas like Cape Coral may be useful for conserving these populations into the future. The last large concentration area considered here is along the western shore of Lake Okeechobee, which includes patches of remnant dry prairie and expansive agricultural lands, both which can provide suitable habitat for Burrowing Owls (Abrahamson and Hartlett 1990). Working in cooperation with private landowners is essential to conserve these isolated prairie remnants and the species dependent upon them, including Florida Burrowing Owls (see also Cox et al. 1994).

Major Populations: Bowen (2000) conducted a metapopulation analysis of Florida Burrowing Owls, which identified eight major subpopulations and 59 metapopulations in Florida (Table A-3). All major subpopulations were in south Florida, but the population on Eglin Air Force Base in the Panhandle is probably large enough to warrant inclusion here. Other central and north Florida metapopulations were present in 26 counties, but these were generally small in size, probably isolated, and had high predicted probabilities of extirpation.

State Status: Species of Special Concern (Millsap 1996; ranked by Millsap et al. 1990, with a Biological Score of 24). Burrowing Owls and their nests are protected by Commission rules (Chapter 39, Florida Administrative Code) and federal rules promulgated under the Migratory Bird Treaty Act (16 U.S.C. 703-712). The Florida Fish and Wildlife Conservation Commission requires that a permit be obtained from the agency before a Florida Burrowing Owl nest burrow can be destroyed.

Natural Heritage Rank: G4/S3 (Rare and uncommon in the state, Florida Natural Areas Inventory 2001)

Habitat Use and Condition: Habitat is best defined as very open well-drained treeless country, with short grassy or herbaceous vegetation maintained by regular and frequent grazing, mowing, or burning. Soil needs to be of a quality for Burrowing Owls to easily dig and maintain burrows. Although burrows of gopher tortoises or large fossorial mammals are used occasionally, in Florida most burrows used are dug by Burrowing Owls themselves.

These requirements were met historically in Florida on the dry prairies of the central peninsula in the vicinity of burns and along the edges of wetlands during dry periods (Howell 1932, Bent 1938, Millsap 1996). Land clearing and extensive drainage of

Table A-3. Distribution and abundance of Florida Burrowing Owls by major subpopulation and county.

Subpopulation	County	Est. population size (no. adults)	Source
Wellington Aerofield and golf course	Palm Beach	63	Bowen (2000)
Boynton Beach subdivisions	Palm Beach	64	Bowen (2000)
Pompano Beach Airport	Broward	69	Bowen (2000)
Ft. Lauderdale Executive Airport	Broward	77	Bowen (2000)
Cooper City, Penbrooke Pines, Davie	Broward	189	Bowen (2000)
Punta Gorda	Charlotte	37	Bowen (2000)
Cape Coral	Lee	756	Bowen (2000)
Marco Island	Collier	47	Bowen (2000)
Eglin Air Force Base	Santa Rosa and Okaloosa	25	Millsap (pers. obs.)

wetlands have led to expansion of habitat especially since the 1940's. Burrowing Owls still occur in remnant patches of dry prairie, but even here they are more often than not associated with canal banks and road berms even in otherwise "natural" habitat. The above habitat conditions are also featured in pastures converted to non-native grasses, airports, golf courses, athletic fields, and partially developed residential and industrial areas where expanses of mowed lawn and ruderal grassland are maintained (Millsap 1996).

Threats: Continued loss of native dry prairie habitat is a serious threat to many endemic taxa in Florida, but cumulative loss of this habitat is mitigated for Florida Burrowing Owls to a degree as they make use of a variety of altered situations. However, these altered habitats may be exposed to increased use of harmful chemicals, increased presence of predators (including domestic as well as feral and native), human harassment, and in some areas fire ants. In developed areas, most documented mortality is associated with vehicular collisions (Mealey 1997, Millsap 2002).

Although there is good evidence that a moderate degree of development in some areas can support large Florida Burrowing Owl populations, too much development leads eventually to population collapse. Habitat set aside programs will be needed to ensure long-term persistence for most of these populations (Millsap 1996).

Millsap (1996) concluded that Florida Burrowing Owls did not appear to warrant further legal protection at that time, but recommended continued or expanded monitoring of local populations, especially in urban-suburban environments. The Florida Fish and Wildlife Conservation Commission will be collecting data to determine if current management actions are maintaining population numbers in Cape Coral, perhaps the most significant subpopulation.

Recommendation on Current Status for the Florida Burrowing Owl: Population trend data are lacking or insufficient for Burrowing Owls in Florida. Limited data indicate that it is decreasing in some areas, but also has stable or increasing populations in others. The Florida Burrowing Owl continues to occupy the majority of its historical range and may have expanded into new areas. However, historical and continuing loss and reduction of dry prairies and an unclear future of urban/suburban population centers are the primary threats to this subspecies in Florida.

Currently, the Burrowing Owl is listed by the USFWS as a Bird of Conservation Concern-2002 (U.S. Fish & Wildlife Service 2002) in the Peninsular Florida and Southeastern Coastal Plain Bird Conservation Regions and in the USFWS Region 4 (Southeast Region). This designation is intended to stimulate collaborative, proactive conservation actions among public and private land managers and other partners. Recommended conservation measures include efforts to more accurately monitor population demographics and trends, and to better understand factors affecting populations now concentrated in urban/suburban areas of Peninsular Florida.

The Migratory Bird Management program of the USFWS recommends retaining the Florida Burrowing Owl on the BCC lists on which it currently appears. The listing of the Florida Burrowing Owl as a Bird of Conservation Concern highlights its potential vulnerability and need for increased monitoring and conservation attention by multiple Federal and State agencies and private organizations. The success of these efforts will be reviewed every five years as the Birds of Conservation Concern list is revised (U.S. Fish & Wildlife Service 2002).

Literature Cited:

Abrahamson, W. G. and D. C. Hartnett. 1990. Pine flatwoods and dry prairies. Pages 103-149 *in* R. L. Myers and J. J. Ewel, editors. Ecosystems of Florida. University of Central Florida Press, Orlando, Florida.

Bent, A. C. 1938. Life histories of North American birds of prey. Part 2. U.S. National Museum Bulletin No. 170.

Bowen, P. 2000. Demographic, distribution, and metapopulation analyses of the burrowing owl (*Athene cunicularia*) in Florida. M.S. Thesis, University of Central Florida, Orlando, FL.

Clark, R. J. 1997. A review of the taxonomy and distribution of the Burrowing Owl (*Speotyto cunicularia*). Journal of Raptor Research Report 9:14-23.

Consiglio, B., and G. Reynolds. 1987. Broward's Burrowing Owl watchers. Florida Naturalist 60:3-5.

Couser, W. D. 1976. A population study of the Burrowing Owl near Tampa, Florida. M.S. Thesis, University of South Florida, Tampa, Florida.

Cox, J., R. Kautz, M. Mac Laughlin, and T. Gilbert. 1994. Closing the gaps in Florida's wildlife habitat conservation system. Florida Game and Fresh Water Fish Commission, Tallahassee, Florida.

Denton, W., Q. Q. Fang, R. Chandler, and B. A. Millsap. *In review.* Genetic variations among populations of Florida borrowing owls using single strand-conformation polymorphism. Georgia Southern University, Statesboro, Georgia.

Florida Game and Fresh Water Fish Commission. 1990. Official lists of endangered and potentially endangered fauna and flora in Florida. 1 August 1990. Tallahassee, Florida.

Florida Natural Areas Inventory. 2001.Tracked species—vertebrates. FNAI, Tallahassee, Florida.

Howell, A. H. 1932. Florida bird life. Coward-McCann, New York, New York.

Kale, H. W., II, B. Pranty. B. Stith, and W. Biggs. 1992. An atlas of Florida's breeding birds. Final Report. Nongame Wildlife Program, Florida Game and Fresh Water Fish Commission, Tallahassee, Florida.

Mealey, B. 1997. Reproductive ecology of the Burrowing Owls, *Speotyto cunicularia floridana*, in Dade and Broward Counties, Florida. Journal of Raptor Research Report 9:74-79.

Millsap, B. A. 1996. Florida Burrowing Owl. Pages 579-587 *in* J. A. Rodgers, Jr., H. W. Kale II, and H. T. Smith, editors. Rare and Endangered Biota of Florida, Vol V. Birds. University Press of Florida, Gainesville, Florida.

Millsap, B. A. 2002. Survival of Florida Burrowing Owls along an urban development gradient. Journal of Raptor Research 36:3-10.

Millsap, B. A., and C. Bear. 1997. Territory fidelity, mate fidelity, and dispersal in an urban-nesting population of Florida Burrowing Owls. Journal of Raptor Research Report 9:91-98.

Millsap, B. A., and C. Bear. 2000. Density and reproduction of Burrowing Owls along an urban development gradient. Journal of Wildlife Management 64:33-41.

Millsap, B. A., J. A. Gore, D. E. Runde, and S. I. Cerulean. 1990. Setting priorities for the conservation of fish and wildlife species in Florida. Wildlife Monographs No. 111.

Nicholson, D. J. 1954. The Florida Burrowing Owl; a vanishing species. Florida Naturalist 27:3-4.

Owre, O. T. 1978. Florida Burrowing Owl. Pages 97-99 *in* H. W. Kale II, ed. Rare and endangered biota of Florida. Volume 2 birds. University Presses of Florida, Gainesville, Florida.

Rhodes, S. N. 1892. The breeding habits of the Florida Burrowing Owl (*Speotyto cunicularia floridana*). Auk:9:1-8.

Ridgway, R. 1914. The birds of North and Middle America. Part IV. U.S. National Museum Bulletin No. 50.

Sauer, J. R., J. E. Hines, and J. Fallon. 2002. The North American Breeding Bird Survey, Results and Analysis 1966-2001. Version 2002.1, U.S. Geological Survey, Patuxent Wildlife Research Center, Laurel, Maryland. http://www.mbr-pwrc. usgs.gov/bbs/bbs2001.html.

Stevenson, H. M., and B. H. Anderson. 1994. The birdlife of Florida. University Press of Florida, Gainesville, Florida.

U.S. Fish & Wildlife Service. 2002. Birds of Conservation Concern 2002. U.S. Department of Interior, Fish and Wildlife Service, Administrative Report, Arlington, Virginia.

Wesemann, T. 1986. Factors influencing the distribution and abundance of Burrowing Owls (*Athene cunicularia*) in Cape Coral, Florida. M.S. Thesis. Appalachian State University, Boone, North Carolina.

Wesemann, T., and M. Rowe. 1987. Factors influencing the distribution and abundance of Burrowing Owls in Cape Coral, Florida. Pages 129-137 *in* L. W. Adams and D. L. Leedy, editors. Integrating man and nature in the metropolitan environment. Proceedings of the national symposium on urban wildlife. National Institute for Urban Wildlife, Columbia, Maryland.

Additional Authors for Florida State Summary:

Brian A. Millsap, Florida Fish and Wildlife Conservation Commission, 620 S. Meridian St., Tallahassee, FL 32399-1600.

(Current address: Division of Migratory Bird Management, U.S. Fish and Wildlife Service, 4401 N. Fairfax Drive MS 634, Arlington, VA 22203)

William C. Hunter, U.S. Fish and Wildlife Service, 1875 Century Blvd., Suite 240, Atlanta, GA 30345.

Idaho

Summary: Burrowing Owls are a locally common summer resident in s. Idaho. The only evidence that the species ever occurred in n. Idaho is a statement by Merriam in 1891 that it was reported by Bendire as nesting at Fort Lapwai (Nez Perce County) (Burleigh 1972). Birds arrive in s. Idaho in early March and young have been observed near natal burrows as early as 10 June and as late as 17 September (Rich 1986). Populations are believed to be generally increasing (K. Steenhof, pers. commun.) Current distribution and relative abundance information has been well documented for several small scale study areas on the Snake River Plain and vicinity. James and Espie (1997) estimated 1,000 to 10,000 pairs in Idaho based on a survey of state wildlife agencies in 1992. Habitat loss and possible impacts to local populations from agricultural activities have been noted (Rich 1986, James and Espie 1997). However, the extent to which agriculture and other habitat disturbances have impacted Burrowing Owl populations is unknown as the species nests in close proximity to cultivated fields in the Snake River Plain, roadsides (Belthoff and King 1997), firing ranges (Lehman et al. 1999), and other disturbed areas in and around sagebrush-steppe habitat (Rich 1986).

BBS: Significantly increasing trends were detected for all survey periods: 1966-2001 (Trend = 19.1, P <0.07, n = 9); 1966-1979 (Trend = 39.2, P <0.03, n = 3), and 1980-2001 (Trend = 28.4, P <0.06, n = 9). Data credibility is low due to small sample sizes and high variance (Sauer et al. 2002).

CBC: N/A

Atlas: Historical and current records of Burrowing Owls in Idaho documented confirmed breeding in 12 out of 29 latilong blocks, predominantly in s. Idaho (Stevens and Struts 1991). Circumstantial evidence of breeding Burrowing Owls is recorded for two additional latilong blocks including the single historical account of a nesting pair in n. Idaho on Fort Lapwai, Nez Perce County as reported in Burleigh (1972).

Research/Monitoring Rich (1986) investigated vegetative and topographical characteristics around 80 occupied Burrowing Owl nest sites in the sagebrush-steppe of sc. Idaho. Burrowing Owls used burrows provided by badgers in open soil. In small lava outcrops, Burrowing Owls exhibited a preference for burrows excavated by yellow-bellied marmots. Cover within a 50-m radius of 80 occupied burrows was mainly bare earth, cheatgrass, rock, and annual forbs. In comparison to randomly chosen sites, occupied sites had a greater cover of cheatgrass, greater habitat diversity, were lower in elevation, and were more frequently located on southerly aspects. Occupied sites had less acreage of farmland and big sagebrush compared to unoccupied sites. Burrow security and prey availability,

especially the proximity to populations of montane voles on farmland, may explain some of the habitat selection observed (Rich 1986).

Gleason and Johnson (1985) found that 75% of the nesting pairs used burrows excavated by badgers and the remainder occupied natural cavities in lava flows. Density was 1 pair/58 km². Average productivity was 3.6 young/nesting pair. Weather and diet influenced productivity with average productivity in a normal precipitation year (1976) and low productivity during drought (1977). Of 22 mortalities (two nestlings, 15 juveniles, and five adults), six (27%) were from vehicle collisions. Badger predation was presumed to be significant prior to emergence of young from nest burrows, but most mortality occurred after fledging when young were most likely vulnerable to starvation. Gleason and Johnson (1985) also found large portions of the study area lacked Burrowing Owls apparently due to factors other than the availability of nest sites.

Lehman et al. (1998, 1999) studied 235 Burrowing Owl nesting attempts between 1991-1994 on the Snake River Birds of Prey National Conservation Area (SRBPNCA), in sw. Idaho. Nest success was studied in relationship to disturbance caused by military training activities in the Orchard Training Area (OTA) in the SRBPNCA. There were no significant differences in nest success between nests located within versus outside of the OTA. Since most military activity occurred after Burrowing Owls established nesting areas and laid eggs, Lehman et al. (1999) suggested that military activity did not play an important direct role in the distribution of raptor nests in the OTA. Furthermore, direct impact to nests was restricted to a relatively small proportion of nesting pairs each year. If confirmation of nesting is made when young emerge from burrows, Mayfield estimates of nest success are likely to be inflated as they were in this study (100%, as all nests found at this stage were successful). Other methods of estimating nest success yielded lower estimates (64-71%, Lehman et al. 1998). Rate of nest reoccupancy in this study was 11% from 1991 to 1992, and 42% from 1993 to 1994.

In sw. and sc. Idaho, Belthoff and King (1997) reported nest success was 94.4% with 4.6 ± 1.8 young/nest in the Kuna Butte area (Ada County) and 92.9% with 5.1 ± 2.4 young/nest the Grand View area (Elmore County). Radio-tagged Burrowing Owls dispersed an average of 1.4 km from natal burrows during the post-fledging period (Belthoff et al. 1995).

Turnover of individuals in the Kuna Butte area appeared to be relatively high based on low rates of return by both adults and young. Of 52 nestling Burrowing Owls banded in the Kuna Butte study area in 1995, two (one male, one female) were detected in the area in 1996. These owls bred 1.8 and 4.8 km from their natal burrows. Of five adult males banded as breeders during 1995, two returned in 1996 and used the same burrows but acquired different mates. Of 14 adult females banded in 1995, two returned to breed in 1996 and used burrows 106 m and 503 m from their 1995 burrows. Mate retention was uncertain with these females. Belthoff and King (1997) felt the difference in return rates between adults was a result of greater female dispersal rather than increased mortality.

Individual burrows were frequently reoccupied in multiple years (Belthoff and King 1997). Of 30 known nest burrows in 1994-95, 50% were reused in a subsequent year. Five burrows were used for nesting in all three years of study and nine others were used for at least two years. Of 10 burrows that fledged young in 1994, 70% were reused at least once. Conversely, burrows tended to remain unoccupied in years following nest failures; six nests remained unused in 1995-96 after failing in 1994 (Belthoff and King 1997).

In another study of nest reoccupancy, Rich (1984) found that 69.4% of previously documented nest burrows were reoccupied. Burrows in rock outcrops were reused 57.5% of the time compared to 31.4% for nests in soil mounds. Outcrop sites also were used more often in consecutive years; 23 were used for two years, and 12 were used for three consecutive years. Fifteen mound nests were used for two years, five were used for three years, and one was used four consecutive years. Greater reuse of outcrop sites was likely related to security; no burrows in outcrops were destroyed while 26 old badger burrows containing nests were filled in by plowing, cattle trampling, drifting sand, dredging, and other unknown causes (Rich 1984). It was unclear why some burrows were not used more regularly, as the changing of burrows could not be attributed to burrow characteristics or to changes in the surrounding habitat. Regardless of an abundance of burrows in suitable habitat, some Burrowing Owls apparently relocate from year to year.

Major Populations: Rich (1986) documented 242 occupied Burrowing Owl nests between 1976-83 in sc. Idaho. Lehman et al. (1999) documented 235 Burrowing Owl nest attempts between 1991-94 on and near the OTA, also on the SRBPNCA. In sw. Idaho (Ada and Elmore counties), Belthoff and King (1997) located 30 Burrowing Owl burrows in 1994-1995. In se. Idaho, Gleason and Johnson (1985) found average densities of 1 pair/58 km^2.

State Status: Protected Nongame Species. No person shall take or possess protected nongame species including nests and eggs at any time or in any manner, subject to fine and possible imprisonment (Idaho Statutes 36-1102 & 36-1402). Habitat protection is not included in State protection law.

Natural Heritage Rank: G4/S3S4 (S3—rare and uncommon in the state, S4—widespread, abundant, and apparently secure in state, with many occurrences, but of long-term concern).

Habitat Use and Condition: On the SRBNCA, 77% of Burrowing Owl nest sites had farmland within a 693 m radius (Rich 1986). Hay was a common crop and variation in cutting dates made rodents readily available throughout the Burrowing Owl breeding season.

Sagebrush is an important habitat type on occupied sites along the Snake River; however, continuous stands of dense sagebrush (10-35% canopy cover) were not occupied by Burrowing Owls (Rich 1986). Also in s. Idaho, 30 of 36 occupied Burrowing Owl nests were located within 100 m of sagebrush (Rich 1986).

Belthoff and King (1997) found that fires did not adversely affect Burrowing Owls in their study area. All nest sites which burned in 1995 were reoccupied in 1996. Several additional burrows within burned areas (but with unknown histories) were occupied by Burrowing Owls in 1996. The fires did not cause direct mortality of adult or juvenile Burrowing Owls (already of fledging age). These owls were repeatedly observed at burned sites for several weeks after fires. Also, juvenile owls from other families dispersed into burned areas immediately following fires in 1995 (Belthoff and King 1997).

Burrowing Owls in sw. Idaho nested in sites close to roads and agricultural fields, and in areas containing exotic plant species such as cheatgrass, tumble mustard, and annual wheatgrass (Belthoff and King 1997). Rich (1986) found that cover within 50 m of the burrows indicated that sites had been disturbed by fire and grazing. However, the dominant plants were not indicative of the highest degree of disturbance possible in sagebrush-steppe habitats (Rich 1986).

Threats: Invasion of shrubby species may contribute to population declines (Rich 1986). Belthoff and King (1997) noted nest burrows destroyed by agriculture and fire rehabilitation. Natural habitat has decreased due to increasing use of irrigation and the growing importance of agriculture in the state (Burleigh 1972). Soil mound nests were destroyed by plowing, cattle trampling, drifting sand, dredging, and other unknown causes (Rich 1984).

Literature Cited:

Belthoff, J. R., R. A. King, J. Doremus, and T. Smith. 1995. Monitoring post-fledging Burrowing Owls in southwestern Idaho. U.S. Bureau of Land Management, Idaho State Office, Technical Bulletin No. 95-8.

Belthoff, J. R., and R. A. King. 1997. Between-year movements and nest burrow use by Burrowing Owls in southwestern Idaho. Technical Bulletin No. 97-3, Idaho Bureau of Land Management.

Burleigh, T. D. 1972. Burrowing Owl. pp. 168-169 *in* Birds of Idaho. Caxton Printers, Ltd., Caldwell, Idaho.

Gleason, R. S., and D. R. Johnson. 1985. Factors influencing nesting success of Burrowing Owls in southeastern Idaho. Great Basin Naturalist 45:81-84.

James, P. C., and R. H. M. Espie. 1997. Current status of the Burrowing Owl in North America: an agency survey. Pages 3-5 *in* J. Lincer and K. Steenhof, editors. The Burrowing Owl, its biology and management including the Proceedings of the First International Burrowing Owl Symposium. Raptor Research Report Number 9.

Lehman, R. N., L. B. Carpenter, K. Steenhof, and M. N. Kochert. 1998. Assessing relative abundance and reproductive success of shrubsteppe raptors. Journal of Field Ornithology 69:244-256.

Lehman, R. N., K. Steenhof, M. N. Kochert, and L. B. Carpenter. 1999. Effects of military training activities on shrub-steppe raptors in southwestern Idaho, USA. Environmental Management 23:409-417.

Rich, T. 1984. Monitoring Burrowing Owl populations: implications of burrow re-use. Wildlife Society Bulletin 12:178-180.

Rich, T. 1986. Habitat and nest-site selection by Burrowing Owls in the sagebrush steppe of Idaho. Journal of Wildlife Management 50:548-555.

Sauer, J. R., J. E. Hines, and J. Fallon. 2002. The North American Breeding Bird Survey, Results and Analysis 1966–2001. Version 2002.1, U.S. Geological Survey, Patuxent Wildlife Research Center, Laurel, Maryland. http://www.mbr-pwrc.usgs.gov/bbs/bbs2001.html.

Stevens, D.A. and S. H. Struts 1991. Idaho Bird Distribution. Idaho Museum of Natural History. Special Publication No. 11.

Iowa

Summary: Northwest Iowa is on the eastern edge of the Burrowing Owl range. There is little to suggest that this species was ever common; the pattern of occurrence suggests periods of range expansion and regression. Some birds nested in the 1960s and 1980s (Dinsmore et al. 1984). Tallgrass prairie in the pre-settlement era was likely too dense for Burrowing Owls. To date, most records have been in pasturelands (J. Dinsmore, pers. commun.).

BBS: N/A

CBC: N/A

Atlas: Only a single record for the Burrowing Owl was reported (J. Dinsmore, pers. commun.).

Research/Monitoring Monitoring is restricted to reports from birdwatchers and incidental observations by biologists. No database for records is known. Not actively monitored by Iowa Department of Fish and Wildlife personnel (D. Howell, pers. commun.).

Conservation Activities: None reported.

Major Populations: None.

State Status: Placed in original Threatened list in 1977 due to low abundance; removed and designated Accidental Breeder in 1994 (D. Howell, pers. commun.).

Natural Heritage Rank: G4/SAB (Accidental breeder)

Habitat Use and Condition: Burrowing Owls are found in grasslands and pastures (Dinsmore et al. 1984). Pasturelands are preferred over ungrazed tallgrass prairie due to excessive cover on the latter. Most native prairie is under intense rowcrop agriculture, and is unsuitable, but no records exist to indicate the species was ever common.

Threats: Remnant tallgrass prairies provide unsuitable habitat due to excessive cover. Potential Burrowing Owl habitat has been lost to rowcrop agriculture (J. Dinsmore, pers. commun.).

Literature Cited:

Dinsmore, J. J., and T. H. Kent, D. Koenig, P. C. Peterson, and D. M. Roosa. 1984. Iowa Birds. Iowa State University Press, Ames, Iowa.

Kansas

Summary: Little data regarding Burrowing Owls in Kansas is available. Reports indicate it was "abundant" and "common" in the late 1800s in c. and w. Kansas. Burrowing Owls are currently considered uncommon summer residents in w. Kansas, but may be common in local areas. Prairie dogs have been nearly extirpated from many counties in c. Kansas, and sightings of Burrowing Owls are very localized. State agencies in 1992 reported the Burrowing Owl populations as between 100 and 1000 pairs, but decreasing due to reduced burrow availability (James and Espie 1997); however, this population estimate is disputed and believed to be in the 1,000 to 10,000 pair category (W. Busby, pers. commun.).

BBS: No significant trends were detected over any survey period (Sauer et al. 2002).

CBC: N/A

Atlas: Burrowing Owls were confirmed in 46 blocks, with probable and possible breeding occurring in 29 and 25 blocks, respectively (Fig. A-4). Burrowing Owls were observed only in the western half of the state where occurrences generally coincided with remaining areas of shortgrass prairie (Busby and Zimmerman 2001).

Research/Monitoring Burrowing Owl research and monitoring in Kansas is limited to natural history accounts and the Breeding Bird Survey which is too imprecise to detect population trends in this state.

Conservation Activities: None documented.

Major Populations: Burrowing Owl populations are highest in the shortgrass prairie region of Kansas. One of the state's largest populations is at Cimarron National Grassland in southwestern Kansas (W. Busby, pers. commun.).

State Status: No special status designated.

Natural Heritage Rank: G4/S3B, SZN (rare and uncommon breeding populations in the state, no non-breeding occurrences).

Habitat Use and Condition: Not reported.

Threats: Prairie dog populations and associated Burrowing Owl habitat appear stable although at levels far below historic levels. In the long term, increases in prairie dog populations are needed to create more Burrowing Owl habitat (W. Busby, pers. commun.).

Literature Cited:

Busby, W. H., and J. L. Zimmerman. 2001 The Kansas Breeding Bird Atlas. University Press of Kansas, Lawrence, Kansas.

James, P. C., and R. H. M. Espie. 1997. Current status of the Burrowing Owl in North America: an agency survey. Pages 3-5 *in* J. Lincer and K. Steenhof, editors. The Burrowing Owl, its biology and management including the Proceedings of the First International Burrowing Owl Symposium. Raptor Research Report Number 9.

Sauer, J. R., J. E. Hines, and J. Fallon. 2002. The North American Breeding Bird Survey, Results and Analysis 1966-2001. Version 2002.1, U.S. Geological Survey, Patuxent Wildlife Research Center, Laurel, Maryland. http://www.mbr-pwrc.usgs.gov/bbs/bbs2001.html.

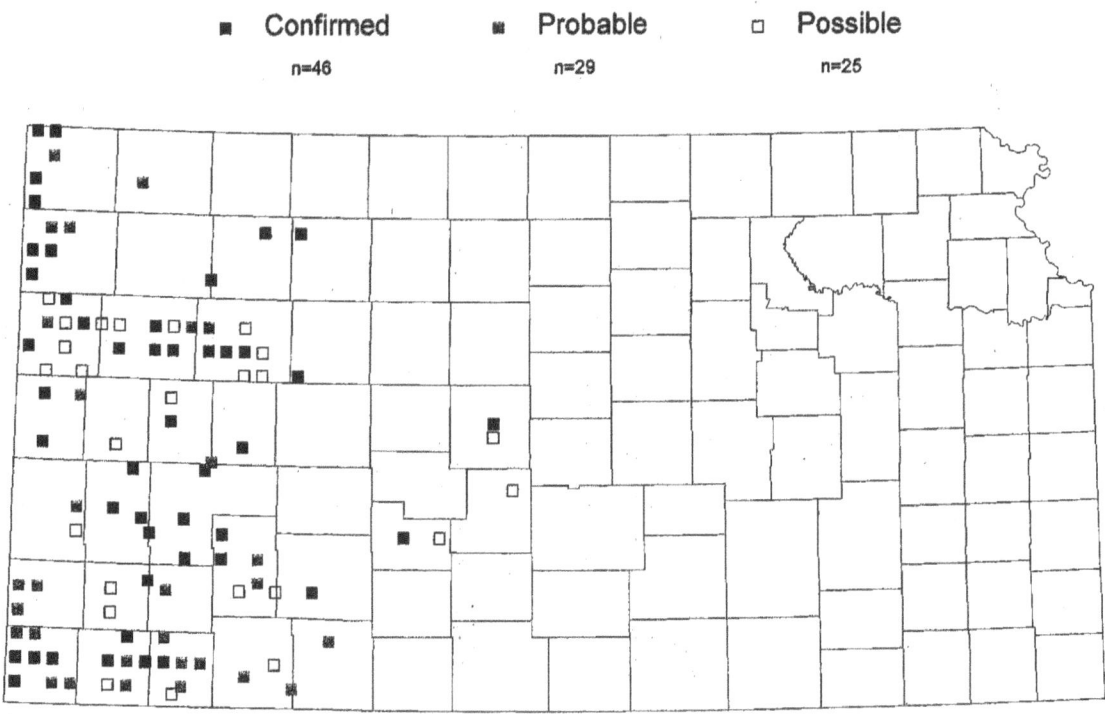

Fig. A-4. Distribution of Burrowing Owls in Kansas from the Kansas Breeding Bird Atlas project (Busby and Zimmerman 2001).

Minnesota

Summary: The Burrowing Owl was a regular to common breeding bird in the prairies of w. Minnesota in the first half of the century, but began to decline between approximately 1940 and 1960. The Burrowing Owl is now considered a very rare or casual resident in the sw. and wc. regions. Only ten documented breeding records exist from 1965-1985 (Janssen 1987, Martell et al. 2001). Reintroduction attempts from 1986-90 were unsuccessful; no returning Burrowing Owls were found in the years subsequent to release. Also, no successful natural nests were documented in 1992-98, despite significant efforts to locate the species (Martell et al. 2001).

BBS: N/A

CBC: N/A

Atlas: Unknown

Research/Monitoring Martell et al. (2001) located 13 natural nests at eight sites in Rock, Pipestone, Travers, and Yellow Medicine Counties, Minnesota during 1986-1990. Mean reproductive success was 3.54 young/pair. Nesting habitats included alfalfa fields (37.5%), pasture, (37.5%), roadside ditch (12.5%), and fenceline (12.5%).

During 1986-1990, 105 pre-flight juvenile Burrowing Owls were released (9 in 1986, 18 in 1987, 21 in 1988, 27 in 1989, and 30 in 1990). Eight fledgling mortalities were documented in the release area. No individuals were relocated after leaving the hack site and no successful nesting attempts were documented 1991-1998 (Martell et al. 2001).

Conservation Activities: Reintroduction of Burrowing Owls was attempted within the historic range in w. Minnesota from 1986-90 (Martell et al. 2001) but discontinued since no owls returned to breed in subsequent years. Land management reported in Martell et al. (2001) focused on protection and enhancement of nesting sites. Landowners were encouraged to maintain fields used by nesting Burrowing Owls in current rotations (e.g., alfalfa) or to enroll those fields in federal agricultural set-aside programs. In 1989, 24 artificial nest burrows were installed near natural burrows to provide alternate nest sites for returning pairs of owls or their offspring. One pair of owls nested and fledged seven young from an artificial burrow the year after their natural burrow collapsed. The artificial structure was located in the same field, approximately 40 m from the original burrow (Henderson 1984, Martell et al. 2001).

No management or research is currently planned beyond protection under current state and federal legislation (e.g., Migratory Bird Treaty Act, Minnesota Endangered Species Act). Should this situation change, habitat protection, management, and public education and cooperation will remain important. Selective use of reintroductions may also be useful in enhancing these efforts (Martell et al. 2001).

Major Populations: None. The Burrowing Owl is considered a very rare or casual resident in the sw. and wc. regions of Minnesota.

State Status: Endangered

Natural Heritage Rank: G4/S1 (Critically imperiled because of extreme rarity or other factor making it especially vulnerable to extirpation)

Habitat Use and Condition: In Minnesota, Burrowing Owls typically select heavily grazed pasture or mixed-grass prairie with colonies of Richardson's ground squirrels (Coffin and Pfannmuller 1988). Martell et al. (2001) reported nesting Burrowing Owls in alfalfa fields, suggesting some potential adaptability to agricultural habitats. Loss of pastures and prairies in western Minnesota has been a factor in the decline of Burrowing Owls in the state. However, some seemingly suitable habitat remains unused.

Threats: Loss of prairie and pasture habitats represent the primary threat to Burrowing Owls in Minnesota (Grant 1965, Martell et al. 2001).

Literature Cited:

Coffin, B., and L. Pfannmuller. 1988. Burrowing Owl. Page 264 *in* Minnesota's Endangered Flora and Fauna. B. Coffin and L. Pfannmuller, editors. University of Minnesota Press, Minneapolis, Minnesota.

Grant, R. A. 1965. The Burrowing Owl in Minnesota. Loon 37:2-17.

Henderson, C. L. 1984. Woodworking for wildlife: homes for birds and mammals. Minnesota Department of Natural Resources, St. Paul, Minnesota.

Janssen, R. B. 1987. Birds in Minnesota. University of Minnesota Press, Minneapolis, MN.

Martell, M. S., J. Schladweiler, and F. Cuthbert. 2001. Status and attempted reintroduction of Burrowing Owls in Minnesota, USA. Journal of Raptor Research 35:331-336.

Montana

Summary: The Burrowing Owl is a rare breeder in Montana. The majority of confirmed Burrowing Owl breeding records are east of the continental divide in association with black-tailed prairie dog and Richardson's ground squirrel colonies. Breeding west of the continental divide is probably associated with badger-enlarged Columbian ground squirrel burrows.

Marti and Marks (1989) reported the Burrowing Owl as common in Montana with a stable population trend from 1977-86. However, no records for number of nesting pairs or number of nest sites were reported. Based on a survey of state wildlife agencies, James and Espie (1997) estimated 100 to 1,000 pairs of Burrowing Owls in Montana in 1992 with a stable population trend. Atkinson (2000) estimated 644 ± 114 Burrowing Owl pairs in known prairie dog colonies in Montana.

BBS: No significant trends were detected over any survey period (Sauer et al. 2002).

CBC: N/A

Atlas: No atlas available. The Montana Bird Distribution shows evidence of breeding in 25 latilongs and indirect evidence in an additional 13 latilongs between 1991-95 (Fig. A-5). Nonbreeding observations encompass another 7 latilongs and there were no records of Burrowing Owls in 2 latilongs (Montana Bird Distribution Committee 1996).

Research/Monitoring Atkinson (2000) derived an estimate of Burrowing Owl population size through analyses of the one-stage stratified random sample obtained from surveys in 1999. Surveyors detected 474 owls with at least 123 pairs; occupancy rate was 38.2% (78 of 204 colonies). Atkinson (2000) estimated the Burrowing Owl population size at 644 ± 114 pairs in known prairie dog colonies in Montana. As supporting evidence, Atkinson (2000) estimated 819 pairs by direct extrapolation of the pair density (123 pairs / 10,079 acres) from surveyed colonies to the known colony acreage statewide (67,080 acres). In identical fashion, he estimated 787 pairs by extrapolating 123 pairs / 209 colonies to 1,337 known colonies. Atkinson (2000) stated that c. Montana, the Charles M. Russell National Wildlife Refuge (NWR), the Custer area in Custer and Prairie counties, s. Chouteau County, and Phillips County were adequately sampled. Parts of Wheatland County, the Northern Cheyenne and Fort Belknap reservations, and Rosebud and s. Custer counties were not adequately sampled in 1999.

A population estimate of 864 Burrowing Owl pairs was derived for four study areas in eastern Montana (Fort Belknap Reservation, South Phillips County, Custer Creek, and Northern Cheyenne Reservation. Restani et al. (2001) documented one Burrowing Owl pair/110 ha of prairie dog town habitat in southeastern Montana in 1998. Prairie dog towns occupied by Burrowing Owls were similar in size to unoccupied towns and no selection was demonstrated for or against towns subjected to recreational shooting or grazing. Occupied nests were closer to active prairie dog burrows than random locations; otherwise Burrowing Owl nest sites were not different than random sites in numerous habitat characteristics (Atkinson 2000, Restani et al. 2001).

Mean Burrowing Owl productivity was 2.6 ± 0.4 young/pair (n = 13) and was not correlated with number of active or inactive burrows, total number of burrows, or town size (Restani et al. 2001). Productivity was not influenced by recreational prairie dog shooting (2.3 young/pair on shot towns; 2.9 young/pair elsewhere).

Prairie dog towns were similar in size and mean burrow density in 1991 and 1998; however, total acreage of prairie dog habitat increased slightly (Restani et al. 2001). Burrowing Owls were present at 16% of prairie dog towns surveyed in 1998 compared to 4% in 1996 (Wittenhagen and Tribby 1996), 14%, in 1991 (Richardson and Tribby 1991), and 27 % in 1978-79 (Restani et al. 2001, Knowles *In review*). Restani et al. (2001) felt the low density of breeding owls, high nearest neighbor distances, and abundant unoccupied habitat suggested the Burrowing Owl population was well below carrying capacity on their study site in southeastern Montana.

Conservation Activities: Indicator colonies will be selected and surveyed on a yearly basis for long-term trends and distribution in addition to randomly selected sites (Atkinson 2000).

Major Populations: Montana's largest prairie dog complex occurs in Phillips and Blaine counties and appears to contain Montana's largest Burrowing Owl complex (currently ~11,336 ha (28,000 ac). Prairie dog colony acreage in this complex appeared to peak in the early 1990s (~21,457 ha (53,000 ac)) (Knowles *In review*).

State Status: Species of Special Concern

Natural Heritage Rank: G4/S3B, SZN (rare and uncommon breeding populations in the state, no non-breeding occurrences).

Habitat Use and Condition: Black-tailed prairie dogs and Richardson's ground squirrel colonies comprise the primary and secondary habitats of Burrowing Owls in Montana. These species are found exclusively east of the Continental Divide and therefore most confirmed Burrowing Owl breeding records are also east of the Divide (Knowles *In review*). Most Burrowing Owls records from west of the Continental Divide are probably associated with badger-enlarged holes in Columbian ground squirrel colonies (Knowles *In review*).

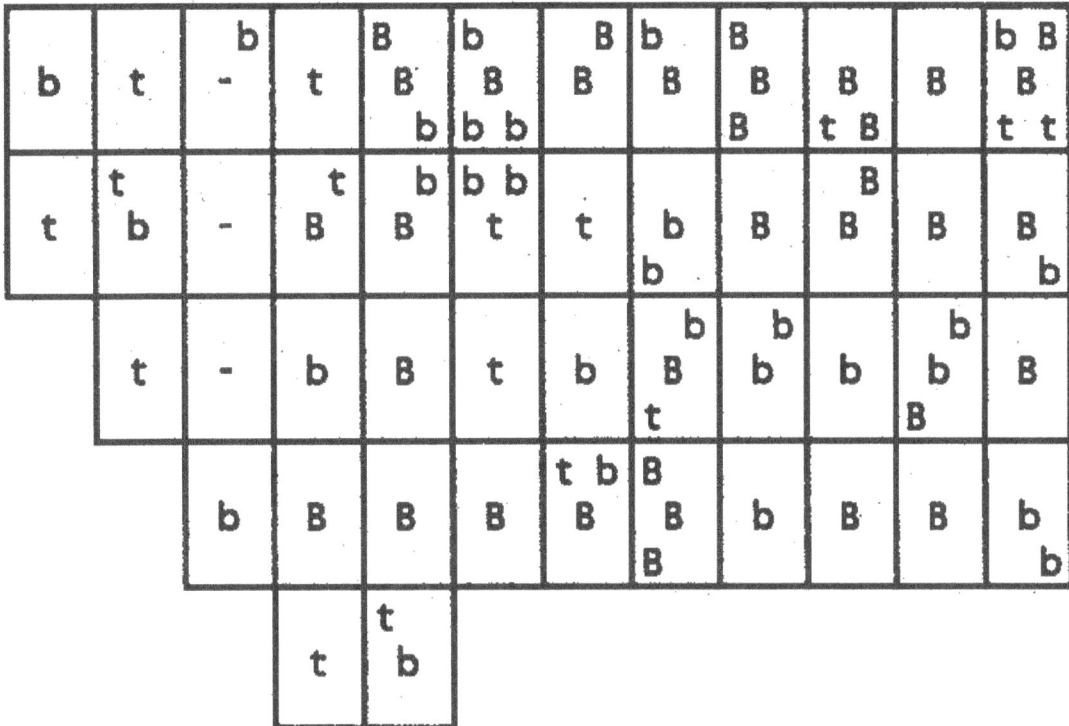

Fig. A-5. Latilong distribution of Burrowing Owls in Montana. B = direct evidence of breeding, b = indirect evidence of breeding, t = species observed, but no evidence of breeding (Montana Bird Distribution Committee 1996).

Most occupied prairie dog habitat in Custer and Harris Creek watersheds (southeast Montana) was on private land (65%), followed by federal (30%) and state lands (5%) (Restani et al 2001). Average town size was 11.0 ± 1.9 ha and 17.3 ± 5.3 ha on private and public lands, respectively. Fifty-four percent of breeding Burrowing Owls were on private land, 23% on state, and the remaining 23% on federal lands.

On the Charles M. Russell NWR in e. Montana, prairie dogs were limited to 283 ha (700 acres) in 1964 (the end of intensive eradication efforts; B. Haglan, pers. commun.). In 1974 prairie dog acreage was 1,807 ha (4,464 acres) and in 1979 acreage had increased to 2,504 ha (6,185 acres). Prairie dog surveys were conducted on the Refuge in 1983, 1988, 1993, and 1997, but data were not reported (Knowles *In review*).

Montana's prairie dog population has declined by 90% or more the 20th century (Flath and Clark 1986). The loss of prairie dogs due to systematic control resulted in a corresponding decline in Burrowing Owls up through at least 1972 when poisoning by the U.S. Fish and Wildlife Service's Animal Damage Control ended on private and public lands (Knowles *In review*). Approximately half of Montana's remaining prairie dog acreage has been

lost during the past decade primarily due to plague (Knowles *In review*). Additional impacts identified for this period included recreational shooting, poisoning, and agricultural land conversions (Knowles *In review*).

Threats: Rodent poisoning, plague, and habitat conversion to cropland have reduced and fragmented prairie dog town habitat in Montana (Flath and Clark 1986). Montana's state agricultural agencies consider prairie dogs vertebrate pests and require systematic suppression (Restani et al. 2001), thereby reducing Burrowing Owl habitat.

Recreational shooting on Montana's prairie dog colonies has the potential to cause direct illegal mortality of Burrowing Owl. Anecdotal data suggests that owls are being shot but the significance of this problem remains undocumented (Knowles *In review*). Restani et al. (2001) found no evidence of Burrowing Owl mortality related to recreational shooting; however, they felt it may disrupted daytime foraging activity of adults. Prairie dog shooting may leave prairie dog carcasses on the surface with significant concentrations of lead, which may be ingested by Burrowing Owls (Knowles *In review*).

Literature Cited:

Atkinson, E. C. 2000. Montana–wide Burrowing Owl Surveys: Description of First Year Results, 1999. Unpublished Report, Marmot's Edge Conservation, Belgrade, Montana.

Flath, D. L., and T.W. Clark. 1986. Historic status of black-footed ferret habitat in Montana. Great Basin Naturalist Memoirs 8:63-71.

James, P. C., and R. H. M. Espie. 1997. Current status of the Burrowing Owl in North America: an agency survey. Pages 3-5 *in* J. Lincer and K. Steenhof, editors. The Burrowing Owl, its biology and management including the Proceedings of the First International Burrowing Owl Symposium. Raptor Research Report Number 9.

Knowles, C. J. *In review*. A Review of Burrowing Owl Observations Recorded in Montana 1964-1999. FaunaWest Wildlife Consultants Rept., Boulder, Montana.

Marti, C. D., and J. S. Marks. 1989. Medium-sized owls. Pages 124-133 *in* B. A. Giron Pendleton, editor. Proceedings of the Western Raptor Management Symposium and Workshop, National Wildlife Federation, Washington, DC.

Montana Bird Distribution Committee. 1996. P.D. Skarr's Montana Bird Distribution. 5th edition. Special publication no. 3. Montana Natural Heritage Program, Helena, MT.

Restani, M., L. R. Rau, and D. L. Flath. 2001. Nesting ecology Of Burrowing Owls occupying prairie dog towns In southeastern Montana. Journal of Raptor Research 35:296-303.

Richardson, R., and D. C. Tribby. 1991. Status of the Black-tailed Prairie Dog in the Custer Creek Complex, Big Dry Resource Area, Miles City District. Bureau of Land Management. U.S. Department of Interior, Technical Report.

Sauer, J. R., J. E. Hines, and J. Fallon. 2002. The North American Breeding Bird Survey, Results and Analysis 1966-2001. Version 2002.1, U.S. Geological Survey, Patuxent Wildlife Research Center, Laurel, Maryland. http://www.mbr-pwrc.usgs.gov/bbs/bbs2001.html.

Wittenhagen, K. W., Jr., and D. C. Tribby. 1996. Status of the Black-tailed Prairie Dog in the Custer Creek Complex, Big Dry Resource Area, Miles City District. Bureau of Land Management. U.S. Department of Interior, Technical Report.

Nebraska

Summary: Burrowing Owls regularly nest in the western two-thirds of Nebraska. Loss of prairie habitat and prairie dog declines have reduced available nesting areas, especially in the eastern part of the state (Ducey 1988). James and Espie (1997) estimated 100 to 1,000 pairs of Burrowing Owls in Nebraska in 1992. The population trend was thought to be decreasing due to habitat loss and pesticide use (James and Espie 1997).

BBS: No significant trends were detected for any survey period (Sauer et al. 2002).

CBC: N/A

Atlas: The Burrowing Owl was previously a common breeder throughout Nebraska; however, breeding is now restricted to the western two-thirds of the state where it is most abundant in the Panhandle (Fig. A-6). Rare observations occur in e. Nebraska, primarily during fall migration (Sharpe et al. 2001).

Research/Monitoring In w. Nebraska, breeding Burrowing Owl pairs declined 63% (91 to 34) from 1990-96 (Desmond et al. 2000). Owl numbers and density of active and inactive prairie dog burrows declined linearly between 1990-96. There was a time-lag in Burrowing Owl response to changes in burrow densities on several prairie dog colonies (Desmond et al. 2000).

Productivity from 1989-93 was low with 1.9 ± 0.1 fledglings/nest (Desmond et al. 2000). Few within-colony variables related to fledging success and a significant colony effect in all five years of productivity study indicated that factors influencing fledging success were at the colony scale. Predation by badgers was significantly lower in high density prairie dog colonies in three of seven years. In one of two years examined, successful nests had an average of 96 active prairie dog burrows within 75 m and unsuccessful nests had only 26 active burrows. This disparity in nesting success may be from enhanced detection of predators by prairie dogs, a dilution effect with abundant alternate prey, reduced vegetation height allowing increased visibility of predators, or presence of alternate burrows for brood dispersal (Desmond et al. 2000).

In w. Nebraska (Banner, Box Butte, Morrill, Scotts Bluff and Sioux counties) Desmond and Savidge (1996) found 85 Burrowing Owl nests in 1989, 109 in 1990, and 103 in 1991. More Burrowing Owls were found in prairie dog communities than in areas with only badger burrows for nesting. Burrowing Owl densities declined between 1989-91 in small prairie dog colonies (<35 ha), but were relatively constant in large colonies ($\geq$ 35 ha). As an indication of density and distribution, nearest-neighbor distance averaged 125 ± 5 m (n = 105, range 46–229 m) for Burrowing Owl nest clusters in large prairie dog colonies. Mean nearest-neighbor distance in small colonies was 105 ± 7 m (n = 118, range 11–434 m) and

240 ± 39 m (n = 20, range 58–588 m) for Burrowing Owls nesting in badger burrows.

Desmond and Savidge (1996) found that Burrowing Owl densities were inversely related to prairie dog town size, active burrow density, inactive burrow density, and total burrow density for at least one of the three years of study. This suggested that burrow availability was not a limiting factor for Burrowing Owls on prairie dog colonies, but they did note that nest sites may be limiting in pastures with only badger burrows. Total Burrowing Owl numbers were positively related to prairie dog town size, but were not related to active, inactive, or total prairie dog burrow densities (Desmond and Savidge 1996). Thus, prairie dog town size, rather than numbers of burrows, was important in determining owl densities and numbers in western Nebraska.

Desmond et al. (1995) hypothesized that if gregarious nesting by Burrowing Owls in prairie dog towns was a response to limited habitat, owl nests should be randomly or regularly distributed throughout the towns with nearest neighbor distance positively related to town size. Alternatively, given sufficient space and burrows, they felt that Burrowing Owls should exhibit a nonrandom spatial nesting pattern. Desmond et al. (1995) found random distributions for Burrowing Owl nests at densities of $\geq$ 0.22 nests/ha which related to prairie dog towns <35 ha in size. Conversely, Burrowing Owls at densities $\leq$ 0.20 nests/ha had clumped distributions (with only one exception) and were related to prairie dog towns $\geq$ 35 ha in size. Within small towns, the nearest neighbor distance between Burrowing Owl nests was positively related to town size; however, this relationship did not occur in large towns. Clumping did not appear to be related to prey abundance or precipitation rates since the spatial patterns of Burrowing Owl nests were similar across the years of study while environmental factors changed. These findings suggest that habitat was limiting on small prairie dog towns and the random distribution was a function of minimum space requirements by Burrowing Owls. Habitat did not appear to be limiting on prairie dog towns $\geq$ 35 ha, as evidenced by lower Burrowing Owl density, clumped distributions, and unoccupied areas of apparently suitable burrows (Desmond et al. 1995). This research further suggested that additional limiting factors, beyond burrow availability, are influencing Burrowing Owl populations in Nebraska, and perhaps elsewhere.

In w. Nebraska, Burrowing Owl chicks preferred to use active versus inactive prairie-dog burrows for satellite burrows (Desmond et al. 1995). The authors cited burrow maintenance by prairie dogs as the primary benefit; inactive burrows degraded quickly (1-3 yrs) and were unsuitable for Burrowing Owls. Family groups used 10 ± 1 (range 0-36) satellite burrows within 75 m of the nest. Twenty-nine broods preferred active satellite burrows, two broods used active burrows less than expected (both were in

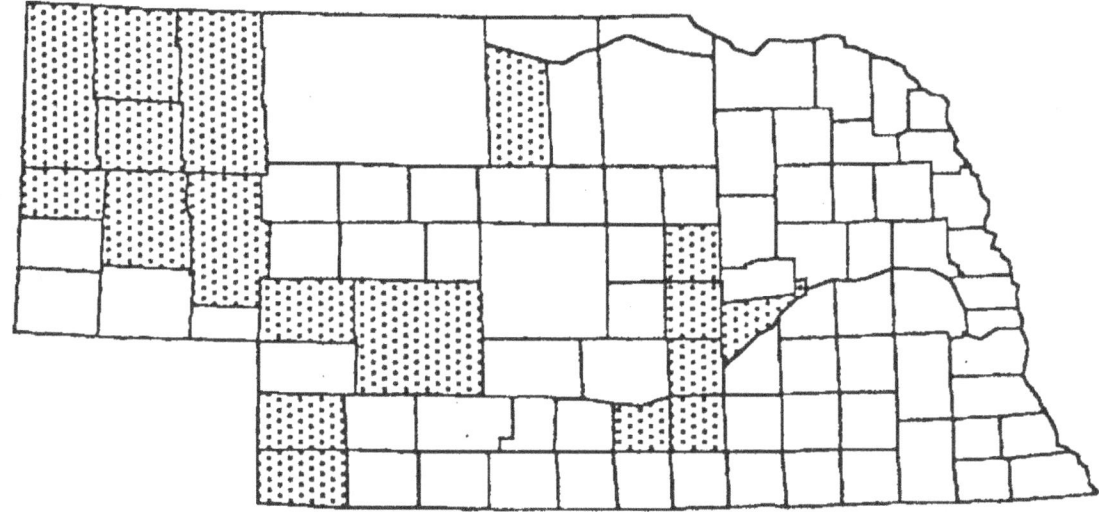

Fig. A-6. Distribution of Burrowing Owls in Nebraska, based on breeding evidence post-1960 (Ducey 1988).

areas with few active burrows due to poisoning), and 11 broods used active burrows in proportion to their availability. Furthermore, seven of the later category had nearly 100% of satellite burrows in active prairie dog burrows. Nine nest burrows had no active prairie-dog burrows within 75 m of the nest (Desmond et al. 1995).

Desmond et al. (1995) found that prairie dog activity in the vicinity of Burrowing Owl nests strongly influenced nest success and attributed this to predator avoidance through prairie dog alarm calls and the "dilution effect" where predators were more likely to target prairie dogs versus the owls. Successful Burrowing Owl nests had more active prairie-dog burrows within a 75-m radius of the nest burrow (Mean = 96 ± 5 m; n = 60) than unsuccessful nests (Mean = 26 ± 4 m; n = 104; Desmond et al. 1995).

Conservation Activities: None identified.

Major Populations: Desmond and Savidge (1996) found 85 Burrowing Owl nests in 1989, 109 in 1990, and 103 in 1991 in 21 prairie dog towns and 17 grassland pastures in Banner, Box Butte, Morrill, Scotts Bluff, and Sioux counties (western Nebraska).

Burrowing Owl surveys were conducted in Banner, Box Butte, Kimball, Morrill, Scotts Bluff and Sioux counties in nw. Nebraska. Of the 92 sites surveyed for prairie dog associates in May/June 2001, 67 contained Burrowing Owls (242 adult Burrowing Owls). Of the 67 Burrowing Owl locations, nine were off-colony sightings and generally only included one or two individuals. In only three of these cases were possible nest burrows observed (all appeared to be old badger or fox dens). The other Burrowing Owls may have been foraging individuals that had

ventured far from their nest sites, though three were located in dense sagebrush habitat where ground burrows were difficult to detect (T. VerCauteren, pers. commun.). Sixty-one additional sites (171 individuals) were observed in Cheyenne, Garden, Keith, and Perkins counties by Z. Roehrs, University of Nebraska (T. VerCauteren, pers. commun.). The majority of these sightings were based on road-side counts and do not represent total populations.

State Status: None.

Natural Heritage Rank: G4/S3 (rare and uncommon in the state).

Habitat Use and Condition: Virtually no information was available on habitat condition. A small amount of habitat related research was conducted in western Nebraska by Desmond (1991); however, this thesis focused primarily on spatial relationships within prairie dog towns and badger burrow areas. The author found Burrowing Owls near both agricultural and range habitats. More nests were located in agricultural areas; however, there was no significant difference in numbers or density of Burrowing Owl pairs between the two habitat types.

Threats: Destruction of black-tailed prairie dogs is the primary threat to Burrowing Owls in Nebraska. Black-tailed prairie dog control in Nebraska in 1990-91 accounted for 50% of the reported prairie dog control activity nationwide, and Nebraska state law required prairie dog eradication on public and private lands until 1995 (Roemer and Forrest 1996, Desmond et al. 2000). Desmond and Savidge (1999) documented reduced burrow availability and increased predation rates in prairie dog town subjected to prairie dog control efforts.

Literature Cited:

Desmond, M. J. 1991. Ecological aspects of Burrowing Owl nesting strategies in the Nebraska panhandle. M.S. Thesis, University of Nebraska, Lincoln, NE.

Desmond, M. J., J. A. Savidge, and T. F. Seibert. 1995. Spatial patterns of Burrowing Owl *(Speotyto cunicularia)* nests in black-tailed prairie dog *(Cynomys ludovicianus)* towns in western Nebraska. Canadian Journal of Zoology 73:1375-1379.

Desmond, M. J. and J. A. Savidge. 1996. Factors influencing Burrowing Owl *(Speotyto cunicularia)* nest densities and numbers In western Nebraska. American Midland Naturalist 136:143-148.

Desmond, M. J., and J. A. Savidge. 1999. Satellite burrow use by Burrowing Owl chicks and its influence on nest fate. Pages 128-130 *in* P. D. Vickery and J. R. Herkert, editors. Ecology and conservation of grassland birds of the western hemisphere. Studies in Avian Biology 19.

Desmond, M. J., J. A. Savidge, and K. M. Eskridge. 2000. Correlations between Burrowing Owl and black-tailed prairie dog declines: a 7-Year analysis. Journal of Wildlife Management 64:1067-1075.

Ducey, J. E. 1988. Nebraska Birds, Breeding Status and Distribution. Simmons-Boardman Books, Omaha, Nebraska.

James, P. C., and R. H. M. Espie. 1997. Current status of the Burrowing Owl in North America: an agency survey. Pages 3-5 *in* J. Lincer and K. Steenhof, editors The Burrowing Owl, its biology and management including the Proceedings of the First International Burrowing Owl Symposium. Raptor Research Report Number 9.

Roemer, D. M., and S. C. Forrest. 1996. Prairie dog poisoning in Northern Great Plains: an analysis of programs and policies. Environmental Management 20:349-359.

Sauer, J. R., J. E. Hines, and J. Fallon. 2002. The North American Breeding Bird Survey, Results and Analysis 1966-2001. Version 2002.1, U.S. Geological Survey, Patuxent Wildlife Research Center, Laurel, Maryland. http://www.mbr-pwrc.usgs.gov/bbs/bbs2001.html.

Sharpe, R. S., W. R. Silcock, J. G. Jorgensen. 2001. Birds of Nebraska: Their Distribution and Temporal Occurrence. University of Nebraska Press, Lincoln, Nebraska.

Nevada

Summary: Burrowing Owls breed throughout Nevada in salt desert scrub, Mojave shrub, and some sagebrush habitat, as well as in agricultural landscapes. It winters most frequently in the southern half of Nevada, but has been recorded throughout the state during all months (Herron et al. 1985). Local declines are noted where habitat is lost to development at the suburban fringe. For example observations suggest a decline of up to 50% in the Lahontan Valley since 1946 (Alcorn 1988). The statewide population was roughly estimated at 1,000 to 10,000 pairs in 1992, based on a survey of state wildlife agencies in 1992 (James and Espie 1997).

BBS: No significant trends were detected for any survey period (Sauer et al. 2002).

CBC: N/A. This species rarely winters in n. Nevada and sparingly in the s. part of the state.

Atlas: Confirmed or suspected breeding in nearly every county (Fig. A-7, Nevada Breeding Bird Atlas, unpublished data, T. Floyd, pers. commun.). No Atlas records for Mineral, Esmeralda, Douglas, Carson City, or Storey counties.

Research/Monitoring Burrowing Owls were intensively monitored on the Nevada Test Site (NTS) in sc. Nevada from 1996-2001 (Hall et al. *In review*, Steen et al. 1997). Three main ecoregions are recognized on the NTS: Great Basin Desert (Great Basin), Mojave Desert (Mojave), and a transitional ecoregion between the two deserts (transition). A total of 114 Burrowing Owl locations, including 84 burrowing sites and 30 sighting locations, were documented on the NTS for a density of 2.4 Burrowing Owls burrows/100 km^2. Sixty-two locations (54%) occurred in the transition, 37 (33%) occurred in the Mojave, nine (8%) occurred in the Great Basin, and six (5%) were at historic, unspecified locations. Most of the locations occurred in areas with disturbances containing partially buried metal culverts and pipes, relatively deep washes with defined banks, mounds of dirt or excavations, or roadcuts.

A total of 19 nest burrows were documented using camera systems from 1999-2001. Breeding was detected during at least one of the three years at 15 sites (10 in transition, 3 in Mojave, two in Great Basin). Breeding during two of the three years occurred at three sites (two in transition, one in Great Basin), and at one site (transition) breeding occurred during all three years. Nest burrows were predominately in metal culverts or metal or plastic pipes. Two nest burrows were in washbanks, two in man-made dirt mounds, two in roadcuts, and one in a desert tortoise burrow (Hall et al. *In review*, Steen et al. 1997).

A total of 26 breeding pairs and 122 young were detected over the three-year period. Seven, eight, and 11 breeding pairs and 24, 43, and 55 young were detected during 1999, 2000, and 2001, respectively. The average number of young per breeding pairs during the entire period was 4.7 (s.d. = 2.0, n = 26). The average number of young per breeding pair by year was 3.4 (s.d = 1.6, n = 7), 5.6 (s.d. = 1.6, n = 8), and 5.0 (s.d. = 2.1, n = 11) during 1999, 2000, and 2001, respectively. The average number of young per breeding pair by ecoregion was 5.0 (s.d. = 1.8, n = 19), 4.5 (s.d. = 3.1, n = 4), and 3.0 (s.d. = 0, n = 3) in the transition, Great Basin, and Mojave, respectively. Twelve (42%) nesting burrows produced young during two or more years between 1999 and 2001. There appeared to be a relationship between the number of young per breeding pair and the amount of precipitation received during the previous October to March. Young were detected between mid-May and early-September. The local population trend appears to be stable. The increase in number of breeding pairs is due to finding new burrows over the three years and does not necessarily reflect a true increase in the population (Steen et al. 1997, Hall et al. *In review*).

Most of the known Burrowing Owls were monitored at least monthly November 1997–July 1998 and November 1998–December 2001. Burrowing Owls were found on the NTS year-round. Generally, Burrowing Owls wintered on the NTS in low numbers with a large influx around mid-March. Owl numbers fluctuated slightly during the spring and summer, increased slightly during September-October, and then steadily declined through late fall and early winter until they reached their lowest point, usually in January (Steen et al. 1997, Hall et al. *In review*).

Burrowing Owls on the NTS appeared to be quite tolerant of disturbance as measured by traffic counters and flushing distance to observers on foot and in a vehicle. Burrowing Owls successfully produced young with few to many vehicles (<1 to 488 per day) passing withing 10 to 269 m of a nest burrow. No apparent relationship was evident between the number of vehicles per day or distance to road and the number of young. Average flushing distance was approximately 31 m (n = 130) to an observer on foot and approximately 29 m (n = 79) to a vehicle (Steen et al. 1997, Hall et al. *In review*).

The Las Vegas Field Station of the U.S. Geological Survey, Biological Resources Division, in cooperation with the National Park Service will initiate a research study on Burrowing Owls at the Lake Mead National Recreation Area (NRA) in s. Nevada, scheduled to begin in 2002. The objective of the study is to determine distribution and abundance of Burrowing Owls inhabiting the Lake Mead NRA, to relate population abundance to environmental variables on a landscape scale to determine area of high to low Burrowing Owl densities, and evaluate reproductive success in relation to habitat and environmental variables (R. Williams, pers. commun.).

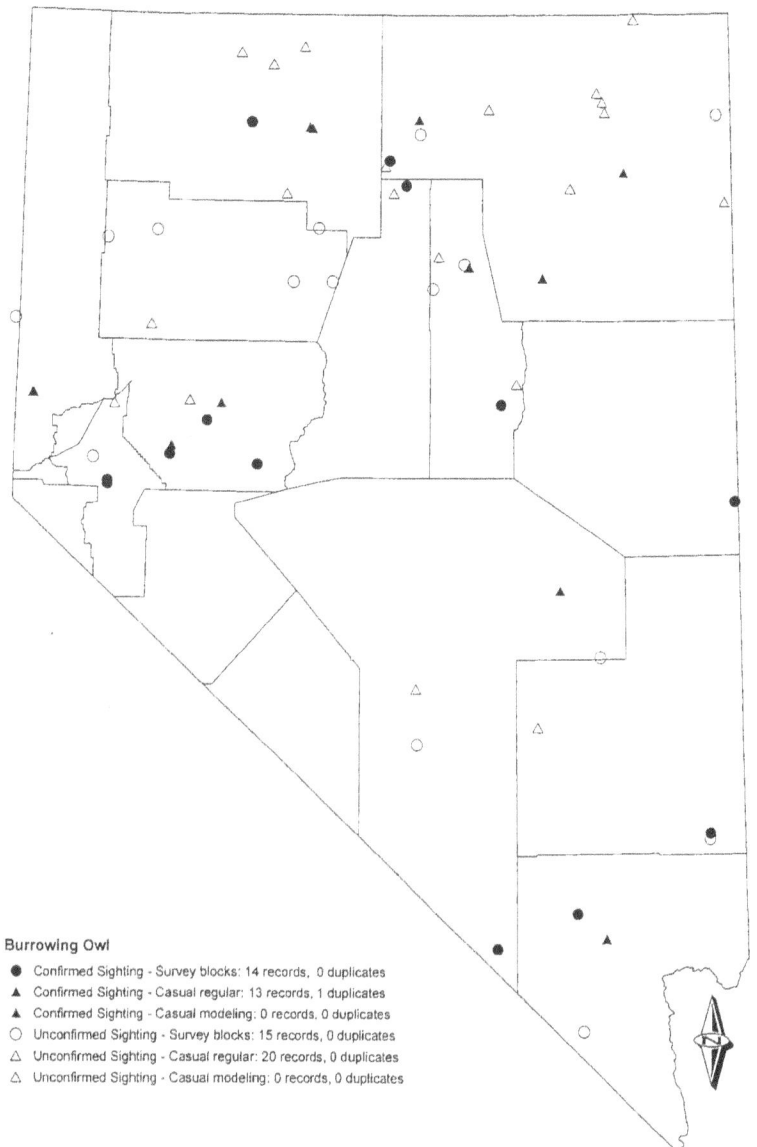

Burrowing Owl

- ● Confirmed Sighting - Survey blocks: 14 records, 0 duplicates
- ▲ Confirmed Sighting - Casual regular: 13 records, 1 duplicates
- ▲ Confirmed Sighting - Casual modeling: 0 records, 0 duplicates
- ○ Unconfirmed Sighting - Survey blocks: 15 records, 0 duplicates
- △ Unconfirmed Sighting - Casual regular: 20 records, 0 duplicates
- △ Unconfirmed Sighting - Casual modeling: 0 records, 0 duplicates

Fig. A-7. Distribution of Burrowing Owls in Nevada from the Nevada Breeding Bird Atlas project (Unpubl. data).

Conservation Activities: The Nevada Partners in Flight Bird Conservation Plan (Neel 1999) outlines conservation measures to improve conditions for Burrowing Owls in the State, and establishes a population objective, to stabilize Burrowing Owl populations by 2004, in each of the 3 habitat types used by Burrowing Owls in Nevada: Agricultural Landscapes, Mojave Scrub, and Salt Scrub.

The Nevada Breeding Bird Atlas proposes to predict the range and breeding locations of Burrowing Owls based on currently known breeding locations and on the distributions of vegetation types within the State. These projections may be used for conservation planning and, with ground-truthing, lead to further investigations of specific habitat conditions favorable for owls.

Major Populations: A total of 114 Burrowing Owl locations, including 19 nest burrows occurred on the NTS in sc. Nevada.

State Status: Species protected under Nevada Revised Statutes 501 and Nevada Administrative Code 503.

Natural Heritage Rank: G4/S3B (rare and uncommon breeding populations in the state).

Habitat Use and Condition: In Nevada, sparsely-vegetated habitats preferred by Burrowing Owls are predominantly found in the salt desert scrub habitat type, which occupies roughly 8.9 million hectares of valley bottoms within the Great Basin physiographic region. Sagebrush habitat was also occupied when artificial burrows were placed in moderately dense sagebrush communities. Burrowing Owls often breed around the fringes of agricultural lands and use crop and pasture lands for foraging during the breeding season. General habitat condition in many of the known nesting territories is poor. Excessive grazing by large ungulates does not seem to decrease nest site suitability, and may be preferred because of increased visibility. Burrowing Owls also nest in open urban areas with open space (e.g., golf courses, airport runways, and industrial areas) if burrows are available. Concrete slabs and other debris left at the old Stead Air Force Base north of Reno, inhabited by California ground squirrels, provided high density nesting habitat for over 40 years (Neel 1999).

Habitat condition of salt desert scrub varies with grazing and fire history. Indian ricegrass was likely much more prevalent historically in this habitat than it is today, and is an important plant for kangaroo rats, a key component in the ecology of this habitat and a prey item for Burrowing Owls. Indiscriminate livestock grazing over the 100-year period following European settlement has tipped the balance toward more durable shrubs, unpalatable forbs, and exotic annual grasses on vast tracts of salt desert scrub.

Invasion of exotic plants such as cheatgrass, halogeton, Russian thistle, and in certain places, tamarisk has compromised native communities (Neel 1999). The effect of this type of habitat conversion on Burrowing Owls has not been measured.

Threats: In general, habitat loss is occurring due to agricultural cultivation and development. Development has placed nesting Burrowing Owls under increasing pressure near Reno, Carson City, and Minden-Gardnerville in particular (Neel 1999). Loss of native components and invasion of exotics in Nevada's shrub habitats may have negative implications for Burrowing Owls (see Habitat Use and Condition).

Literature Cited:

Alcorn, J. R. 1988. The Birds of Nevada. Fairview West Publishing, Fallon, Nevada.

Hall, D. B., P. D. Greger, and A. V. Housewright. *In review*. Burrowing owl ecology on the Nevada Test Site. DOE/NV/11718–701. U.S. Department of Energy, National Nuclear Security Administration, Nevada Operations Office, Las Vegas, Nevada.

Herron, G. B., C. A. Mortimore, and M. S. Rawlings. 1985. Nevada Raptors: Their biology and management. Nevada Department of Wildlife.

James, P. C., and R. H. M. Espie. 1997. Current status of the Burrowing Owl in North America: An agency survey. Pages 3-5 in J. Lincer and K. Steenhof, editors. The Burrowing Owl, its biology and management including the Proceedings of the First International Burrowing Owl Symposium. Raptor Reserarch Report Number 9.

Neel, L. 1999. Nevada Partners in Flight Bird Conservation Plan. Nevada Partners in Flight. http://www.blm.gov/wildlife/plan/pl-nv-10.pdf

Sauer, J. R., J. E. Hines, and J. Fallon. 2002. The North American Breeding Bird Survey, Results and Analysis 1966–2001. Version 2002.1, U.S. Geological Survey, Patuxent Wildlife Research Center, Laurel, Maryland. http://www.mbr-pwrc.usgs.gov/bbs/bbs2001.html.

Steen, D. C., D. B. Hall, P. D. Greger, and C. A. Wills. 1997. Distribution of the chuckwalla, western burrowing owl, and six bat species on the Nevada Test Site. DOE/NV/11718–149. U.S. Department of Energy, Nevada Operations Office, Las Vegas, Nevada.

New Mexico

Summary: Burrowing Owls are found in Great Basin shrub-steppe with open to dense stands of shrubs and low trees, including big sagebrush, saltbush, greasewood, or creosote bush. They are also found in Chihuahuan Desert scrub with open stands of creosote bush and large succulents, Mojave Desert scrub, annual grassland, and farms (New Mexico Dept. Game and Fish 2000). Numerous anecdotal accounts of distribution and relative abundance exist for New Mexico, but no quantitative data are available other than on small study sites. Based on a survey of biologists, James and Espie (1997) estimated 1,000 to 10,000 pairs in New Mexico in 1992 with a stable population trend.

BBS: A significant decline (Trend = –3.8, P <0.03, n = 6) was detected for the 1966-1979 subinterval. No other significant trends were detected. Moderate data deficiencies were noted (sample sizes <14, sub-interval trends significantly different from each other) (Sauer et al. 2002).

CBC: Detected on only three CBCs with regularity, with the largest numbers recorded at Las Cruces, the primary wintering area in the state. No detectable trend (Sauer et al. 1996), although local declines have been noted on the Roswell CBC, due probably to the elimination of a sizeable prairie dog town in that area.

Atlas: Commenced in 2000. Data not yet available.

Research/Monitoring: Botelho and Arrowood (1996) found Burrowing Owl pairs nesting in human-altered areas had significantly more nestlings and fledged significantly more young than pairs nesting in natural areas. They speculated that lower reproductive rates of natural-area pairs was due to increased inter-owl disturbance and/or to increased predation (Botelho and Arrowood 1996).

In 1996-97, Johnson et al. (1997) also found a predominance of nests in areas of heavy human activity on Holloman Air Force Base. Owls were attracted to these areas for a variety of reasons, including soil disturbance and insect-attracting lighting. They found 18 nest burrows in 1996 and 19 in 1997, for a total of 37 nests; 21 in areas of high disturbance and 11 in areas of low disturbance (five nests were not included in the analyses due to reoccupancy). The mean number of young fledged from all successful nests was 2.1 (range 1-4) in 1996 and 2.7 (range 1-5) in 1997. Nest success was 64% (n = 11) for 1996 and 77% (n = 13) for 1997. Nests in high disturbance areas were closer to high perches, closer to roads, further from shrubs, and had lower shrub cover than nests in low disturbance areas. Despite a preference to breed in these areas, and contrary to the findings of Botelho and Arrowood (1996), high rates of abandonment were noted in disturbed areas. Sixty-four percent of nests disturbed by human activity or natural events were abandoned. Of 11 nests disturbed by human activity alone, 55% (6) were abandoned (Johnson et al. 1997). Forty-five artificial burrows were installed on Holloman Air Force Base in 2000-2001 to replace natural burrows that had collapsed (C. Finley, pers. commun.).

Martin (1973) studied 15 breeding pairs of Burrowing Owls three miles south of Albuquerque, NM, in the Tijeras Arroyo and a railway cut in desert grassland. Burrowing Owls exclusively used rock squirrel burrows since no prairie dogs were present in the study area. Mean reproductive success was 4.9 young per pair. The lowest possible mean clutch size was 5.2 eggs based on 78 young seen.

Martin (1973) banded nine breeding males and nine females in 1970. Six males and two females returned in 1971. All returning males selected the same burrow they had inhabited in 1970, unless the burrow had been destroyed. Of banded birds, no pair combinations were retained in 1971, suggesting low intra-pair fidelity. It was unknown whether low female return rates were due to higher mortality or to lower site fidelity. Martin (1973) determined that few Burrowing Owls remained resident on the study area during winter. Fall departure was from August through September and earliest spring arrival was mid-March. Pair formation in some Burrowing Owls apparently occurred before arrival.

Hawks Aloft, Inc. has been monitoring breeding success in nests on Kirtland Air Force Base in Albuquerque since the late 1990's. Numbers declined significantly in 2000 and 2001 for unknown reasons (C. Finley, pers. commun.). Monitoring is continuing.

On Holloman Air Force Base, six of 18 (33%) nesting burrows were occupied by Burrowing Owls during the winter, in addition to two newly occupied winter burrows (Johnson et al. 1997). Similarly, most males and a few female Burrowing Owls overwinter at burrows they used for breeding on the campus of New Mexico State University in Las Cruces (Arrowood et al. 2000), while all fledglings leave the area. Few banded owls ever return to the study area. However, some owls return after several years of absence.

Arrowood et al. (2000) found that resident male Burrowing Owls produced more nestlings (mean = 3.5 ± 2.6) than migrant males (mean = 2.5 ± 1.9). Area-experienced females produced more nestlings than area-inexperienced females (mean = 2.2 ± 2.3). More nestlings were produced by resident males paired with area-experienced females than were produced by other pair types. Most females were migratory, although it is unknown what factors influence females to overwinter or to migrate.

Arrowood et al. (2001) reported that in some areas of New Mexico, Burrowing Owl populations were stable or increasing, although decreasing populations were reported in other areas. Stable and increasing populations were associated with the presence of suitable habitat and increased precipitation and food availability. Decreasing populations were associated with loss of suitable habitat, due to declining prairie dog populations and urban sprawl.

Conservation Activities: The New Mexico Burrowing Owl Working Group (NMBOWG) was formed in response to population declines at some sites in New Mexico (Hawks Aloft, Inc. 2002). The NWBOWG is a collaborative effort of non-profit organizations, government agencies, private enterprises and individuals. The goals of the working group are to (1) facilitate communication, (2) establish a statewide monitoring effort, (3) maintain a web page to educate the public, promote the NMBOWG, and provide on-line data forms, (4) promote the NMBOWG through public outreach, (5) develop a review committee to determine sighting accuracy, (6) enter sightings into a database and share the database with contributing organizations, (7) create a map showing general locations in New Mexico, (8) over time, determine the population trends of Burrowing Owls in New Mexico, and (9) develop conservation recommendations based on monitoring results. The NMBOWG currently supports on-going research projects at four sites: Holloman and Kirtland Air Force Bases, New Mexico State University, and the Turner Ranch. The NMBOWG has initiated a volunteer monitoring system to collect data on Burrowing Owl populations in the state (C. Finley, pers. commun., Hawks Aloft, Inc. 2002).

Major Populations: Burrowing Owls have been documented as permanent residents at the White Sands National Monument in Dona Ana and Otero counties (White Sands National Monument 1993), Grulla National Wildlife Refuge (USFWS 1994), Holloman Air Force Base (Mesilla Valley Audubon Society 1996), Gray Ranch in Hidalgo County (Black 1997), and the Las Cruces/New Mexico State University area (W. Howe, pers. commun.). Burrowing Owls are uncommon spring and fall migrants and common breeders at the El Malpais National Monument and National Conservation Area (Hvenegaard 1989), Sevilleta National Wildlife Refuge (USFWS 1992), and Fort Bliss (Fort Bliss Directorate of Environment 1995) (New Mexico Dept. Game and Fish 2000). A minimum of 475 Burrowing Owls were detected in sc. Quay county, Curry county, and n. Roosevelt County in 2002, where 63% of surveyed prairie dog colonies were occupied by Burrowing Owls (L. Sager and C. Rustay, pers. commun.). Kirtland AFB in Albuquerque has one of the largest populations of Burrowing Owls in New Mexico with 40-50 pairs present in some years.

State Status: No special designation.

Natural Heritage Rank: G4/S4B, S4N (widespread, abundant, and secure in the state, but of long-term concern during breeding and non-breeding seasons).

Habitat Use and Condition: The grasslands of southern New Mexico have been invaded by mesquite and creosote bush (Gardner 1951, York and Dick-Peddie 1960), reducing habitat suitability in much of this region.

Best (1969) studied Burrowing Owls in Dona Ana and Luna counties of south-central New Mexico from 1964-67, including nine colonies ranging from 9-19 birds. Burrowing Owls used a broad range of macro and micro-habitats. Single breeding pairs were found in small isolated areas of open habitat, and colonies were restricted to yucca grassland with burrows of banner-tailed kangaroo rats. The largest colonies found during the study were in areas occupied by cattle.

Fire affects Burrowing Owls by altering vegetation and prey base. Frequent fire can maintain or improve Burrowing Owl habitats by reducing plant height and cover around burrows and by controlling woody plant invasion. Periodic fire in grasslands probably increases prey diversity for Burrowing Owls, and may increase overall prey density (New Mexico Dept. Game and Fish 2000).

Threats: Prairie dog eradication, increased urbanization and human disturbance during the breeding season represent primary threats to Burrowing Owls in New Mexico (Arrowood et al. 2001).

Literature Cited:

Arrowood, P. C., C. A. Finley, C. Blood, B. Thompson, and E. S. Botelho. 2000. Residency, return, and reproduction by Burrowing Owls (*Athene cunicularia*) in southern New Mexico, U.S.A. Poster presentation; Owls 2000—The Biology, Conservation, and Cultural Significance of Owls. Australian National University, Canberra, Australia.

Arrowood, P. C., C. A. Finley, and B. C. Thompson. 2001. Analyses of Burrowing Owl populations in New Mexico. Journal of Raptor Research 35:362-370.

Best, T. R. 1969. Habitat, annual cycle, and food of Burrowing Owls in southcentral New Mexico. M.S. Thesis, New Mexico State University, Las Cruces, New Mexico.

Black, C. 1997. Animas Foundation Gray Ranch Bird List. Animas Foundation, Animas, New Mexico.

Botelho, E. S., and P. C. Arrowood. 1996. Nesting success of western Burrowing Owls in natural and human-altered environments *in* Bird, D., D. Varland, and J. Negro, editors. Raptors in Human Landscapes. Academic Press, Ltd., London.

Botelho, E. S., and P. C. Arrowood. 1998. The effect of burrow site use on the reproductive success of a partially migratory population of western Burrowing Owls *(Speotyto cunicularia hypugaea)*. Journal of Raptor Research 32:233-240.

Conservation Division, Fort Bliss Directorate of Environment. 1995. Checklist of Birds, Fort Bliss, Texas [and New Mexico].

Hawks Aloft, Inc. 2002. New Mexico Burrowing Owl Working Group web page. http://www.hawksaloft.org/burrowingowl.html.

Hvenegaard, G. T. 1989. A checklist of the birds of El Malpais National Monument a Conservation Area. Southwest Parks and Monuments Association.

James, P. C., and R. H. M. Espie. 1997. Current status of the Burrowing Owl in North America: an agency survey. Pages 3-5 *in* J. Lincer and K. Steenhof, editors. The Burrowing Owl, its biology and management including the Proceedings of the First International Burrowing Owl Symposium. Raptor Research Report Number 9.

Johnson, K., L. DeLay, P. Mehlhop, and K. Score. 1997. Distribution, Habitat, and Reproductive Success of Burrowing Owls on Holloman Air Force Base. Unpublished Report, New Mexico Natural Heritage Program.

Martin, D. J. 1973. Selected aspects of burrowing owl ecology and behavior. Condor 75:446-456.

Mesilla Valley Audubon Society. May 1996. Checklist of Birds Holloman Airforce Base.

New Mexico Department of Game and Fish. 2000. Species List / Species Accounts: Burrowing Owl. Biota Information System of New Mexico (BISON-M), New Mexico Department Of Game And Fish, Santa Fe, New Mexico. http://151.199.74.229/states/nmex_main/species/041320.htm (Version 1/2000).

Sauer, J. R., J. E. Hines, and J. Fallon. 2002. The North American Breeding Bird Survey, Results and Analysis 1966-2001. Version 2002.1, U.S. Geological Survey, Patuxent Wildlife Research Center, Laurel, Maryland. http://www.mbr-pwrc.usgs.gov/bbs/bbs2001.html.

U.S. Fish and Wildlife Service. 1992. Birds of Sevilleta National Wildlife Refuge. U.S. Fish and Wildlife Service. http://www.npwrc.usgs.gov/resource/othrdata/chekbird/r2/sevillet.htm (Version 22 May 99).

U.S. Fish and Wildlife Service. 1994. Grulla National Wildlife Refuge. U.S. Fish and Wildlife Service. http://www.npwrc.usgs.gov/resource/othrdata/chekbird/r2/grulla.htm (Version 22 May 98).

White Sands National Monument. 1993. Checklist of Birds.

North Dakota

Summary: Burrowing Owl nesting was documented throughout North Dakota from the 1800s until the 1950s. From approximately 1950 to 1970, the range contracted and the species was no longer found in the eastern one-third to one-fifth of the state. From 1970 to 1999, the range further contracted and Burrowing Owls are currently rare north and east of the Missouri River. Literature reviews indicate no breeding records for e. North Dakota since the 1980s. James and Espie (1997) estimated 100 to 1,000 Burrowing Owl pairs in North Dakota with a stable population trend.

Extensive Burrowing Owl surveys from 1994-99 found very low occupancy rates at historically abundant sites (Murphy et al. 2001). Data sources are very current and reliable for trend information east and north of the Missouri River. West of the Missouri River the population trend is less clear, but is tied to the status of the black-tailed prairie dog, which has decreased significantly in recent decades.

BBS: A significant decline in Burrowing Owl relative abundance was noted for 1980-99 (Trend = –15.8, P <0.00, n = 9). No additional significant trends were detected. Data credibility is low due to small sample sizes and high variance (Sauer et al. 2002).

CBC: N/A.

Atlas: No breeding bird atlas is published for North Dakota. Stewart (1975) stated that Burrowing Owls were fairly common on the Northwestern Drift Plain; uncommon on the Missouri Coteau, Southwestern Slope, and Southern Drift Plain; and rare in the Agassiz Lake Plain and the Northeastern Drift Plain (Fig. A-8).

Research/Monitoring: Igl et al. (1999) compared Burrowing Owl abundance on 128 randomly selected plots (quarter-sections) from 1967 (Stewart and Kantrud 1972) and 1992-93 (Igl and Johnson 1997). Burrowing Owl frequency of occurrence on survey plots (% of plots with owls) did not change over the survey period; frequency was 1.6% in 1976 compared to 2.3% and 1.6% in 1992 and 1993, respectively. The statewide population estimate was 7,000 breeding pairs in 1967 compared to 7,000 and 5,000 pairs in 1992 and 1993, respectively.

Murphy et al. (2001) conducted three different Burrowing Owl surveys throughout much of w. and c. North Dakota between 1994-99. They (1) randomly sampled 20% of two intensive study areas in Divide and Kidder counties, (2) searched for Burrowing Owls within 500 m of 35 historic (1976-87) nesting areas in northwestern North Dakota, and (3) surveyed for Burrowing Owls in prairie dog towns on the Little Missouri National Grassland (LMNG; Billings, Slope, Golden Valley, and McKenzie counties of southwestern North Dakota). They found very few Burrowing Owls in random surveys of Divide

County; the maximum density was 3.2 pairs/100 km^2 in 1998. The maximum density based on suitable habitat was 7.2 pairs/100 km^2. Also, no Burrowing Owls were detected during surveys of historic breeding areas throughout nw. North Dakota. They felt the decline in Burrowing Owl abundance in Divide County may be from loss of burrowing animals and grassland habitat. Due to the presence of what appeared to be unoccupied suitable habitat, Murphy et al. (2001) felt that additional factors may also be influencing Burrowing Owl populations in nw. North Dakota. Murphy et al. (2001) failed to locate Burrowing Owls during intensive random surveys of Kidder County in 1998, where the species was fairly common until the 1970s. Area resource staff noted declines in number of breeding Burrowing Owls since the mid-1980s. Burrowing Owls also have disappeared from Ward County in nc. North Dakota.

In 1991, De Smet et al. (1992) found Burrowing Owls at 45% of prairie dog towns surveyed on the LMNG, but felt the occupancy rate was underestimated due to poor survey conditions. Murphy et al. (2001) found Burrowing Owls at 39% of the same towns which were still active in 1996. Additionally, Burrowing Owls were detected on <50% of prairie dog towns during other spring and summer surveys (1998) reported in Murphy et al. (2001), despite anticipated higher detection rates for summer surveys

Murphy et al. (2001) also selected 10 prairie dog towns which had been documented as occupied by Burrowing Owls in 1991 (De Smet et al. 1992) for reoccupancy surveys in 1995-98. They found 5-7 of these were used by Burrowing Owls annually, and all but one town were occupied for more than one year. Higher occupancy rates of recently used prairie dog towns (<5 yr) indicate short-term site fidelity for the species. Non-use of available habitat within years may suggest the Burrowing Owl is below carrying capacity in North Dakota.

Conservation Activities: A program under the North American Waterfowl Management Plan and Ducks Unlimited exists to permanently protect native prairie through perpetual easements. This has some positive ramifications for Burrowing Owl habitat conservation but overlooks some important, historical owl habitats (R. Murphy, pers. commun.).

The U.S. Forest Service expects to implement a proposed Land and Resource Management Plan in the near future. The preferred alternative currently includes objectives to double prairie dog town acreage and protective measures for Burrowing Owl nest sites (D. Freed, pers. commun.).

North Dakota Game and Fish Department has solicited funding for compiling Burrowing Owl nesting records and provided financial assistance for the research conducted in Murphy et al. (2001) and to the Canadian Wildlife Service for a Burrowing Owl migration telemetry project (R. Murphy, pers. commun.).

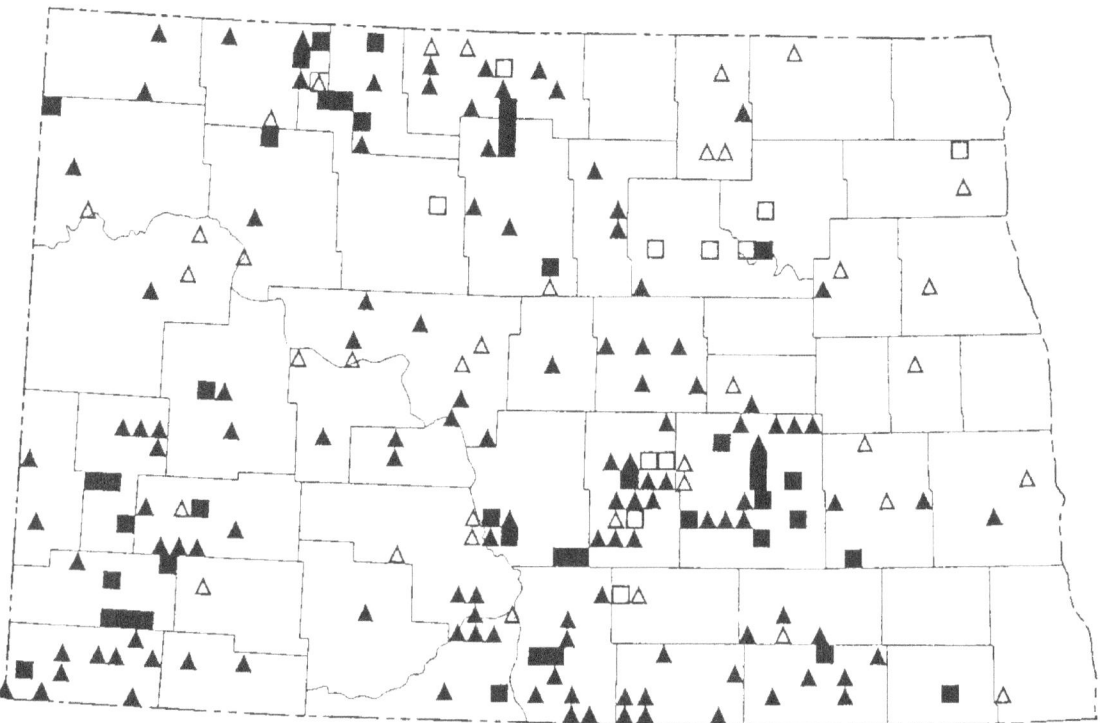

Fig. A-8. Distribution of Burrowing Owls in North Dakota, prior to 1972. Filled squares = nest or dependent young recorded from 1950 to 1972. Empty squares = nests or dependent young recorded prior to 1950. Filled triangles = territorial males or pairs recorded from 1950 to 1972. Empty triangles = territorial males or pairs recorded prior to 1950 (Stewart 1975).

Major Populations: Population estimate on the LMNG was 82 breeding pairs in 1999 (D. Freed, unpubl. data). Major populations also occur on tribal lands in Sioux County (Murphy et al. 2001).

State Status: No official state list for North Dakota.

Natural Heritage Rank: G4/SU (unrankable, possibly in peril in the state, but status not certain).

Habitat Use and Condition: Overall, about 75% of North Dakota mixed-grass prairie has been lost, primarily to agricultural cropland, with decreases being particularly great in the Drift Plain, the largest physiographic subregion in North Dakota (Samson and Knopf 1994, Murphy et al. 2001). Conversion of native prairie continues along with invasion of introduced and woody vegetation (Samson and Knopf 1994, Murphy et al. 2001). Burrowing Owls no longer occur on National Wildlife Refuges in North Dakota (Murphy et al. 2001) due to refuge management practices favoring tall, dense vegetation (Murphy 1993).

Burrowing Owls are closely associated with tracts of mixed-grass prairie that are heavily grazed by both livestock and prairie dogs. Burrowing Owls concentrate in grasslands with colonies of burrowing mammals, particularly colonies of black-tailed prairie dogs west of the Missouri River and colonies of Richardson's ground squirrels elsewhere (Stewart 1975). Murphy et al. (2001) felt the decline in Burrowing Owl abundance in w. North Dakota may be from loss of burrowing animals and grassland habitat. Native prairie around historic Burrowing Owl nest sites declined 33% in Divide County since the 1960s, from 15.5 ± 2.5 (SE) ha within 500 m of nests in 1969 to 9.5 ± 2.2 ha in 1998. Loss of breeding Burrowing Owls in c. North Dakota may be linked to declines in Richardson's ground squirrels, the primary burrow provider in this region. Murphy et al. (2001) seldom observed Richardson's ground squirrels, burrows, or heavily grazed native prairie in and near Kidder County. They felt ground squirrel abundance was negatively influenced by increased vegetation height in recent years (1993-99).

In sw. North Dakota, the black-tailed prairie dog is largely restricted to the LMNG and tribal lands in Sioux County. The remaining area is dominated by agriculture with few active towns. Acreage of prairie dog towns decreased 93% from 1939-72 in and near the LMNG (from 5,512 ha to 403 ha; Bishop and Culbertson 1976); and currently occupies only 0.2% of LMNG (Murphy et al. 2001). Acreage of prairie dog towns on the LMNG is believed to be stable to increasing slightly, while the status of prairie dog habitat outside the LMNG is unknown (D. Freed, pers. commun.). Prairie dogs are, however, considered a noxious pest in North Dakota and private landowners are required to eradicate them (North Dakota Century Code 63-01.1-02, subsec. 12; Murphy et al. 2001).

Threats: Loss of habitat is the primary threat to Burrowing Owls in North Dakota. Recent declines in Richardson's ground squirrels in c. and e. North Dakota may be influencing Burrowing Owls populations. Murphy et al. (2001) noted decreases in ground squirrel abundance coinciding with increased vegetation height in Kidder County (c. North Dakota). Livestock ranching, especially sheep grazing, has decreased in some east river counties in recent years. Burrowing Owl habitat quality is probably declining in part due to these changes. Large-scale plague events in prairie dog populations may result in long-term habitat loss for Burrowing Owls (D. Freed, unpubl. data).

Predation on Burrowing Owls has been exacerbated by increases in numbers of Red-tailed Hawks and Great Horned Owls due to increases in trees because of succession, shelter-belt planting, and fire suppression (Clayton and Schmutz 1999, Murphy 1993). Mammalian predation pressure likely has increased due to fragmentation of habitat and major change in composition and distribution of predator communities (Sargeant et al. 1993, Murphy et al. 2001).

Literature Cited:

Bishop, N. G and J. L. Culbertson. 1976. Decline of prairie dog towns in southwestern North Dakota. Journal of Range Management 29:217-220.

Clayton, K. M. and J. K. Schmutz. 1999. Is the decline of Burrowing Owls (*Speotyto cunicularia*) in prairie Canada linked to changes in Great Plains ecosystems? Bird Conservation International 9:163-185.

De Smet, K. D., G. Mcmaster, and K. Mazur. 1992. Cooperative surveys and reintroductions of Burrowing Owls between Manitoba and North Dakota, 1991. Manitoba Natural Resource Report.

Igl, L. D., D. H. Johnson. 1997. Changes in breeding bird populations in North Dakota: 1997 to 1992-93. Auk 114:74-92.

Igl, L. D., D. H. Johnson, and H. A. Kantrud. 1999. Uncommon breeding birds in North Dakota: population estimates and frequencies of occurrence. Canadian Field Naturalist 113:646-651.

James, P. C., and R. H. M. Espie. 1997. Current status of the Burrowing Owl in North America: an agency survey. Pages 3-5 *in* J. Lincer and K. Steenhof, editors. The Burrowing Owl, its biology and management including the Proceedings of the First International Burrowing Owl Symposium. Raptor Research Report Number 9.

Murphy, R. K. 1993. History, nesting biology, and predation ecology of raptors in the Missouri Coteau of northwestern North Dakota. Ph.D. Dissertation, Montana State Univ., Bozeman, Montana.

Murphy, R. K., K. W. Hasselblad, C. D. Grondahl, J. G. Sidle, R. E. Martin, and D. W. Freed. 2001. Status of the Burrowing Owl in Minnesota. Journal of Raptor Research 35:322-330.

Samson, F., And F. Knopf. 1994. Prairie conservation in North America. Bioscience 44:418-421.

Sargeant, A. B., R. J. Greenwood, M. A. Sovada, and T. L. Shaffer. 1993. Distribution and abundance of predators that affect duck production—Prairie Pothole Region. U.S. Fish and Wildlife Service Resource Publication 194.

Sauer, J. R., J. E. Hines, and J. Fallon. 2002. The North American Breeding Bird Survey, Results and Analysis 1966-2001. Version 2002.1, U.S. Geological Survey, Patuxent Wildlife Research Center, Laurel, Maryland. http://www.mbr-pwrc.usgs.gov/bbs/bbs2001.html.

Stewart, R. E. 1975. Breeding Birds of North Dakota. Tri-College Center For Environmental Studies, Fargo, North Dakota.

Stewart, R. E., and H. A. Kantrud. 1972. Population estimates of breeding birds in North Dakota. Auk 89:766-788.

Oklahoma

Summary: Burrowing Owls in Oklahoma occur primarily in association with prairie dog towns in short- and mixed-grass prairies and mesquite savannahs in the w. third of the state and are primarily restricted to the panhandle (Sheffield and Howery 2001). During the breeding season some owls are found away from prairie dog towns in shortgrass prairie. Burrowing Owls occasionally winter in w. and c. Oklahoma in the vicinity of prairie dog towns, airports, and areas with short grass (Sheffield and Howery 2001). Based on a survey of biologists, James and Espie (1997) estimated 100 to 1,000 pairs in Oklahoma with a stable population trend. Sheffield and Howery (2001) estimated a breeding population of 800-1000 individuals in the state.

BBS: A significant negative trend was noted for 1966-2001 (Trend = –11.5, P <0.00, n = 10). No other significant trends were detected. Data credibility is low due to small sample sizes and high variance (Sauer et al. 2002).

CBC: N/A; <1% of the summer population remains resident during the winter in Oklahoma.

Atlas: Unknown

Research/Monitoring: In Beaver and Texas counties on the Oklahoma panhandle, Butts and Lewis (1982) found 66% (n = 359) of adult owls were associated with prairie dog colonies even though this habitat comprised only 0.16% of the study area. This was equivalent to a density of 0.52 Burrowing Owls/ha or 1 pair/1.9 ha. The estimated population outside 1.6 km from prairie dog colonies was 92 pairs (34%; 0.0002 Burrowing Owls/ha or 1 pair/4,604 ha). The average brood size was 4.7 (range 2-9, n = 54) and nest success was 79%. Survival of young owls from the fledgling stage through July was 89% (n = 38) (Butts 1971). Most of this population migrated from Oklahoma in October; about 0.05% of the total population remained resident (Butts and Lewis 1982). In a survey of prairie dog colonies and their associated vertebrates in Oklahoma, Shackford and Tyler (1991) recorded at least one Burrowing Owl on at least one prairie dog colony in every county with ≥ 7 prairie dog colonies (n = 11), but no Burrowing Owls in any county with ≤ 2 prairie dog colonies (n = 10).

Currently there are no on-going research projects in Oklahoma which specifically target Burrowing Owls. A project is underway to monitor prairie dog town numbers, acreage, and distribution and could potentially also address Burrowing Owls (M. Howery, pers. commun.).

Conservation Activities: The USFWS attempted reintroduction of Burrowing Owls to a prairie dog town on the Wichita Mountains National Wildlife Refuge. The reintroduction effort failed to establish a breeding population. An Oklahoma state management plan is currently being developed for the black-tailed prairie dog. The plan could have indirect benefits for the Burrowing Owl (M. Howery, pers. commun.).

Major Populations: Based on BBS data, other breeding records, and personal observations, Sheffield and Howery (2001) estimated the total breeding population in Oklahoma as 800-1,000 individuals. The majority of the breeding individuals are limited to the panhandle counties of Cimmaron, Texas, and Beaver. The wintering range of the Burrowing Owl in Oklahoma is limited primarily to the western half of the state, with periodic extra-limital records further east (Sheffield and Howery 2001).

State Status: Species of Special Concern, Category II (native species identified by technical experts as possibly threatened or vulnerable to extirpation but for which little, if any, evidence exists to document the population level, range, or other factors pertinent to its status).

Natural Heritage Rank: G4/S2 (imperiled in the state because of extreme rarity or because of some factor(s) making it especially vulnerable to extirpation from the state).

Habitat Use and Condition: Beaver and e. Texas counties in the panhandle of Oklahoma had 50-60% of the area cultivated with the remainder used primarily for cattle grazing. Most prairie dog towns were located in linear strips of remaining habitat along drainages (Butts 1971). Butts and Lewis (1982) found 66% (n = 359) of adult owls were associated with these prairie dog colonies even though this habitat comprised only 0.16% of the study area. Within colonies, Burrowing Owl nests were distributed randomly, concentrated along the edges of colonies, and clumped. Nests outside dog towns were in badger dens but never in the more numerous burrows of thirteen-lined ground squirrels, spotted ground squirrels, or Ord's kangaroo rats. Of approximately 300 nests, all but six were in heavily grazed, short grass; the exceptions were five nests on field edges with vegetation clipped short by prairie dogs and one nest in a mowed pasture. Burrowing Owls did not exhibit any preference for soil type. Eradication of prairie dogs resulted in rapid declines in numbers of burrows available (<3 yr), and consequently Burrowing Owls rarely used inactive towns. Burrowing Owls did not nest in areas where prairie dogs were eradicated. Areas with light cattle grazing were used occasionally for feeding and escape. The use of satellite burrows by the male and broods indicated a requirement met only in prairie dog towns (Butts and Lewis 1982). They believed non-prairie dog habitat in Oklahoma was marginal breeding habitat for Burrowing Owls. Prairie dog populations should be maintained if conservation of Burrowing Owls is desired (Butts and Lewis 1982).

Oklahoma historically had millions of hectares of prairie dog towns, but by 1968 this had declined to 3,856 ha (Tyler 1968). Butts (1973) documented a decrease of 7% in acreage and 12% in numbers of active prairie dog towns in his study area (Oklahoma panhandle) from 1967 through 1970. Formation of four new dog towns and a 9.5 % increase in acreage

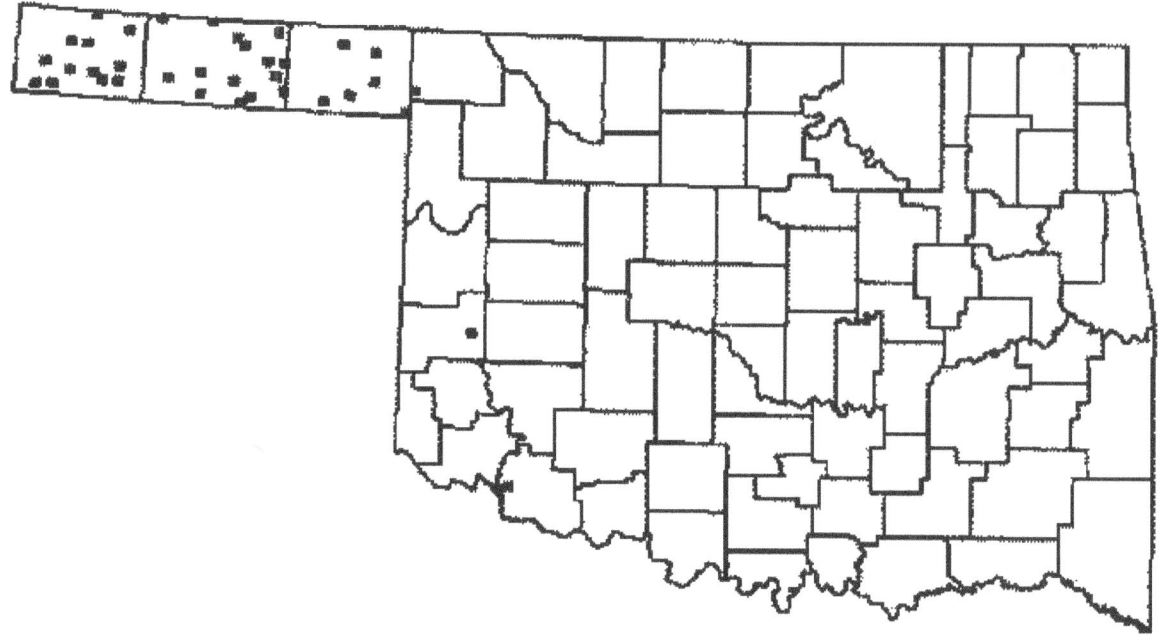

Fig. A-9. Distribution of Burrowing Owls in Oklahoma (Oklahoma Breeding Bird Atlas Project, D. Reinking, pers. commun.).

of existing towns tempered the net loss. Prairie dog eradication generally eliminated or reduced to a few individuals distinct colonies or colony segments (Butts 1973). Conversion of grassland to cropland (especially irrigated cropland) also caused a decrease in the availability and persistence of suitable nest burrows that could have adversely affected owl populations (Butts 1973). Tyler (1968) surveyed prairie dog colonies and associated vertebrates, and approximately 20 years later Shackford and Tyler (1991) repeated the survey. Comparison of the two studies showed a drastic decrease in both prairie dog colonies and Burrowing Owl numbers in the majority of the state (excluding the panhandle).

Threats: Conversion of grassland to cropland (especially irrigated cropland) has caused a decrease in the availability and persistence of suitable nest burrows that could adversely affect owl populations (Butts 1973). Continued habitat loss and loss of prairie dog to plague and direct eradication are also detrimental to Burrowing Owls.

Literature Cited:

Butts. K. O. 1971. Observations on the ecology of Burrowing Owls in western Oklahoma. A preliminary report. Proceedings of the Oklahoma Academy of Science 51:66-74.

Butts, K. O. 1973. Life history and habitat requirements of Burrowing Owls in western Oklahoma. M.S. Thesis, Oklahoma State University, Stillwater, Oklahoma.

Butts, K. O., and J. C. Lewis. 1982. The importance of prairie dog towns to Burrowing Owls in Oklahoma. Proceedings of the Oklahoma Academy of Science 62:46-52.

James, P. C., and R. H. M. Espie. 1997. Current status of the Burrowing Owl in North America: an agency survey. Pages 3-5 *in* J. Lincer and K. Steenhof, editors. The Burrowing Owl, its biology and management including the Proceedings of the First International Burrowing Owl Symposium. Raptor Research Report Number 9.

Sauer, J. R., J. E. Hines, and J. Fallon. 2002. The North American Breeding Bird Survey, Results and Analysis 1966-2001. Version 2002.1, U.S. Geological Survey, Patuxent Wildlife Research Center, Laurel, Maryland. http://www.mbr-pwrc.usgs.gov/bbs/bbs2001.html.

Shackford, J. S., and J. D. Tyler. 1991. Vertebrates associated with black-tailed prairie dog colonies in Oklahoma. Final Report, Oklahoma Department of Wildlife Conservation, Oklahoma City, Oklahoma.

Sheffield, S. R., and M. Howery. 2001. Current status, distribution, and conservation of the Burrowing Owl in Oklahoma. Journal of Raptor Research 35:351-356.

Tyler, J. D. 1968. Distribution and vertebrate associates of the black-tailed prairie dog in Oklahoma. Ph.D. Dissertation, University of Oklahoma, Norman, Oklahoma.

Oregon

Summary: East of the Cascades, the Burrowing Owl breeds in all or nearly all counties. As it was historically, it is now most common in Wasco, Morrow, Umatilla, Malheur, Harney, and Lake counties (Gabrielson and Jewett 1940, Adamus et al. 2001). West of the Cascades it bred in the Rogue River Valley (Jackson County) until the late-1970's or early 1980's (C. Cwiklinski, pers. commun). It is a rare winter visitor in the Rogue and Willamette valleys, along the coast, and occasionally in e. Oregon (Marshall et al. 1996). The population was estimated to be between 1,000 and 10,000 pairs in 1992 (James and Espie 1997). Burrowing Owl populations are generally thought to be stable in se. Oregon, possibly increasing with conversion of shrub-steppe to annual grasses in Malheur County, but significant trend data is lacking. Habitat loss has been greatest in the Columbia Basin (ne. Oregon) due to cultivation (Marshall et al. 1996).

BBS: No significant trends were detected over any survey period. Data credibility is low due to small sample size and high variance (Sauer et al. 2002).

CBC: Limited data available; rare winter records are from west of the Cascades, mostly interior valleys; some records from the coast.

Atlas: The Oregon Breeding Bird Atlas (Adamus et al. 2001) shows Burrowing Owls breeding throughout three se. counties: Malheur, Harney, and Lake (Fig. A-10). Additionally Burrowing Owls were reported in se. Deschutes and s. Crook counties, between the Wallowa and Blue Mountains in Baker and Union counties and east of the Columbia River Gorge in Wasco, Sherman, Gilliam, Morrow, and Umatilla counties. Breeding has been confirmed in s. Klamath County west of the Cascades, and Linn County. At this site, a pair was seen entering a burrow over the course of several weeks, but neither eggs nor chicks were observed and the birds did not return in subsequent years (P. Adamus, pers. commun.). Another summer sighting of a single individual on a culvert in this county suggests that Burrowing Owls might be re-established west of the Cascades if proper habitat conditions existed.

Research/Monitoring: In nc. Oregon (Gilliam, Morrow, and Umatilla counties) Burrowing Owl nest success was 57% for 63 nests in 1980 and 50% for 76 nests in 1981. Desertion was the major cause (32%; 45/139 nesting attempts) of nest failures and was related to the proximity of other nesting pairs (see below). Predation was the next most frequent cause of nest failure (14%; 20/139 attempts), and 90% (18/20) of depredation events were caused by badgers (Green and Anthony 1989).

Green and Anthony (1989) found a significant difference in nearest-neighbor distances for successful and deserted Burrowing Owl nests. In all cases where inter-nest distance was <110 m, at least one of the two nests was deserted in mid-nesting cycle (both nests abandoned when <60 m apart, n = 3). Only three of 21 (14%) pairs with inter-nest distances >110 m abandoned one or both nests. Many desertions occurred after hatching (Green and Anthony 1989). Apparently, clumped distributions of badger burrows and limited burrow availability in preferred habitat forced pairs close together; inter-pair competition for food presumably intensified as chick demand grew, available prey switched from small rodents to insects, and foraging bouts were conducted increasingly close to the nest (Green and Anthony 1989).

Green and Anthony (1989) also documented that 72% (23/32) of successful nests were lined with cow dung, while only 13% (2/15) of unsuccessful nests were lined. Presumably, dung masks the scent of the birds and thus lining nests with dung appears to be an adaptation to escape detection by predators.

Of five habitat types surveyed for Burrowing Owls, sites dominated by snakeweed, cheatgrass, and antelope bitterbrush were used by owls. Sites dominated by grasses (primarily needlegrass, Sandberg bluegrass, and bluebunch wheatgrass), or rabbitbrush were not used, despite having nearly twice the number of available badger burrows. Over-grazed snakeweed habitat was preferred, where burrows were surrounded with little grass cover conveying greater horizontal visibility than at less grazed sites. The success of Burrowing Owls nesting in the Columbia Basin appears to be dependent on a combination of the availability of properly-spaced badger burrows in preferred habitat, shifting prey resources during the nesting season, and on predation pressure by badgers (Green and Anthony 1989).

In the Malheur Resource Area, BLM personnel conducted Burrowing Owl surveys two to three times per year for 10 years along three to four survey routes. These data have not been analyzed, however the observers believe no major changes have occurred over the past 10 years (A. Bamman, pers. commun.).

Conservation Activities: In 1982, 13 Burrowing Owls were reintroduced by "hacking" at four artificial burrows in the Agate Desert of Jackson County, Oregon. Birds were obtained for reintroduction from nests in the Klamath Valley. The young were fed for about two months before full release. No reintroduced Burrowing Owls were detected in subsequent years (C. Cwiklinski, pers. commun.). Artificial nest burrows are being installed in areas of historic nesting by Burrowing Owls in Jackson County at the Rogue Valley International Airport and on private land with the goal of providing wintering habitat and stimulating summer use as well (C. Cwiklinski, pers. commun.). Twenty artificial burrows were installed in e. Oregon (Umatilla and Morrow counties) in the spring and summer of 1979

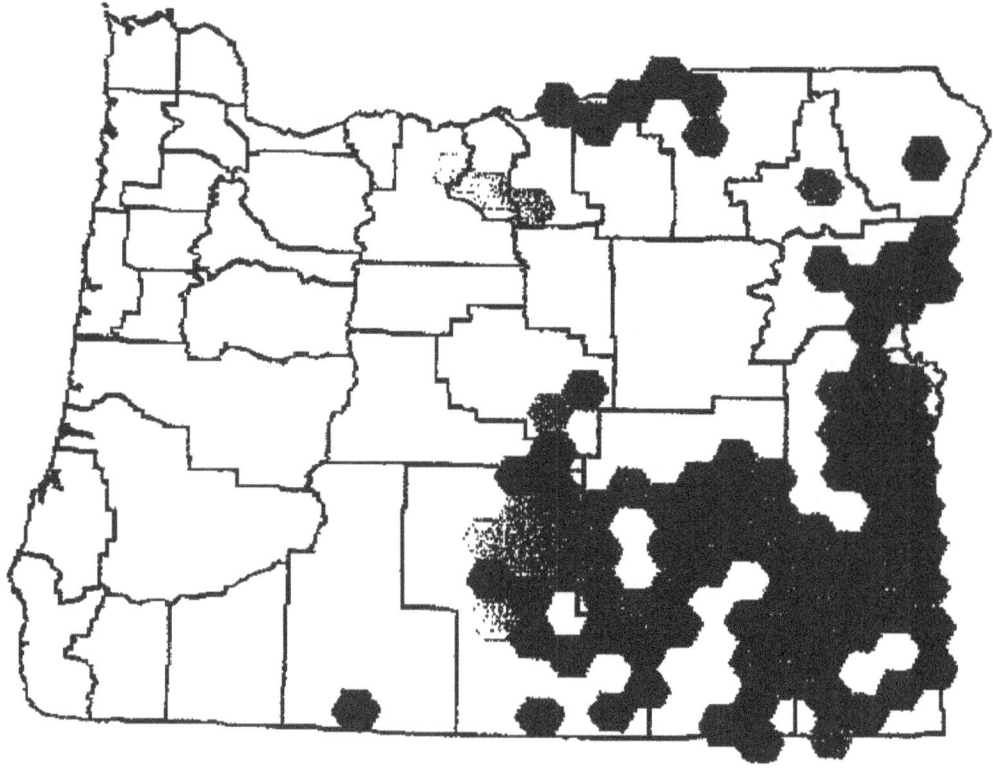

Fig. A-10. Distribution of confirmed (n = 49), probable (n = 9), and possible (n = 37) breeding activity of Burrowing Owls in Oregon from the Oregon Breeding Bird Atlas project (Adamus et al. 2001).

to facilitate research of the species (Henny and Blus 1981). No information was available on the continuation of this project.

In burned shrub-steppe, BLM is now to trying to replant with seed mixes that include sagebrush and other shrubs, and to rehabilitate cheatgrass dominated sites by a combination of prescribed fire, herbicide application and re-seeding with a mix of bunch grasses and shrubs. These efforts to restore the natural vegetation of the area may decrease the quality of habitat preferred by Burrowing Owls. However, BLM is also engaged in land exchanges to consolidate and expand contiguous parcels of Federal land; this probably has a beneficial effect on Burrowing Owls and other wildlife by securing the future ownership of larger blocks of habitat, reducing the chance of future habitat conversion (A. Bamman, pers. commun.).

Major Populations: The Oregon Breeding Bird Atlas (Adamus et al. 2001) shows the bulk of the state's Burrowing Owl population in se. Oregon counties, where they historically occurred (Gabrielson and Jewett 1940); however current and historic densities and numbers of breeding Burrowing Owls are unknown.

State Status: Critical (T&E status pending, or possible if conservation measures are not taken), in the Willamette Valley and Klamath Mountains, High Plains, Columbia Basin, and Blue Mountain physiographic provinces (ODFW 1997).

Natural Heritage Rank: G4/S2?B (imperiled during breeding season because of rarity or other factors making the species very vulnerable to extirpation; (?) indicates uncertainty about rank).

Habitat Use and Condition: Found in sagebrush-steppe, grasslands, pastures, roadsides, and even airports where vegetation is sparse and terrain is level. Also found where soil and/or vegetation has been disturbed through overgrazing, fire, construction, or farming; or at sites where vegetation has been heavily clipped or grazed by ground squirrels (Marshall et al. 1996). Burrows, such as those left by ground squirrels and badgers, are a necessity for breeding.

The areas of high Burrowing Owl populations are lower elevation flat to gently rolling hills with fine grain, deep soils. These areas are at the edge of farmlands where past range fires have repeatedly burned off the sagebrush and heavy grazing apparently resulted in exotic annual grasses and forbs becoming the dominant plant species. This habitat contains moderate to high rodent numbers and suitable burrows, and is grazed most years. These conditions occur on both private and public lands. Individual Burrowing Owl breeding sites occasionally are found in sagebrush covered areas (A. Bamman, pers. commun.).

Threats: Extirpation of Burrowing Owls through loss of habitat to urbanization and irrigated agriculture has been documented in the Rogue River Valley (Marshall et al. 1996). Habitat conversions of this type are probably more of a threat in n. Oregon than se. Oregon.

Green and Anthony (1989) found predation accounted for 20% of nest failures in n. Oregon (see Research/Monitoring above). Occasional shooting by the public probably has a only a small, local impact.

USDA/APHIS/Wildlife Services poisons ground squirrels and gophers, and traps badgers; these activities could affect burrow availability. USDA/APHIS/Plant Protection and Quarantine conducts grasshopper control operations on a local basis during years when grasshopper populations are exceptionally high. Although direct poisoning is highly unlikely given the pesticides used and methods of application, loss of prey base might affect some pairs of birds some years. The effects of farmer-applied pesticides on birds nesting near and foraging in agricultural fields has not been documented.

Additional threats listed by Altman and Holmes (2000) include: domestic predators (cats and dogs); destruction of burrows through livestock trampling in sandy soils and human disturbance (e.g., ATV use) near nest burrows.

Literature Cited:

Adamus, P. R., K. Larsen, G. Gillson, and C. R. Miller. 2001. Oregon Breeding Bird Atlas. Oregon Field Ornithologists, Eugene, Oregon.

Altman, B. and A. Holmes. 2000. Conservation strategy for landbirds in the Columbia Plateau of eastern Oregon and Washington. Oregon-Washington Partners in Flight. http://community.gorge.net/natres/pif/con_plans/columbia.html

Gabrielson, I. N. and S. G. Jewett. 1940. Birds of the Pacific Northwest. Oregon State College.

Green, G. A., and R. G. Anthony. 1989. Nesting success and habitat relationships of Burrowing Owls in the Columbia Basin, Oregon. Condor 91:347-354.

James, P. C., and R. H. M. Espie. 1997. Current status of the Burrowing Owl in North America: an agency survey. Pages 3-5 in J. Lincer and K. Steenhof, editors. The Burrowing Owl, its biology and management including the Proceedings of the First International Burrowing Owl Symposium. Raptor Research Report Number 9.

Henny, C. J., and L. J. Blus. 1981. Artificial burrows provide new insight into Burrowing Owl nesting biology. Journal of Raptor Research 15:82-85.

Marshall, D. B., M. W. Chilcote, and H. Weeks. 1996. Species at risk: sensitive, threatened and endangered vertebrates of Oregon. 2nd edition. Oregon Department of Fish and Wildlife, Portland, Oregon.

ODFW. 1997. Oregon Department of Fish and Wildlife, Sensitive Species. Web page: http://www.dfw.state.or.us/ODFWhtml/InfoCntrWild/Diversity/senspecies.pdf

Sauer, J. R., J. E. Hines, and J. Fallon. 2002. The North American Breeding Bird Survey, Results and Analysis 1966–2001. Version 2002.1, U.S. Geological Survey, Patuxent Wildlife Research Center, Laurel, Maryland. http://www.mbr-pwrc.usgs.gov/bbs/bbs2001.html.

South Dakota

Summary: Burrowing Owls were previously considered a locally common summer resident in South Dakota west of the Missouri River (except rare in the Black Hills), uncommon to the east, and casual in the winter (South Dakota Ornithologist Union 1991). Based on a survey of biologists, James and Espie (1997) estimated 100 to 1,000 pairs in South Dakota in 1992 with a stable population trend

BBS: A significant negative trend in relative abundance was detected from 1980-2001 (Trend = –11.4, P <0.08, n = 10). No significant trends were noted for other survey periods. Deficiencies in data quality were moderate (sample sizes <14, sub-interval trends significantly different from each other) (Sauer et al. 2002).

CBC: N/A.

Atlas: According to results of the South Dakota Breeding Bird Atlas (Peterson 1995), the Burrowing Owl is now "uncommon and scattered." Concentrations were noted in and near Buffalo Gap National Grassland, Badlands National Park, and the following counties: River Falls, Custer, Pennington, Meade, and Shannon in sw. South Dakota, and McPherson, Edmunds, Faulk, and Hand in nc. South Dakota (Fig. A-11). During field work for the South Dakota Breeding Bird Atlas, Burrowing Owls were found in 12.1% of random bocks with totals of 1 bird observed in each of 10 random blocks and 2-10 birds detected in each of five blocks (Peterson 1995). Of reported Burrowing Owl locations, 87 were from prairie dog towns and 42 from were from upland grassland sites (Peterson 1995).

Research/Monitoring: In 1991, Martell et al. (1993) documented a density of 1 pair/68 ha (0.015 pairs/ha) on prairie dog towns in Badlands National Park (Pennington and Jackson counties) in sw. South Dakota. In 1992, density on the same five towns was 1 pair/41 ha (0.024 pairs/ha) and density on three additional towns was 1 pair/48.5 ha. (0.021 pair/ha). The increase in Burrowing Owls detected from 1991-92 was partially due to increases in the area surveyed (from 819 ha to 1506 ha); however, for towns surveyed both years, increases were noted in the number of pairs (from 14 to 20 pairs), young (29 to 62 young), and average brood size (2.07 young/pair to 3.10 young/pair) indicating actual population increases between years.

Martell et al. (1993) applied the area-occupied technique of relative abundance estimation (Iverson and Fuller 1989) to Burrowing Owls on prairie dog towns in Badlands National Park. They determined the proportion of the area surveyed that was occupied by Burrowing Owls was 0.34 (SE = 0.07) in 1991. In 1992 the proportion of the area occupied increased to 0.57 (SE = 0.07). The probability of detection was 0.486 (SE = 0.056) for all study areas combined.

In the Conata Basin of Buffalo Gap National Grassland (Pennington and Jackson counties), Martell et al. (1993) documented 14 Burrowing Owl broods in 1991 and 11 Burrowing Owl broods in 1992, but did not provide a description of study area boundaries or density estimates. MacCracken et al. (1985) found that Burrowing Owls in the Conata Basin used burrows in early stages of plant succession (high forb and buffalograss cover, and reduced blue grama and perennial plant cover) where vegetation height was lower than the surrounding prairie.

Conservation Activities: Burrowing Owls are monitored as a sensitive species by the South Dakota Natural Heritage Program. Known information about nesting sites is included in environmental review comments on projects submitted for comment to the Heritage Program.

The Crow Creek Sioux Tribe plans to maintain the current number of prairie dogs and prairie dog towns through a Candidate Conservation Agreement with the U.S. Fish & Wildlife Service (L. Fredrickson, pers. commun.).

Major Populations: Concentrations of Burrowing Owl observations were noted in and near Buffalo Gap National Grassland, Badlands National Park, and the following counties: River Falls, Custer, Pennington, Meade, and Shannon in sw. South Dakota, and McPherson, Edmunds, Faulk, and Hand in nc. South Dakota (Peterson 1995).

State Status: None

Natural Heritage Rank: G4/S3S4B, SZN (S3—rare and uncommon breeding populations in the state, S4—widespread, abundant, and apparently secure in state, with many occurrences, but of long-term concern, no non-breeding occurrences).

Habitat Use and Condition: Results from the South Dakota Breeding Bird Atlas supported the importance of prairie dog towns to nesting Burrowing Owls. The majority of black-tailed prairie dogs presently occur on federal or tribal lands, although smaller colonies on private lands are undoubtedly important Burrowing Owl nesting areas as well. Prairie dog numbers and acreage are stable on the Lower Brule Sioux Tribal lands (S. Grassel, pers. commun.).

Threats: Any threats to black-tailed prairie dogs will impact Burrowing Owls in South Dakota. At present, the prairie dog population appears stable, although no systematic surveys are conducted on nesting Burrowing Owls (E. Dowd-Stukel and D. Backlund, pers. commun.). Rapid reductions in Richardson's ground squirrel abundance on private lands are also causing loss of potential Burrowing Owl habitat (R. Peterson, per. commun.)

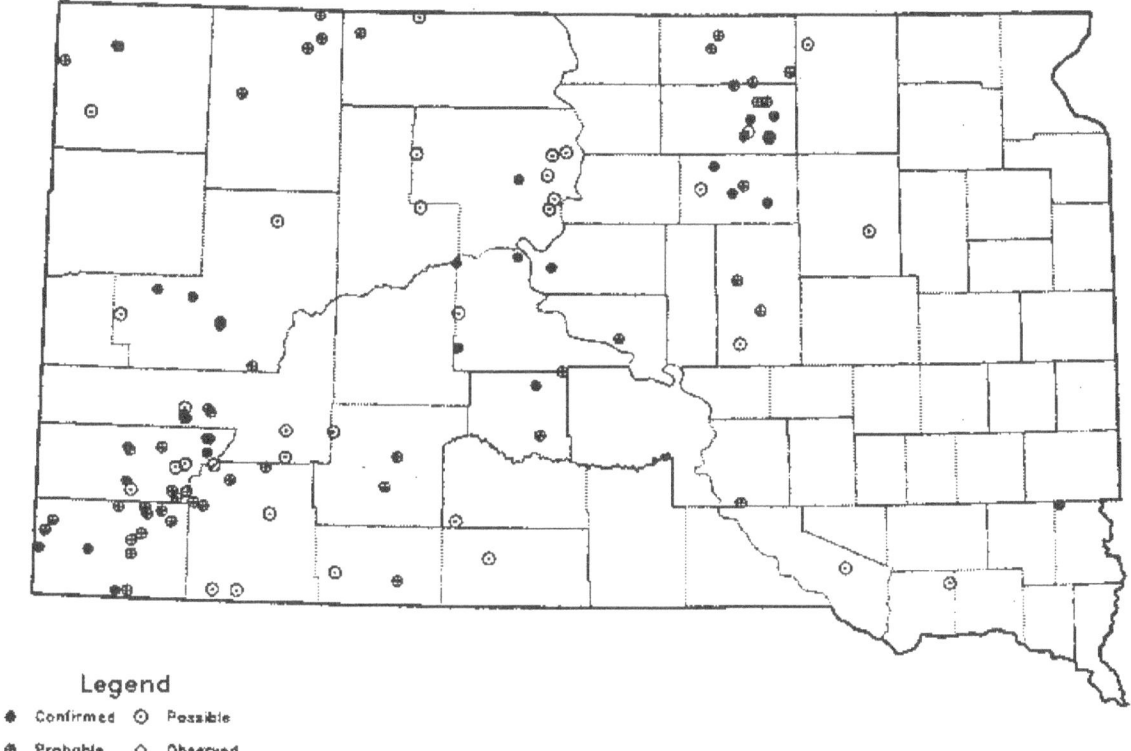

Legend

* Confirmed   ⊙ Possible

⊛ Probable   ○ Observed

Fig. A-11. Distribution of Burrowing Owl breeding activity and observation in South Dakota from the South Dakota Breeding Bird Atlas project (Peterson 1995).

Literature Cited:

Iverson, G. C. and M. R. Fuller. 1989. Area-occupied survey techniques for nesting woodland raptors. Pages 118-124 *in* Proceedings of the Midwest Raptor Management Symposium and Workshop. National Wildlife Federation, Washington, DC

James, P. C., and R. H. M. Espie. 1997. Current status of the Burrowing Owl in North America: an agency survey. Pages 3-5 *in* J. Lincer and K. Steenhof, editors. The Burrowing Owl, its biology and management including the Proceedings of the First International Burrowing Owl Symposium. Raptor Research Report Number 9.

MacCracken, J. G., D. W. Uresk, and R. M. Hansen. 1985. Vegetation and soils of Burrowing Owl nest sites in Conata Basin, South Dakota. Condor 87:152-154.

Martell, M. S., P. T. Redig, and J. Nibe. 1993. Demography of the Burrowing Owl in Badlands National Park: Final Report. The Raptor Center, Univ. of Minnesota, St. Paul, Minnesota.

Peterson, R. A. 1995. South Dakota Breeding Bird Atlas. South Dakota Ornithologists' Union, Aberdeen, South Dakota.

Sauer, J. R., J. E. Hines, and J. Fallon. 2002. The North American Breeding Bird Survey, Results and Analysis 1966-2001. Version 2002.1, U.S. Geological Survey, Patuxent Wildlife Research Center, Laurel, Maryland. http://www.mbr-pwrc. usgs.gov/bbs/bbs2001.html.

South Dakota Ornithologists' Union. 1991. The Birds of South Dakota, Second Edition Aberdeen, South Dakota.

Texas

Summary: Burrowing Owls are an uncommon to common resident on the open prairies of the western half of the state, east to Wilbarger County. It is a rare migrant and winter visitor east to coastal Texas (Texas Ornithological Society 1995). In winter, Burrowing Owls are locally fairly common to uncommon in the c. and s. Panhandle, but usually withdraw from the n. Panhandle. Based on a survey of biologists in 1992, James and Espie (1997) estimated more than 10,000 pairs in Texas.

BBS: No significant trends were detected over any survey period (Sauer et al. 2002).

CBC: No significant trend detected over the survey period (1959-88) (Sauer et al. 1996).

Atlas: Unknown.

Research/Monitoring: In s. Texas (primarily the Corpus Christi area) a monitoring effort sponsored by the Canadian Wildlife Service, U.S. Geological Survey-Texas Gulf Coast Field Research Station, and the Texas A&M University-Corpus Christi was begun in the winter of 1998-99 and continues to the present. This cooperative project currently is focused on documenting range, numbers, and habitat use throughout agricultural areas of s. Texas and to determine the response to installation of artificial burrows. Plans are underway to trap, band, and place radio transmitters on Burrowing Owls to monitor over-winter movements and survival. Ongoing collection of pellets and feathers in Texas will continue for diet and isotope studies. (C. Shackelford, pers. commun.).

Conservation Activities: None documented.

Conservation Recommendations: None documented.

Major Populations: Mackenzie State Park in Lubbock. This population is currently threatened by the city of Lubbock's plan to eradicate prairie dogs from the area. No other major populations documented.

State Status: None

Natural Heritage Rank: G4/S3B (rare and uncommon breeding populations in the state).

Habitat Use and Condition: Habitat includes culverts along roads adjacent to plowed fields or cleared pastures. Areas immediately around occupied culverts have short and/or sparse vegetation. Most of these habitats occur on private lands. County roads allow visual sightings of many of the birds; however, numbers of Burrowing Owls wintering on large private ranches are unknown (C. Shackelford, pers. commun.).

Threats: Loss of traditional grassland habitats and associated natural burrows to agriculture and development are a primary threat. Vehicle collisions due to use of roadside culverts for burrows and ingestion of pesticides from prey associated with agricultural fields are also threats (C. Shackelford, pers. commun.).

Literature Cited:

James, P. C., and R. H. M. Espie. 1997. Current status of the Burrowing Owl in North America: an agency survey. Pages 3-5 *in* J. Lincer and K. Steenhof, editors. The Burrowing Owl, its biology and management including the Proceedings of the First International Burrowing Owl Symposium. Raptor Research Report Number 9.

Sauer, J. R., J. E. Hines, and J. Fallon. 2002. The North American Breeding Bird Survey, Results and Analysis 1966-2001. Version 98.1, U.S. Geological Survey, Patuxent Wildlife Research Center, Laurel, Maryland. http://www.mbr-pwrc.usgs.gov/bbs/bbs2001.html.

Sauer, J. R., S. Schwartz, and B. Hoover. 1996. The Christmas Bird Count Home Page. Version 95.1 U.S. Geological Survey, Patuxent Wildlife Research Center, Laurel, Maryland. http://www.mbr.nbs.gov/bbs/cbc.html.

Texas Ornithological Society. 1995. Checklist of the birds of Texas 3rd edition. Capital Printing, Inc. Austin, Texas.

Utah

Summary: The Burrowing Owl is an uncommon permanent resident with localized occurrence (Behle and Perry 1975). Populations appear to have declined across the range; its distribution has been localized in many areas of Utah (Utah Division of Wildlife Resources 1998). Based on a survey of state biologists, James and Espie (1997) estimated 1,000 to 10,000 pairs in Utah in 1992 with a decreasing population trend.

BBS: No significant trends were detected for any survey period (Sauer et al. 2002).

CBC: The Burrowing Owl is a casual wintering resident in s. Utah.

Atlas: Unknown.

Research/Monitoring: Little published research was identified for Utah.

Conservation Activities: None identified.

Major Populations: None identified.

State Status: Species of Special Concern.

Natural Heritage Rank: G4/S3B (rare and uncommon breeding populations in the state).

Habitat Use and Condition: Not documented.

Threats: None documented

Literature Cited:

Behle, W. H., and M. L. Perry. 1975. Utah birds: check-list, seasonal and ecological occurrence charts and guides to bird finding. Utah Museum of Natural History, Univ. of Utah, Salt Lake City, Utah.

James, P. C., and R. H. M. Espie. 1997. Current status of the Burrowing Owl in North America: an agency survey. Pages 3-5 *in* J. Lincer and K. Steenhof, editors. The Burrowing Owl, its biology and management including the Proceedings of the First International Burrowing Owl Symposium. Raptor Research Report Number 9.

Sauer, J. R., J. E. Hines, and J. Fallon. 2002. The North American Breeding Bird Survey, Results and Analysis 1966-2001. Version 2002.1, U.S. Geological Survey, Patuxent Wildlife Research Center, Laurel, Maryland. http://www.mbr-pwrc.usgs.gov/bbs/bbs2001.html.

Utah Division of Wildlife Resources. 1998. Utah Sensitive Species List. Utah Division of Wildlife Resources homepage (http://www.nr.state.ut.us/dwr/sensppl.htm#bird). October, 2000.

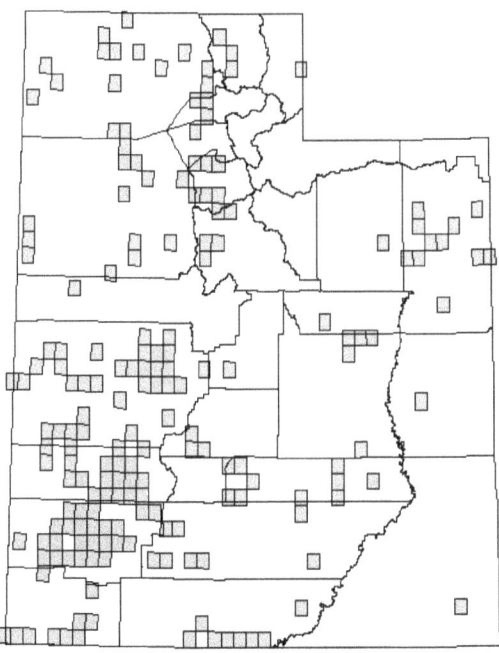

counties
burrowing owl

Fig. A-12. Distribution of Burrowing Owl observations in Utah (Utah Natural Heritage Program, A. Axel, pers. commun.).

Washington

Summary: Burrowing Owls are local and uncommon in shrub-steppe and grassland habitats east of the Cascades. It is widespread in the southern part of this region, but numbers fluctuate and breeders are limited to areas with suitable burrow sites. West of the Cascades, the Burrowing Owl was historically a rare migrant and winter resident of the n. Puget Sound region. It perhaps once nested in the vicinity of Bellingham, south of Tacoma, and Grays Harbor (Jewett et al. 1953). Smith et al. (1997) stated that in most areas numbers are seriously declining, and that losses are especially pronounced in the channeled scablands, Okanogan Valley, and se. Washington. This statement is supported by nest site occupancy analyses by Washington Department of Fish and Wildlife (WDFW), Wildlife Resources Data System (unpubl. data).

BBS: No significant trends were detected over any survey period (Sauer et al. 2002).

CBC: N/A.

Atlas: No breeding bird atlas is available for Washington; information regarding distribution is from the Washington Wildlife Resources Data System (Fig. A-13). Confirmed breeding records are concentrated in sc. Washington (east of the Cascades), in sw. Adams, extreme w. Walla Walla, Franklin, Grant, Benton, e. Yakima, and s. and e. Klickitat counties. Also in w. Whitman, c. Lincoln, sw. and n. Douglas, and s. Okanogan counties. There are no recent breeding records or suitable habitat west of the Cascades (Smith et al. 1997).

Research/Monitoring: WDFW surveys in 1987, 1999, and 2000 and occasional incidental observations of nest locations since 1960 show that the most significant change in distribution from pre-1987 to post-1987 is the apparent loss of owls from c. Okanogan County along the Okanogan River plain. GAP analysis also shows no remaining potential habitat for owls in this region (Smith et al. 1987). Other range changes are not as striking but involve the loss of burrow sites in se. Yakima County and s. Lincoln County (WDFW, Wildlife Resources Data System, unpubl. data).

The 1987 WDFW study was originally conducted to assess the status of the Washington State population, and its ability to absorb losses from a transplant program designed to re-establish Burrowing Owls in British Columbia. Additional nest information was collected, however, and follows (Radke 1987). The study was concentrated in a relatively small area of Grant (south of Ephrata), w. Adams, and nw. Franklin counties. Of the 117 nests found, 39% (46/117) were on county roadside rights-of-way ($\leq$ 10 feet to the road). These data may be biased as they were predominantly conducted while driving roads. Only 13% (15/117) of the nests were in areas considered 'natural'. The remaining 45% (52/117) were roughly equally divided between pasture, canal and ditch banks, and vacant lots. Of all nests, 74% were within 50 feet of roads. By far the greatest disturbance to nests was vehicles or recreational uses (100 nests), followed by disturbance from agricultural operations (from cattle operations, 17 nests; grain crop activities, 10 nests; truck crop activities, 9 nests). Disturbance from development, industrial, and residential activities affected 16 nests altogether. Natural burrows accounted for 72% (84/117) of the nests; the rest were in culverts or irrigation pipes (21%, 25/117) or in artificial nest burrows (7%, 8/117).

In 1999 and 2000 WDFW surveyed approximately 80% of all previously documented Burrowing Owl nesting sites in Washington. All nest sites visited were classified as either occupied, unoccupied, destroyed, or not found (Table A-4, WDFW, Wildlife Resources Data System, unpubl. data).

Conservation Activities: Prairies and steppe, and shrub-steppe habitats are listed as "Priority Habitats" by WDFW under the Priority Habitat and Species (PHS) Program. This designation facilitates consideration of conservation needs and measures during state and local land use planning. WDFW is currently developing management guidelines to promote the conservation of all priority habitats and species identified under the PHS Program. This will include conservation guidelines for prairies and steppe, and shrub-steppe habitats and species management guidelines for the conservation of Burrowing Owls. WDFW also plan to conduct a state status assessment for Burrowing Owls and searches for Burrowing Owls will be intensified in se. Washington (E. Cummings, pers. commun.).

Radke (1987) and Smith et al. (1997) mentioned that artificial nest burrows have been placed by conservation groups. No concerted or systematic nest box programs are known, however.

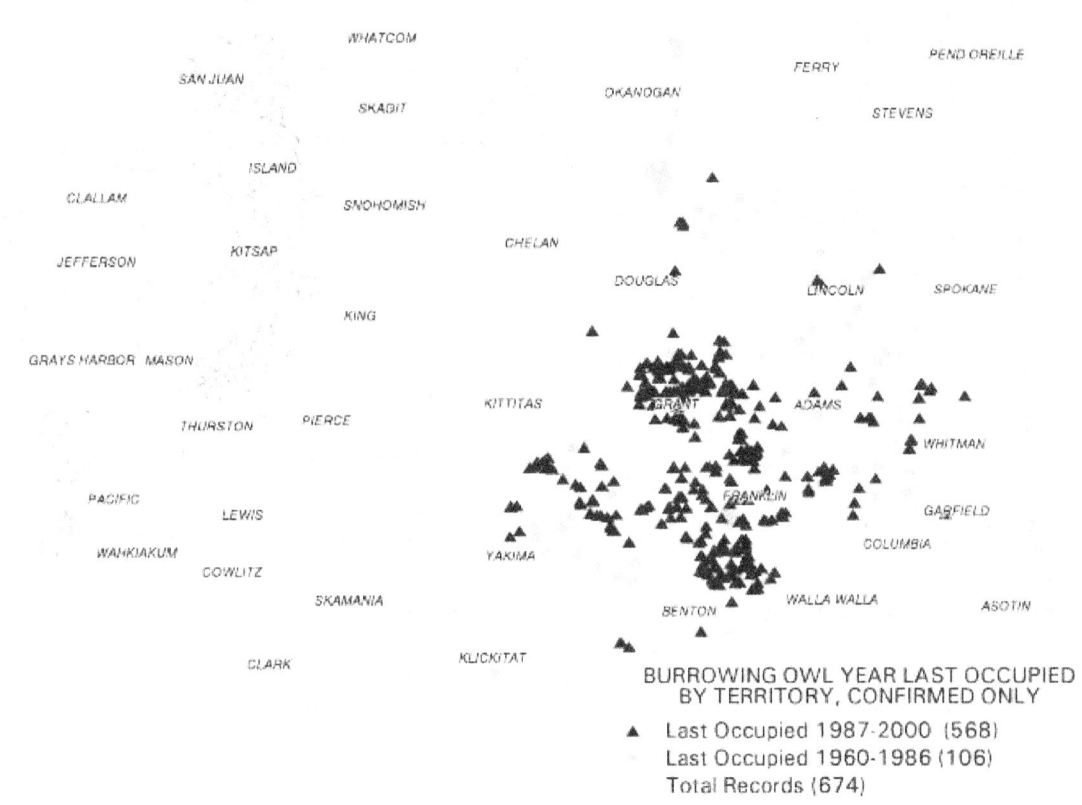

BURROWING OWL YEAR LAST OCCUPIED
BY TERRITORY, CONFIRMED ONLY

▲ Last Occupied 1987-2000 (568)
Last Occupied 1960-1986 (106)
Total Records (674)

Fig. A-13. Distribution of Burrowing Owls burrows in Washington (Washington Department of Fish and Wildlife, Wildlife Resources Data System, J. Brookshier, pers. commun.).

Table A-4. Number of occupied, unoccupied, destroyed, and not found Burrowing Owl nests located in Washington during Washington Department of Fish and Wildlife surveys in 1999 and 2000.

Year	Occupied	Unoccupied	Destroyed	Not Found	Total # Sites Visited
1999	170	100	44	141	455
2000	195	220	54	130	599

Major Populations: Grant and Franklin counties hold over half (55%) of nest sites in the State, occupied or historical (WDFW, Wildlife Resources Data System, unpubl. data 2001).

State Status: Candidate for listing as State Endangered, Threatened, or Sensitive.

Natural Heritage Rank: G4/S3B (rare and uncommon breeding populations in the state)

Habitat Use and Condition: Most nest sites located by Radke (1987) were near agricultural areas, and 21% were in artificial burrows of some sort, such as culverts and irrigation pipes. About 75% of nests found were within 50 feet of roads. Thus, disturbed, artificial situations are often used by these birds in Washington.

Threats: Loss of historic nest sites to agricultural conversion has been documented in Walla Walla County (Smith et al. 1997). However, agriculture has provided habitat in some areas (E. Cummings, pers. commun.).

The Burrowing Owl is currently a candidate for listing as Threatened, Endangered, or Sensitive in Washington. This designation serves to facilitate consultation with WDFW regarding state and local land use planning but no specific regulatory protection is afforded beyond that of other native wildlife species in Washington

Literature Cited:

Jewett,S. G., W. P. Taylor, W. T. Shaw, and J. W. Aldrich. 1953. Birds of Washington State. Univ. of Washington Press, Seattle, Washington.

Radke, M. 1987. Burrowing Owls in the Columbia Basin, Washington, 1987. British Columbia Conservation Foundation Report. June 28, 1987.

Sauer, J. R., J. E. Hines, and J. Fallon. 2002. The North American Breeding Bird Survey, Results and Analysis 1966-2001. Version 2002.1, U.S. Geological Survey, Patuxent Wildlife Research Center, Laurel, Maryland. http://www.mbr-pwrc.usgs.gov/bbs/bbs2001.html.

Smith, M. R., P. W. Mattocks, Jr., and K. M. Cassidy. 1997. Breeding birds of Washington State. Volume 4 *in:* K.M. Cassidy, C.E. Grue, M.R. Smith, and K.M. Dvornich, editors. Washington State Gap Analysis—Final Report. Seattle Audubon Society Publications in Zoology No. 1, Seattle, Washington.

Wyoming

Summary: Burrowing Owls occur statewide in grasslands and open areas of shrub-steppe regions. Burrowing Owls have been documented in all latilong blocks in the state but are considered uncommon (Wyoming Game and Fish Dept. 1997). Marti and Marks (1989) listed Burrowing Owls as common in Wyoming with an unknown population trend. They listed more than 200 nesting pairs and more than 200 nest sites from 1977-86, based on a National Wildlife Federation survey of state wildlife agencies in 1987. Based on a survey of state biologists, James and Espie (1997) estimated 1,000 to 10,000 pairs in Wyoming in 1992 with a stable population trend.

BBS: Significant negative declines were detected 1966-2001 (Trend = –23.7, P <0.04, n = 11). No significant trends were detected for other survey periods. Deficiencies in data quality were moderate (sample sizes <14, sub-interval trends significantly different from each other) (Sauer et al. 2002).

CBC: N/A

Atlas: No breeding bird atlas is available for Wyoming. Burrowing Owls were recorded as breeding in 24 of 28 latilongs and observed in all latilongs (Wyoming Game and Fish Dept. 1997). The Wyoming Natural Diversity Database (WYNDD) maintains a database of historic and current Burrowing Owl observations throughout Wyoming. Records are from various sources such as the Wyoming Game and Fish Dept. Wildlife Observation System (WOS), agency surveys, university research projects, and personal observations; all of which are scrutinized for credibility (D. Keinath pers. commun.).

Research/Monitoring: Martin (1983) recorded Burrowing Owl observations while conducting day and night searches for black-footed ferrets in sc. and sw. Wyoming from June through September of 1978-82. He found 86 Burrowing Owls on 34 of 426 (8.0%) white-tailed prairie dog colonies. This included 14,349 ha searched on 16 colonies in Sweetwater, 14 in Carbon, three in Uinta, and one in Lincoln counties. Nest burrows with young were documented on 10 (2.4%) colonies (2.7 ± 0.5 young / nest, range 1-5). Burrowing Owl density on white-tailed prairie dog colonies was one adult/172.5 ha. Low Burrowing Owl density was attributed to taller vegetation and less open habitat on white-tailed versus black-tailed prairie dog colonies (Martin 1983). Colonies occupied by Burrowing Owls averaged 72.8 ± 13.2 ha (n = 33; range 0.8-325.1) with 31.6 ± 6.9 burrows / ha (n = 25; range 4.7-167.2). Colonies with owl nests averaged 74.0 ± 12.8 ha (n = 10; range 27.5-147.8) with 20.0 ± 2.7 burrows / ha (n = 9; range 7.2-34.3; Martin 1983).

The WYNDD (June 2000) has documented 43 Burrowing Owl occurrences in the state. An "occurrence" is a locality where multiple Burrowing Owls or confirmed breeding/nesting behavior have been documented. An occurrence generally represents an established prairie dog town that reliably contains several nesting pairs of owls each year (Keinath pers. commun.).

In 1999 and 2000, the Rocky Mountain Bird Observatory (RMBO) conducted roadside surveys of potential Burrowing Owl habitat in se. Wyoming including most of Platte, Goshen, and Laramie counties, and extreme s. Niobrara County. In 1999, RMBO located 71 colonies of Burrowing Owls, totaling 180 individuals (Hutchings et al. 1999). In 2000, they located 107 sites with 575 Burrowing Owls; site reoccupancy was 66% between 1999 and 2000 (T. VerCauteren pers. commun.).

In 1998, the U.S. Forest Service conducted surveys for Burrowing Owls on black-tailed prairie dog towns within the Great Plains National Grasslands (Sidle et al. 2001). In the n. Great Plains (including Wyoming), 196 (59%) of 330 active towns were occupied by Burrowing Owls, and 12 (25%) of 48 inactive towns had owls. However, only 16% of prairie dog towns on Thunder Basin National Grassland in northeastern Wyoming had owls. Furthermore, Sidle et al. (2001) noted that surveys in 1995 failed to locate Burrowing Owls on Thunder Basin, but did not provide information on the extent or conditions of surveys.

Korfanta et al. (2001) examined Burrowing Owl sightings in the WOS. Burrowing Owl sightings were broadly distributed throughout Wyoming, with the highest concentrations occurring in the southern half of the state (Fig. A-14). Two trends were evident from the WOS data (Figure A-15): numbers of records generally increased between 1974-80, while record numbers decreased between 1981-97. There was a significant, negative linear relationship (P =0.002, r^2 = 0.64) between numbers of Burrowing Owl sightings and time for the 1986-97 subset of the WOS data (Fig. A-15). However, there may be potential reporting bias in the WOS, which might obscure real population trends.

Korfanta et al. (2001) surveyed 103 historic sites and 85 random sites selected on the basis of vegetation in eastern Wyoming in 1999. A total of 37 Burrowing Owls were seen at 16 sites; 36 on WOS historical sites (n = 103), one on a "high probability" site (n = 55), and none on "low probability" sites (n = 30). High probability sites were comprised of northern mixed- or short-grass prairie while low probability sites contained sub-optimal Burrowing Owl habitat such as sagebrush or open ground. A total of 43% of occupied sites (n = 16) and 10% of unoccupied sites (n = 168) were also occupied by black- or white-tailed prairie dogs. Twenty-percent of the occupied sites were currently or recently (within the previous year) grazed by cattle, sheep, or buffalo.

Conservation Activities: Burrowing Owls are monitored and managed within the vicinity of surface mines as mandated by the federal Surface

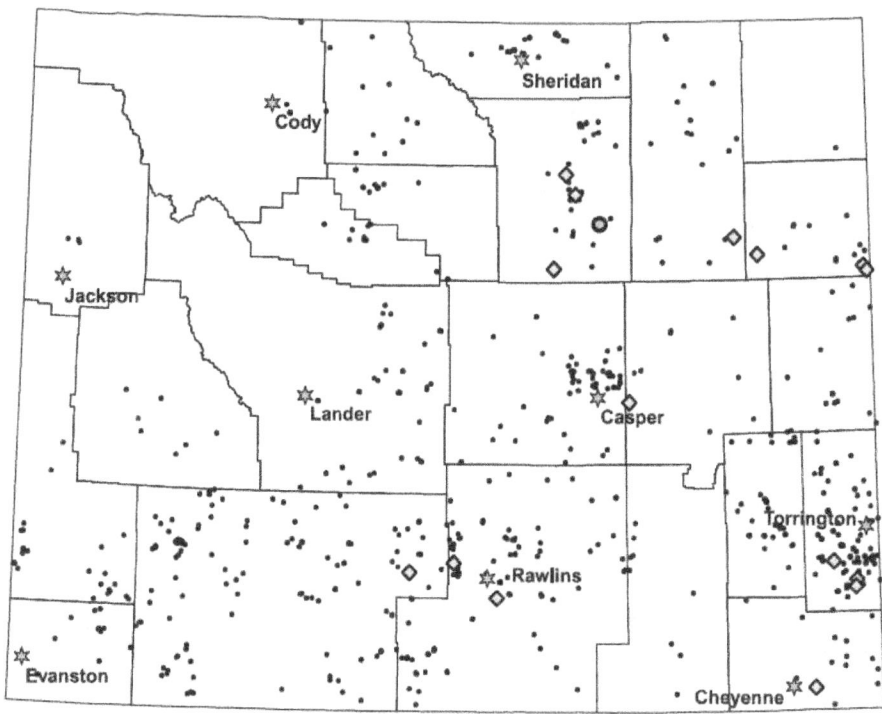

Fig. A-14. Historic Burrowing Owl records (dots) from the Wyoming Game and Fish Department Wildlife Observation System and reoccupancy survey sites with Burrowing Owls (diamonds) in 1999 (from Korfanta et al. 2001).

Fig. A-15. Numbers of Burrowing Owl records per year in the Wyoming Game and Fish Department Wildlife Observation System. The trend line for the 1986 – 1997 period represents a period of presumed consistent search effort (from Korfanta et al. 2001).

Mining Control and Reclamation Act of 1977 (30 U.S.C. 1201).

Major Populations: Burrowing Owl sightings are distributed primarily in e. and s. Wyoming with higher concentrations around Torrington, Sheridan, and Rawlins (Fig. A-14) although this may reflect a reporting bias in WOS data whereby owls are more readily detected near population centers (Korfanta et al. 2001). Hutchings et al. (1999) found 107 sites with Burrowing Owls in Platte, Goshen, Laramie, and s. Niobrara counties in 2000. Significant potential habitat exists on Thunder Basin National Grassland; however, few Burrowing Owls were documented during 1995 and 1998 surveys of prairie dog towns within the Grassland (Sidle et al. 2001).

State Status: Species of Special Concern (Category 4)

Natural Heritage Rank: G4/S3B, SZN (rare and uncommon breeding populations in the state, no non-breeding occurrences)

Habitat Use and Condition: During re-occupancy surveys of historic nest sites in e. Wyoming, Korfanta et al. (2001) found 43% of Burrowing Owls observed in 1999 were associated with prairie dog colonies. Only one Burrowing Owl was located during surveys of 85 random sites in the same region, which included 55 high probability sites in northern mixed- or short-grass prairie and 30 low probability sites with sagebrush, irrigated croplands, or desert shrub as the dominant cover type.

Only 1.9% of the Great Plains National Grasslands deemed suitable for prairie dogs was inhabited by the species (Sidle et al. 2001). The U.S. Forest Service estimated Thunder Basin National Grassland contains 1,013 ha of active prairie dog towns at approximately 121 burrows/ha. National Grasslands in general are fragmented, making active prairie dog management difficult, and there is no concerted effort to restore prairie dog towns. Despite this, Great Plains National Grasslands offer abundant potential habitat for prairie dogs and therefore, Burrowing Owls (Sidle et al. 2001).

Threats: Destruction of prairie dog habitat and rodent control are believed to have reduced Burrowing Owl numbers in the state (Wyoming Game and Fish 1977, Martin 1983, Sidle et al. 2001). Sylvatic plague outbreaks in prairie-dog populations have also reduced available Burrowing Owl habitat in Wyoming (USFWS 2000). Recreational shooting of prairie dogs may also significantly influence population size and therefore, available Burrowing Owl habitat in portions of Wyoming.

Literature Cited:

Hutchings, S., M. Carter, E. Atkinson, T. VerCauteren, C. Finley, S. Gillihan, and J. Nocedal. 1999. Prairie Partners: Promoting stewardship of shortgrass prairie. Unpubl. Rep., Colorado Bird Observatory, Brighton, Colorado.

Korfanta, N. M., L. W. Ayers, S. H. Anderson, and D. B. McDonald. 2001. A preliminary assessment of Burrowing Owl population status in Wyoming. Journal of Raptor Research 35:337-343.

James, P. C., and R. H. M. Espie. 1997. Current status of the Burrowing Owl in North America: An agency survey. Pages 3-5 *in* J. Lincer and K. Steenhof, editors. The Burrowing Owl, its biology and management including the Proceedings of the First International Burrowing Owl Symposium. Raptor Research Report Number 9.

Marti, C. D., and J. S. Marks. 1989. Medium-sized owls. Pp. 124-133 *In:* B. A. Giron Pendleton, editor. Proceedings of the Western Raptor Management Symposium and Workshop, National Wildlife Federation, Washington, DC

Martin, S. J. 1983. Burrowing Owl occurrence on white-tailed prairie dog colonies. Journal of Field Ornithology 54:422-423.

Sauer, J. R., J. E. Hines, and J. Fallon. 2002. The North American Breeding Bird Survey, Results and Analysis 1966-2001. Version 2002.1, U.S. Geological Survey, Patuxent Wildlife Research Center, Laurel, Maryland. http://www.mbr-pwrc.usgs.gov/bbs/bbs2001.html

Sidle, J. G., M. Ball, D. Weber, J. Chynoweth, G. Foli, R. Hodorff, G. Moravek, and R. Peterson, D. Svingen. 2001. Occurrence of Burrowing Owls in prairie dog towns on Great Plains. Journal of Raptor Research 35:316-321.

U.S. Fish and Wildlife Service. 2000. Endangered and threatened wildlife and plants: 12-month finding for a petition to list the black-tailed prairie dog as Threatened. Proposed Rules. Federal Register 65:5476-5488 (Feb. 4, 2000).

Wyoming Game and Fish Dept. 1997. Atlas of Birds, Mammals, Reptiles, and Amphibians in Wyoming. Wyoming Game and Fish Dept., Wildlife Division, Biological Services Section, Lander, Wyoming.

Arkansas, Illinois, Missouri, Wisconsin

Summary: IL, MO, WI: Vagrant; AR: Irregular migrant and winter resident

BBS: N/A

CBC: N/A

Atlas: N/A

Research/Monitoring: No research identified.

Conservation Activities: No conservation activities reported.

Major Populations: None.

State Status:

AR: State—None. There are a few scattered, records in the 1960's in Lonoke County. Single birds have been reported in Arkansas, Craighead, Cross, Crittenden, Jefferson, Mississippi, Pope, and Prairie counties (James and Neal 1986)

IL: Status—Nongame Protected. The Burrowing Owl is a very rare spring vagrant in n. and c. Illinois (Illinois Natural Resources Information Network 2000). No breeding records exist.

MO: Status—None. The Burrowing Owl is transient in w. Missouri and accidental in eastern Missouri during migration. It is an accidental summer and winter resident with one confirmed breeding record.

WI: State—None. The Burrowing Owl is a vagrant in Wisconsin. Undocumented historic observations suggest potential isolated breeding. There were 12 accepted state records between 1939 and 1992 (R. Domagalski, pers. commun.).

Natural Heritage Rank: AR: Unknown; IL: SA (Accidental in State); MO, WI: S? (Unranked in State).

Habitat Use and Condition: Unknown

Threats: Unknown

Literature Cited:

Illinois Natural History Information Network. 2000. Illinois Birds: Burrowing Owl (*Athene cunicularia*). Illinois Natural History Survey webpage (http://www.inhs.uiuc.edu/chf/pub/ifwis/birds/index.html) version August, 2000.

James, D. A., and J. C. Neal. 1986. Arkansas Birds: Their distribution and Abundance. University of Arkansas Press, Fayetteville, Arkansas.

Appendix B: Summary of Conservation Recommendations for Burrowing Owls

Below is a summary of conservation recommendations from western states gleaned from the literature, State wildlife agencies, Partners in Flight Bird Conservation Plans, and researchers in the field. Sources of the summarized conservation recommendations for each state are listed at the end of this section. Discussion of on-going conservation activities in each state can be found in Appendix A. There is considerable variability in the recommendations, but they are generally organized into six categories (Table B-1). No recommendations were found for Arizona, New Mexico, Oklahoma, Texas, or Utah.

Statewide Management Strategies

A statewide management strategy was suggested for Burrowing Owls in California, addressing ground squirrel control policies, fire management and agricultural practices, and land management on golf courses, airports, and private lands. Additionally, it was recommended the State relocate Burrowing Owls threatened by development, while striving to maintain populations encircled by development.

Recommendations in Nevada included development of Best Management Practices for rangeland pesticides and minimizing use, particularly in areas of high Burrowing Owl density. The impacts of off-road vehicles could be mitigated by adjustment of sanctioned event routes and closure of casual use in Burrowing Owl breeding centers, presumably regulated by State and Federal agencies.

Artificial Burrows

Artificial Burrows as a means of maintaining current populations or encouraging populations to immigrate to new sites was recommended in California, Idaho, and Nevada. Care was suggested in Nevada to place artificial burrows, whether used as mitigation or not, in protected areas suitable to support owls. The suggestion of a "Burrowing Owl trail," as with bluebirds, was made in Minnesota.

Relocation

Relocation of colonies away from impending development was suggested in California, where development pressure in several areas of the state is especially great, although most relocations were unsuccessful.

Surveys and Research

Surveys were recommended in California, Minnesota, Nebraska, Nevada (Mojave Desert region), North Dakota, and South Dakota, either to locate new nest sites, monitor known sites, or both. Survey recommendations in North Dakota included the development of a database of incidental sightings in the State. Research recommendations in North Dakota included detailed studies of Burrowing Owl reproductive success and survival (particularly on prairie dog colonies). In Nevada, research on the impacts of rangeland pesticides and off-road vehicles on Burrowing Owls, and on the degree to which populations are reliant on agriculture was recommended.

Education

Education of people who shoot ground squirrels and prairie dogs was recommended in Colorado, Minnesota, and Montana. Farmers and off-road vehicle enthusiasts are suggested targets of education in Nevada. In Nevada, it was suggested that USDA Natural Resource Conservation Service (NRCS) extension services could help to educate the farming community regarding the benefits of field margins as wildlife habitat, the effects of the indiscriminate use of insecticides and rodenticides, and the advantages of maintaining high raptor populations to control pests on crop and pasture lands.

Table B-1: General categories of conservation recommendations for Burrowing Owls from states for which recommendations were found[1].

	CA	ID	MN	MT	NE	NV	ND	OR	SD	WA	WY
Statewide Management Strategy	♦					♦					
Artificial Burrows	♦	♦	♦			♦					
Relocate Owls	♦										
Surveys & Research	♦		♦		♦	♦	♦		♦		
Education			♦	♦		♦					
Habitat Protection & Management, & Burrowing Animal Management		♦	♦	♦	♦	♦	♦	♦	♦	♦	♦

[1]–No recommendations were found for Arizona, Colorado, New Mexico, Oklahoma, Texas, or Utah.

Habitat Protection

Habitat protection and management, and protection and management of burrowing mammals was suggested in several states. Recommendations included the following: introduce fire in shrub-steppe to increase grassland near cropland, reduce the conversion of grasslands and pasture to cultivation, and maintain pesticide- and herbicide-free zones of 600-m radius around burrows (Idaho); leave drain ditches unburned and ditch banks and turnrows undisturbed (Nevada); protect burrow sites (Colorado, Idaho, and Nevada); establish conservation easements with private landowners to secure good owl habitats (Nevada); maintain open ground cover >40%, and native grass cover <40% and <40 cm tall on average, and maintain a 200-m buffer around nest burrows where human activities are prohibited (Oregon and Washington); maintain 100-300 m buffers around nest burrows (Colorado); preserve shortgrass habitat and manage for ground squirrels and badgers (Minnesota); preserve salt desert scrub habitat and its burrowing mammal community (Nevada); manage plague in prairie dog towns and change regulations regarding shooting of prairie dogs and ground squirrels (Montana); survey prairie dog colonies for burrowing owls and reevaluate hunting of prairie dogs (Nebraska and South Dakota); manage habitats for prairie dogs (North Dakota) and restore former prairie dog colonies on National Grasslands (Wyoming); preserve habitat for burrow providers (Oregon and Washington); and work with developers in urban and suburban areas to preserve open space within developments for Burrowing Owls (Nevada).

Sources of Conservation Recommendations

California
California Burrowing Owl Consortium
http://www2.ucsc.edu/scpbrg/owls.htm

J. Barclay, pers. commun.

Colorado
Coloardo Partners in Flight Bird Conservation Plan. 2000. http://rmb.wantjava.com/bcp/index.htm

Idaho
Belthoff, J. R., and R. A. King. 1997. Between-Year Movements and Nest Burrow Use by Burrowing Owls in Southwestern Idaho. Technical Bulletin No. 97-3, Idaho Bureau of Land Management.

Leptich, D. J. 1994. Agriculture development and its influence on raptors in southern Idaho. Nothwest Science 68:167-171.

Rich, T. 1984. Monitoring Burrowing Owl populations: implications of burrow re-use. Wildlife Society Bulletin 12:178-180.

Rich, T. 1986. Habitat and nest-site selection by Burrowing Owls in the sagebrush steppe of Idaho. Journal of Wildlife Management 50:548-555.

Minnesota
Coffin, B. and L. Pfannmuller. 1988. Minnesota's Endangered Flora & Fauna. University of Minnesota Press.

Martell, M. S., J. Schladweiler, and F. Cuthbert. 2001. Status and attempted reintroduction of Burrowing Owls in Minnesota. Journal of Raptor Research 35:331-336.

Montana
Knowles, C. J. *In review*. A Review of Burrowing Owl Observations Recorded in Montana 1964-1999. FaunaWest Wildlife Consultants Rept., Boulder, Montana.

Restani, M., L. R. Rau, and D. L. Flath. 2001. Nesting ecology Of Burrowing Owls occupying prairie dog towns in southeastern Montana. Journal of Raptor Research 35:296-303.

Nebraska
Desmond, M. J., and J. A. Savidge. 1999. Satellite burrow use by Burrowing Owl chicks and its influence on nest fate. Pages 128-130 *in* P. D. Vickery and J. R. Herkert, editors. Ecology and conservation of grassland birds of the western hemisphere. Studies in Avian Biology 19.

Nevada
Neel, L. 1999. Nevada Partners in Flight Bird Conservation Plan. Nevada Partners in Flight. http://www.blm.gov/wildlife/plan/pl-nv-10.pdf

North Dakota
R. Murphy, pers. commun.

Oregon
Altman, B., and A. Holmes. 2000. Conservation strategy for landbirds in the Columbia Plateau of eastern Oregon and Washington, version 1.0. Oregon-Washington Partners in Flight.

South Dakota
E. Dowd Stukel and D. Backlund, pers. commun.

Washington
Altman, B., and A. Holmes. 2000. Conservation strategy for landbirds in the Columbia Plateau of eastern Oregon and Washington, version 1.0. Oregon-Washington Partners in Flight.

Wyoming
Korfanta, N. M., L. W. Ayers, S. H. Anderson, and D. B. McDonald. 2001. A preliminary assessment of Burrowing Owl population status in Wyoming. Journal of Raptor Research 35:337-343.

Sidle, J. G., M. Ball, T. Byer, J. J. Chynoweth, G. Foli, R. Hodorff, G. Moravek, R. Peterson, and D. Svingen. 2001. Occurrence of Burrowing Owls in black-tailed prairie dog colonies of Great Plains National Grasslands. Journal of Raptor Research 35:316-321.

Appendix C: Distribution List for the Burrowing Owl Status Assessment and Conservation Plan

Allen, Harriet
Wildlife Management Program
Washington Dept. of Fish and Wildlife
600 Capitol Way N.
Olympia, WA 98501-1901
Ph: (360) 902-2200

Alvaro, Jaramillo
San Francisco Bay Bird Observatory
1290 Hope Street, P.O. Box 247
Alviso, CA 95002-0247
Ph: (408) 946-6548

Anderson, David
Fisheries and Wildlife Department
University of Minnesota
200 Hodson Hall
St. Paul, MN 55108
Ph: (612) 626-1222
E-mail: dea@fw.umn.edu

Anderson, Stanley
Wyoming Cooperative Fish and Wildlife Research
University of Wyoming
Box 3166, University Station
Laramie, WY 82071

Arrowwood, Patricia
Department of Fish & Wildlife Sciences
NMSU, P.O. Box 30003, Campus Box 4901
Las Cruces, NM 88003-0003
Ph: (505) 526-9427
E-mail: Parrowoo@nmsu.edu

Atkinson, Eric
Marmot's Edge Conservation
4580 E. Baseline Road
Belgrade, MT 59714
Ph: (406) 586-1585
E-mail: sawwhet@mcn.net

Axel, Anne, Information Manager
Utah Natural Heritage Program
Division of Wildlife Resources
1594 West North Temple
Salt Lake City, UT 84114-6301
Ph: (801) 538-4759
E-mail: anneaxel@utah.gov

Bammann, Albert, Wildlife Biologist
Bureau of Land Management
100 Oregon Street
Vale, OR 97918
Ph: (541) 473-6283
E-mail: al-bammann@or.blm.gov

Banasch, Ursula
1223 85th Street
Edmonton, AB T6K 1X7
Canada
Ph: (780) 951-8678
E-mail: ursula.banasch@ec.gc.ca

Barclay, Jack
Albion Environmental, Inc.
1414 Soquel Avenue, No. 205
Santa Cruz, CA 95062
Ph: (831) 426-6847
E-mail: jbarclay@albionenvironmental.com

Beauvais, Gary, Heritage Zoologist
Wyoming Natural Diversity Database
1604 Grand Avenue, Suite 2
Laramie, WY 82070-4332
Ph: (307) 766-3023
E-mail: beauvais@uwyo.edu

Belthoff, Jim
Department of Biology
Boise State University
Boise, ID 83725-1515
Ph: (208) 426-4033
E-mail: Jbeltho@boisestate.edu

Benz, Carl, Assistant Field Supervisor
U.S. Fish and Wildlife Service, South Coast/Desert
2493 Portola Road, Suite B
Ventura, CA 93003
Ph: (805) 644-1766
E-mail: Carl_Benz@r1.fws.gov

Bildstein, Keith
Hawk Mountain Sanctuary
1700 Hawk Mountain Road
Kempton, PA 19529-9449
Ph: (610) 756-6961
E-mail: bildstein@say.acnatsci.org

Bird, David
Avian Science & Conservation Center
McGill University
21111 Lakeshore Road
Ste. Anne De Bellevue, QC H9X 3V9
Canada
Ph: (514) 398-7760
E-mail: bird@nrs.mcgill.ca

Botelho, Eugene
58 Ohio Street
New Bedford, MA 02745
Ph: (508) 995-1633
E-mail: 110310.1752@compuserve.com

Brechtel, Steve
Alberta Fish & Wildlife Division
9945-108 Street
Edmonton, AB T5K 2G6
Canada
Ph: (780) 422-9535
E-mail: steve.brechtel@gov.ab.ca

Britten, Mike
National Park Service
12795 Alameda Parkway
Denver, CO 80225
Ph: (303) 987-6705
E-mail: Mike_Britten@nps.gov

Brown, Nikolle, Wildlife Biologist
7779 N. Leonard
Clovis, CA 93611
Ph: (559) 298-8574
E-mail: black-catnik@worldnet.att.net

Brunson, Ken, Nongame Coordinator
Kansas Department of Wildlife and Parks
512 SE 25th Avenue
Pratt, KS 67124-8174
Ph: (316) 672-0792
E-mail: kenb@wp.state.ks.us

Burkett, Ester
California Department of Fish & Game
Wildlife Management Division
1416 Ninth Street
P.O. Box 944209
Sacramento, CA 95814

Busby, Bill, Associate Scientist
Kansas Biological Survey
2041 Constant Avenue
Lawrence, KS 66047
Ph: (785) 864-7692
E-mail: w.busby@falcon.cc.ukans.edu

Butts, Ken, Refuge Manager
U.S. Fish and Wildlife Service
Bitter Lake NWR
P.O. Box 7
Roswell, NM 88202-0007
Ph: (505) 622-6755 ext. 19
E-mail: Kenneth_Butts@fws.gov

Byer, Tim
Thunder Basin National Grassland
2250 E. Richards Street
Douglas, WY 82633
E-mail: tbyer/r2_mbr@fs.fed.us

Campbell, Erick, Wildlife Specialist
Bureau of Land Management
1340 Financial Boulevard, P.O. Box 12000
Reno, NV 89520-0006
Ph: (775) 861-6471
E-mail: Erick_Campbell@nv.blm.gov

Cannings, Dick
Bird Studies Canada
1330 Debeck Road, S. 11, C. 96, RR#1
Naramata, BC V0H 1N0
Canada
Ph: (250) 496-4049
E-mail: cannings@vip.net

Cerovski, Andrea, Nongame Bird Biologist
Wyoming Game & Fish Department
260 Buena Vista
Lander, WY 82520
Ph: (307) 332-7723 x232
E-mail: acerov@state.wy.us

Chavez-Ramirez, Felipe
Platte River Whooping Crane Maintenance Trust
6611 W. Whooping Crane Dr.
Wood River, NE 68883
Ph: (308) 384-4633
E-mail: fchavezramirez@aol.com

Chew, Lincoln
University of Lethbridge
4401 University Drive
Lethbridge, AB T1K 3M4
Canada
Ph: (403) 329-2245

Chynoweth, James, Wildlife Biologist
Cimarron National Grassland, US Forest Service
P.O. Box J
Elkhard, KS 67950
E-mail: jchynoweth/r2_psicc@fs.fed.us

Clayton, Kort
Thunderbird Wildlife Consulting, Inc.
P.O. Box 437
Wright, WY 82732-0437
Ph: (307) 464-6757
E-mail: clayton@vcn.com

Collister, Douglas, President
URSUS Ecosystem Management Ltd.
3426 Lane Crescent SW
Calgary, AB T3E 5X2
Canada
Ph: (403) 246-2697
E-mail: collis@telusplanet.net

Conrad, Shawn
Comanche National Grassland
P.O. Box 127
Springfield, CO 81073

Conway, Courtney
Arizona Cooperative Fish and Wildlife
    Research Unit
104 Bio Science East
University of Arizona
Tucson, AZ 85721
Ph: (520) 626-3775
E-mail: cconway@ag.arizona.edu

Corman, Troy, Neotropical Migratory Bird
    Coordinator
Arizona Game and Fish Department
2221 West Greenway Road
Phoenix, AZ 85023-4399
Ph: (602) 789-3508
E-mail: tcorman@gf.state.az.us

Cox, Nancy
4426 San Isidro NW
Albuquerque, NM 87107
Ph: (505) 345-2385
E-mail: sora@flash.net

Craig, Gerald
Colorado Division of Wildlife
317 West Prospect
Fort Collins, CO 80526-2003
Ph: (303) 297-1192
E-mail: Gerald.craig@state.co.us

Culbert, Doug
Alberta Environmental Protection, Natural
    History Section
Main Floor, North Tower, Petroleum Plaza
9945–108 Street
Edmonton, AB T5K 2G6
Canada
Ph: (403) 427-6750

Cummins, Eric
Washington Department of Fish & Wildlife
600 Capitol Way North
Olympia, WA 98501-1091

Dawson, Neil, Wildlife Assessment Program Leader
Ontario Ministry of Natural Resources, NW Region
25th Side Road, RR# 1
Thunder Bay, ON P7C 4T9
Canada
Ph: (807) 939-3120
E-mail: neil.dawson@mnr.gov.on.ca

Davis, Stephen
Acting Director
Watershed Monitoring & Assessment
SK Watershed Authority
101-2022 Cornwall St.
Regina, SK S4P 2K5
Ph: (306) 787-0711
E-mail: sdavis@wetland.sk.ca

DeSante, David, President
Institute for Bird Populations
P.O. Box 1346
Point Reyes Station, CA 94956
Ph: (415) 663-2052
E-mail: ddesante@birdpop.org

DeSmet, Ken, Endangered Species Biologist
Manitoba Natural Resources, Wildlife Branch
Box 520
Melita, MB R0M 1L0
Canada
Ph: (204) 522-3719
E-mail: kdesmet@gov.mb.ca

Desmond, Martha, Assistant Professor
Dept. of Fishery and Wildlife Sciences
NMSU, Campus Box 4901
P.O. Box 30003
Las Cruces, NM 88003-0003
Ph: (505) 646-1217
E-mail: mdesmond@nmsu.edu

Dillon, Jeff
U.S. Fish and Wildlife Service–ES
Oregon Fish and Wildlife Office
2600 S.E. 98th Avenue, Suite 100
Portland, OR 97266-1398
Ph: (503) 231-6179

Dinan, John J., Nongame Bird Program
Manager
Nebraska Game and Parks Commission
2200 N. 33rd Street, P.O. Box 30370
Lincoln, NE 68503-0370
Ph: (402) 471-5440
E-mail: jdinan@ngpc.state.ne.us

Dinsmore, Jim
Iowa State University
Department of Animal Ecology
Aimes, IA 50011
Ph: (515) 294-7669
E-mail: Oldcoot@iastate.edu

Dose, Jennifer L.
Comanche National Grassland
P.O. Box 127
Springfield, CO 81073

Dowd Stukel, Eileen
South Dakota Dept. of Game, Fish & Parks
523 East Capitol Avenue
Pierre, SD 57501-3182
Ph: (605) 773-4229
E-mail: dowdstukel@state.sd.us

Dunning, Jr., John B.
Department of Forestry & Natural Resources
Purdue University
West Layfayette, IN 47907
Ph: (765) 494-3565
E-mail: bdunning@fnr.purdue.edu

Duxbury, Jason M.
Department of Renewable Resources
751 General Service Building
University of Alberta
Edmonton, AB T6J 4T8
Canada
Ph: (403) 951-8671
E-mail: Jason.duxbury@ec.gc.ca

Dyer, Orville
British Columbia Dept. of Environment & Parks
3547 Skaha Lake Road
Penticton, BC V2A 7K2
Canada
Ph: (604) 490-8244
Email: orville.dyer@gems4.gov.bc.ca

Eliason, Bonita
Minnesota Department of Natural Resources
500 Lafayette Road, Box 7
St. Paul, MN 55155
Ph: (612) 297-2276

Enderson, James H.
Department of Biology, Colorado College
Colorado Springs, CO 80903
Ph: (719) 389-6400
Email: Jenderson@cc.colorado.edu

Erickson, Carol
Fort Pierre National Grassland
124 S. Euclid Avenue, Box 417
Pierre, SD 57501

Espie, Rick, Wildlife Biologist
Saskatchewan Environment & Res. Mgmt.
Fish and Wildlife Branch, Room 436
Regina, SK S4S 5W6
Canada
Ph: (306) 787-2461
E-mail: rick.espie.erm@govmail.gov.sk.ca

Ethier, Thomas
Saskatchewan Museum of Natural History
Regina, SK S4P 3V
Canada
E-mail: tom.ethier@gems9.gov.bc.ca

Felskie, Heather
Saskatchewan Burrowing Owl Interpretive Center
Box 1467
Moose Jaw, SK S6H 4R3
Canada
Ph: (306) 692-8710
E-mail: sboic@sask.compatico.ca

Finley, Carol
Hawks Aloft, Inc.
P.O. Box 10028
Albuquerque, NM 87184

Finn, Jeff, Wildlife Biologist
California Department of Fish and Game
13515 Schooner Hill Drive
Gross Valley, CA 95945
Ph: (530) 477-0308
E-mail: jfinn@dfg.ca.gov

Foli, Gary
Little Missouri National Grassland
Box 8
Watford City, ND 58854
E-mail: gfoli/r1_dakotaprairie@fs.fed.us

Fox, Glen
877 Ridley Blvd.
Ottawa, ON K2A 3P4
Canada
Ph: (819) 997-6076
E-mail: glen.fox@ec.gc.ca

Fraser, James
Department of Fish & Wildlife Science
Virginia Polytechnic Institute
Blacksburg, VA 24061
Ph: (540) 231-6064
E-mail: fraser@vt.edu

Fredrickson, Larry, Wildlife Biologist
Department of Natural Resources
Crow Creek Sioux Tribe
P.O. Box 48
Fort Thomas, SD 57339
Ph: (605) 245-2187
E-mail: wildlife@rapidnet.com

Freilich, Jerry, Science Director
The Nature Conservancy
258 Main St., Suite 200
Lander, WY 82520
Ph: (307) 332-2973 ext. 3008
E-mail: jfreilich@rmisp.com

Fyfe, Richard
P.O. Box 3263
Fort Saskatchewan, AB T8L 2T2
Canada
Ph: (403) 998-9552
E-mail: fyferl@connect.ab.ca

Garza, Alfredo
Instituto de Ecologia
Centro Regional Durango
Apartado Postal 632
34000 Durango, DGO
Mexico

Gelvin-Innvaer, Lisa
Minnesota Department of Natural Resources
Nongame Wildlife Program (Region 4)
261 Hwy 15 South
New Ulm, MN 56073
Ph: (507) 359-6033
E-mail: lisa.gelvin-innvaer@dnr.state.mn.us

Gervais, Jennifer
Department of Fisheries and Wildlife
104 Nash Hall
Oregon State University
Corvallis, OR 97331

Geupel, Geoff, Landbird Program Coord.
Point Reyes Bird Observatory
4990 Shoreline Hwy.
Stinson Beach, CA 94970
Ph: (415) 868-1221
E-mail: ggeupel@prbo.org

Gifford, Dan, Wildlife Biologist
California Department of Fish and Game
1701 Nimbus Road
Rancho Cordova, CA 95670-4599
Ph: (916) 369-8851
E-mail: dgifford@dfg.ca.gov

Gilmer, David
USGS-BRD
6924 Tremont Road
Dixon, CA 95620
Ph: (707) 678-0682 ext. 614
E-mail: dave_gilmer@usgs.gov

Gilmore, Doug
Ontario Ministry of Natural Resources
Box 5003
Red Lake, ON P0V 2M0
Canada
Ph: (807) 727-1336
E-mail: doug.gilmore@mnr.gov.on.ca

Gould, Gordon
California Department of Fish & Game
Wildlife Management Division
P.O. Box 944209
Sacramento, CA 95814

Graham, Gary
Texas Parks and Wildlife Department
3000 IH 35 South, Suite 100
Austin, TX 78704

Grassel, Shaun, Wildlife Biologist
Lower Brule Sioux Tribe
Dept. of Wildlife, Fish, and Recreation
P.O. Box 246
Lower Brule, SD 57548
Ph: (605) 473-5666
E-mail: lbwfr@wcenet.com

Green, Mike, Landbird Biologist
US Fish and Wildlife Service
911 N.E. 11th Avenue
Portland, OR 97232
Ph: (503) 231-6164
E-mail: Michael_Green@fws.gov

Grensell, William
Nongame Bird and Mammal Section
California Department of Fish and Game
Wildlife Management Division
1416 Ninth Street
Sacramento, CA 95814
Ph: (916) 654-3828

Grettenberger, John
U.S. Fish and Wildlife Service
Endangered Species Consultation and Technical
    Asst. Branch
510 Desmond Drive SE, Suite 102
Lacey, WA 98503
Ph: (360) 753-6044
E-mail: John_Grettenberger@r1.fws.gov

Grissley, Kerry, Manager
Operation Grassland Community
Alberta Fish & Game Association
6924-104th St.
Edmonton, AB T6H 2L7
Canada
Ph: (780) 437-2342
E-mail: office@afga.org

Grondahl, Chris
North Dakota Game and Fish Department
100 N. Bismark Expressway
Bismark, ND 58501-5095
Ph: (701) 328-6612
E-mail: Cgrondah@state.nd.us

Haley, Katherine
Department of Fisheries and Wildlife
104 Nash Hall
Oregon State University
Corvallis, OR 97331

Hanebury, Lou, Wildlife Biologist
U.S. Fish and Wildlife Service
2900–4th Ave. N., Suite 301
Billings, MT 59101-1228
Ph: (541) 737-1957
E-mail: Lou_Hanebury@fws.gov

Harvey, Dwight
U.S. Fish and Wildlife Service, Listing Branch
Sacramento Fish and Wildlife Office
2800 Cottage Way, Room W-2605
Sacramento, CA 95825
Ph: (916) 414-6644
E-mail: Dwight_Harvey@fws.gov

Haug, Elizabeth, Biologist
P.O. Box 54, E R.R. 5
Saskatoon, SK S7K 3J8
Canada
Ph: (306) 975-9194
E-mail: Didiuka@sprint.ca

Hawkins, Cole
3612 Washoe Street
Davis, CA 95616-5087
Ph: (530) 753-1927
E-mail: chawkins@dcn.davis.ca.us

Hays, **Dave**, Endangered Species Specialist
Washington Department of Fish and Wildlife,
    Wildlife Diversity Division
600 Capitol Way N.
Olympia, WA 98501-1091
Ph: (360) 902-2366
E-mail: HAYSDWH@dfw.wa.gov

Hays, Loren
U.S. Fish and Wildlife Service, Listing and
    Recovery
2730 Loker Avenue West
Carlsbad, CA 92008
Ph: (760) 431-9440
E-mail: Loren_Hays@r1.fws.gov

Henderson, Carrol
Minnesota Department of Natural Resources
Nongame Wildlife Program
Box 7, 500 Lafayette Road
St. Paul, MN 55155
Ph: (651) 296-0700
E-mail: carro.henderson@dnr.state.mn.us

Herron, John
Texas Parks and Wildlife Department
3000 IH 35 South, Suite 100
Austin, TX 78704

Hetrick, Mindy
U.S. Fish & Wildlife Service
Rocky Mountain Arsenal NWR, Bldg. 120
Commerce, City CO 80022
Ph: (303) 289-0232
E-mail: mhetrick@rma.army.mil

Hickman, Melynda
Oklahoma Dept. of Wildlife Conservation
1801 North Lincoln Blvd.
Oklahoma City, OK 73105
Ph: (405) 521-4619

Hilliard, Mark, Wildlife Specialist
Bureau of Land Management
1387 South Vinnell Way
Boise, ID 83709-1657
Ph: (208) 373-4000
E-mail: Mark_Hilliard@blm.gov

Hinam, Heather
Department of Zoology
University of Manitoba
Winnipeg, MB R3T 2N2
Canada
Ph: (204) 253-7115
E-mail: umhinamh@cc.umanitoba.ca

Hjertaas, Dale
15 Olson Place
Regina, SK S4S 2J6
Canada
Ph: (306) 584-2835
E-mail: dale.hjertaas.erm@govmail.gov.sk.ca

Hodorff, Robert, Wildlife Biologist
Buffalo Gap National Grassland
Fall River Ranger District, U.S. Forest Service
209 N. River Street
Hot Springs, SD 57747
Ph: (605) 745-4107
E-mail: rhodorff@fs.fed.us

Holmes, Aaron
PRBO
4990 Shoreline Hwy.
Stinson Beach, CA 94970
Ph: (415) 868-1221

Holroyd, Geoffrey
Canadian Wildlife Service
4123–122 Street
Edmonton, AB T6J 1Z1
Canada
Ph: (780) 951-8689
E-mail: geoffrey.holroyd@ec.gc.ca

Holt, Denver
Owl Research Institute
P.O. Box 39
Charlo, MT 59824-0039
Ph: (406) 549-7626
E-mail: owl@montana.com

Howe, Frank, Nongame Avian Program
Coordinator
Utah Division of Wildlife Resources
1594 W. North Temple, Suite 2110
P.O. Box 146301
Salt Lake City, UT 84114-6301
Ph: (801) 538-4764
E-mail: fhowe@state.ut.us

Howery, Mark, Nat. Res. Biologist
Oklahoma Dept. of Wildlife Conservation
Wildlife Diversity Program
1801 North Lincoln Blvd.
Oklahoma City, OK 73105
Ph: (405) 521-4619
E-mail: mhowery@odwc.state.ok.us

Hunt, W. Grainger
Predatory Bird Research Group
Marine Lab, University of California
Long Beach, CA 95064
Ph: (408) 459-2466
E-mail: grainger@cats.ucsc.edu

Hunter, Chuck
U.S. Fish and Wildlife Service
1875 Century Boulevard, Suite 420
Atlanta, GA 30345
Ph: (404) 679-7130
E-mail: Chuck_Hunter@fws.gov

Hutchings, Scott, Prairie Partner Coord.
Rocky Mountain Bird Observatory
13401 Piccadilly Road
Brighton, CO 80601
Ph: (303) 659-4348
E-mail: Scott.Hutchings@cbobirds.org

Ireland, Terry
Fish and Wildlife Enhancement
764 Horizon Drive, South Annex A
Grand Junction, CO 81506-3946
Ph: (970) 243-2778

Jacobson, Susan
U.S. Fish and Wildlife Service
P.O. Box 1306
Albuquerque, NM 87103
Phone: (505) 248-6655
E-mail: Susan_Jacobson@fws.gov

Jakubos, Bonnie
Bureau of Land Management
100 Oregon Street
Vale, OR 97918
Ph: (503) 473-3144

James, Paul
Saskatchewan Museum of Natural History
2340 Albert Street,Wascana Park
Regina, SK S4P 3V7
Canada
Ph: (306) 787-2798
E-mail: paul.james.erm@govmail.gov.sk.ca

Jaramillo, Alvaro
San Francisco Bay Bird Observatory
1290 Hope Street
P.O. Box 247
Alviso, CA 95002-0247
Ph: (408) 946-6548
E-mail: admin@sfbbo.org

Johnson, Douglas
USGS, Grasslands Ecosystem Initiative
Northern Prairie Wildlife Research Center
8711–37th Street, SE
Jamestown, ND 58401-7317
E-mail: Douglas_H_Johnson@usgs.gov

Kaltenecker, Greg, Director
Idaho Bird Observatory
Boise State University
Department of Biology
1910 University Drive
Boise, ID 83725-1515
Ph: (208) 426-3262

Knowles, Craig
Fauna West Wildlife Consultants
P.O. Box 113
Boulder, MT 59632
Ph: (406) 225-3221 or (406) 225-9118
E-mail: FaunaWest@aol.com

Kochert, Mike
USGS, Snake River Field Station
Forest/Rangeland Ecosystem Science Center
970 Lusk Street
Boise, ID 83706
Ph: (208) 426-5201
E-mail: mkochert@eagle.boisestate.edu

Korfanta, Nicole
School of Environment and Natural Resources
University of Wyoming
Laramie, WY 82071-3971
Ph: (307) 766-2068
E-mail: korfanta@uwyo.edu

LeCaptain, Leonard
U.S. Fish and Wildlife Service
Ecological Services
6610 Washburn Way
Klamath Falls, OR 97603

Leupin, Ernest
Centre for Applied Conservation, U.B.C.
1405 Cariboo Hwy.
Williams Lake, BC V2G 2W3
Canada
Ph: (250) 392-2358
E-mail: leupin@direct.ca

Lewis, Steve A., Project Leader
Klamath Falls Fish and Wildlife Office
6610 Washburn Way
Klamath Falls, OR 97603-9365
Ph: (541) 885-8481

Lewis, Steve J.
Nongame Migratory Bird Coordinator
U.S. Fish and Wildlife Service
Federal Building, 1 Federal Drive
Ft. Snelling, MN 55111-4056
Ph: (612) 713-5473
E-mail: Steve_J_Lewis@fws.gov

Lorentzen, Ed
Bureau of Land Management
2800 Cottage Way
Sacramento, CA 95825-1886
Ph: (916) 978-4646
E-mail: Edward_Lorentzen@ca.blm.gov

Low, Dave
Ministry of Environment
British Columbia Government, Lands and Parks
1259 Dalhousie
Kamloops, BC V2C 5Z5
Canada
Ph: (250) 371-6243
E-mail: dlow@kamloops.env.gov.bc.ca

Lutz, Scott, Assistant Professor
Department of Wildlife Ecology
University of Wisconsin, 226 Russell Labs
1630 Linden Drive
Madison, WI 53706-1598
Ph: (608) 263-8979
E-mail: rslute@facstaff.wisc.edu

Martell, Mark, Cons. Programs Coord.
The Raptor Center
College of Veterinary Medicine
St. Paul, MN 55108
Ph: (612) 624-9790
E-mail: marte006@tc.umn.edu

Marti, Carl, Raptor Research Center
Boise State University
Boise, ID 83725
Ph: (208) 426-6996

Martin, Catrina, Assistant Field Supervisor
U.S. Fish and Wildlife Service, North Coast
2493 Portola Road, Suite B
Ventura, CA 93003
Ph: (805) 644-1766
E-mail: Catrina_Martin@r1.fws.gov

Martin, Roy
California Dept. of Parks & Recreation
Resource Protection Division
P.O. Box 450
Sacramento, CA 94296
Ph: (916) 653-3591

Mazur, Kurt
Grassland and Forest Bird Project
Partners in Flight Manitoba
200 Saulteaux Cresent, Box 24
Winnipeg, MB R3J 3W3
Canada
Ph: (204) 945-6816
E-mail: kmazur@nr.gov.mb.ca

McCluskey, Cal, Sr. Wildlife Specialist
BLM, Fish, Wildlife and Forests Group
1387 S. Vinnell Way
Boise, ID 83709
Ph: (208) 373-4042
E-mail: cmcclusk@id.blm.gov

McKeever, Katherine
The Owl Foundation
4117 21st. Street
Vineland Station, ON L0R 2E0
Canada
Ph: (905) 562-5986

Mealey, Brian Keith
Miami Museum of Science
3280 South Miami Avenue
Miami, FL 33129
Ph: (305) 854-4247 ext. 256
E-mail: 6mealey@miamisci.org

Mehlman, David, Dir. of Cons. Programs
Wings of the Americas
322 Tyler Road NW
Albuquerque, NM 87107
Ph: (505) 344-1732
E-mail: dmehlman@tnc.org

Mele, Gary
4536 Alpine Road
Portola Valley, CA 94028

Melquist, Wayne
Idaho Department of Fish and Game
600 South Walnut, P.O. Box 25
Boise, ID 83707
Ph: (208) 334-2676
E-mail: Wmelquis@idfg.state.id.us

Mesta, Robert, Coordinator
USFWS, Sonoran Desert Joint Venture
12661 E. Broadway Blvd.
Tucson, AZ 85748
Ph: (520) 722-4289
E-mail: Robert_Mesta@fws.gov

Miller, Edwin J.
Kansas Department of Wildlife & Parks
5089 Co. Road 2925
Independence, KS 67301

Miller, Jeff
Center for Biological Diversity
P.O. Box 40090
Berkley, CA 94704
Ph: (510) 841-0812
E-mail: jmiller@biologicaldiversity.org

Millsap, Brian
Division of Migratory Bird Management
U.S. Fish and Wildlife Service
4401 N. Fairfax Drive MS 634
Arlington, VA 22203
E-mail: Brian_Millsap@fws.gov

Moravek, Glen
Fort Pierre National Grassland
124 S. Euclid Avenue, Box 417
Pierre, SD 57501
E-mail: gmoravek/r2_nebraska@fs.fed.us

Murphy, Robert, Wildlife Biologist
U.S. Fish and Wildlife Service
Lostwood National Wildlife Refuge
8315 Highway 8
Kenmare, ND 58746-9046
Ph: (701) 848-2722
E-mail: Bob_Murphy@fws.gov

Neal, Larry
Nevada Division of Wildlife
1100 Valley Road
Reno, NV 89512-2817

Nevada Breeding Bird Atlas
Great Basin Bird Observatory
One East First Street, Suite 500
Reno, NV 89501
Ph: (775) 348-2644
E-mail: gbbo@altavista.com

Nugent, Martin
Oregon Department of Fish and Wildlife
Wildlife Diversity Program
2501 SW First Avenue, P.O. Box 59
Portland, OR 97207
Ph: (503) 872-5260 x5346
E-mail: Martin.Nugent@state.or.us

Oakleaf, Bob, Nongame Coordinator
Wyoming Game and Fish Department
260 Buena Vista
Lander, WY 82520
Ph: (307) 332-2688
E-mail: roakle@missc.state.wy.us

Oliphant, Lynn
Department of Vet. Anatomy
University of Saskatchewan
Saskatoon, SK S7N 0W0
Canada

Olson, Mike
U.S. Fish and Wildlife Service, Ecological Services
3425 Miriam Avenue
Bismarck, ND 58501-7926
Ph: (701) 250-4481
E-mail: Michael_Olson@fws.gov

Ortega-Rubio, Alfredo
Centro de Investigaciones Biologicas, Div. Biol. Terr.
APDO Postal 128
La Paz, B.C.S. 23000
Mexico

Palermo, Kerrie, State Office Biologist
Bureau of Land Management
P.O. Box 2965
Portland, OR 97208
Ph: (503) 952-6382
E-mail: OSO_Wildlife_Biologist_Mail@or.blm.gov

Parrish, Jim, Coordinator
Utah Partners in Flight Program
Utah Division of Wildlife Resources
1594 West North Temple, Suite 2222
Salt Lake City, UT 84116
Ph: (801) 538-4788
E-mail: Nrdwr.jparrish@state.ut.us

Pence, Diane
US Fish and Wildlife Service
300 Westgate Center Drive
Hadley, MA 01035
Ph: (413) 253-8577
E-mail: Diane_Pence@fws.gov

Peregrine Fund
566 W Flying Hawk Lane
Boise, ID 83709
Ph: (208) 362-3716

Pezzolesi, Linda
Department of Biological Sciences
Binghamton University
P.O. Box 6000
Binghamton, NY 13902-6000
Ph: (607) 777-2438

Plumpton, David, Wildlife Biologist
H.T. Harvey & Associates
3150 Almaden Expressway, Suite 145
San Jose, CA 95118
Ph: (408) 448-9450 ext. 204
E-mail: dplumpton@harveyecology.com

Poulin, Ray G.
Department of Biology
University of Regina
Regina, SK S4S 0A2
Canada
Ph: (306) 585-4562
E-mail: poulinr@uregina.ca

Priestley, Lisa
Bird Studies Canada
Environment Canada
Room 200
4999-98 Avenue
Edmonton, Alberta, T6B 2X3 Canada

Quinlan, Richard
Regional Biologist
Species at Risk Program
Alberta Fish and Wildlife
2nd Flr, YPM Place 530 – 8 St. S.
Lethbridge, Alberta, T1J 2J8
Ph: (403) 381-5397
E-mail: Richard.Quinlan@gov.ab.ca

Rangel-Salazar, Jose-Luis
Museo de Zoologica Iztacala
ENEP UNAM IZTACALA
Apartado Postal 314
Tlalnepantla, 54090
Mexico
E-mail: Penrique@yahoo.com

Ratcliff, Brian
307 Dog Lake Road, RR #12, Site 15-22
Thunderbay, ON P7B 5E3
Canada
Ph: (807) 768-8408
E-mail: brat@nomin.norlink.net

Ratti, John
Department of Wildlife Resources
University of Idaho
Moscow, ID 83844-1136
Ph: (208) 885-7741

Rau, Larry
Bureau of Land Management
111 Garryowen Road
Miles City, MT 59301
E-mail: Larry_Rau@blm.gov

Reinking, Dan, Atlas Coordinator
Sutton Avian Research Center
P.O. Box 2007
Bartlesville, OK 74005-2007
Ph: (918) 336-7778
E-mail: www.suttoncenter.org

Restani, Marco
Ecosystem Science & Conservation Div.
University of Washington
College of Forest Resources, Box 352100
Seattle, WA 98195-2100
Ph: (206) 543-2764
E-mail: restani@u.washington.edu

Rodrigues-Estrella, Ricardo
Centro de Investigaciones Biologicas
Div. Biol. Terr.,
Apartado Postal 128
La Paz, B.C.S. 23000
Mexico

Ronan, Noelle
Department of Fisheries and Wildlife
104 Nash Hall
Oregon State University
Corvallis, OR 97331

Roscoe, Terry, Wildlife Biologist
1701 Nimbus Road
Rancho Cordova, CA 95670-4599
Phone: (916) 358-2876
E-mail: troscoe@dfg.ca.gov

Rosenberg, Daniel K.
Department of Forest, Range, and Wildlife Sciences
Utah State University
5230 Old Main Hill
Logan, UT 84322-5230
Phone: (435) 797-8167
E-mail: dan.rosenberg@usu.edu

Ruckeles, Ann
Colorado Natural Heritage
850 37th Street
Boulder, CO 80303

Sallabanks, Rex
Idaho Department of Fish & Game
600 S. Walnut
Boise, ID 83707

Sample, David
Wisconsin DNR
1350 Femrite Drive
Monona, WI 53716

Saslaw, Larry, Wildlife Mgmt. Biologist
Bureau of Land Management
3801 Pegasus Drive
Bakersfield, CA 93308
Ph: (661) 391-6000
E-mail: Lawrence_Saslaw@ca.blm.gov

Schlafmann, Deb
U.S. Fish and Wildlife Service
2800 Cottage Way, Room W-2605
Sacramento, CA 95825
Ph: (916) 414-6600
E-mail: Debra_Schlafmann@fws.gov

Scobie, Dave, Principle
Avocet Environmental Inc.
P.O. Box 1644
Brooks, AB T1R 1C5
Canada
Ph: (403) 793-8500
E-mail: avocet@eidnet.org

Sebesta, Dawn
HawkWatch International
2466 Meadows Drive
Park City, UT 84060-7032
Ph: (435) 649-3024
E-mail: stoney@pcfastnet.com

Shackelford, Clifford, Nongame Ornithologist
Texas Parks and Wildlife Department
3000 IH 35 South, Suite 100
Austin, TX 78704
Ph: (512) 912-7045
E-mail: clifford.shackelford@tpwd.state.tx.us

Shackford, John
429 Oak Cliff Drive
Edmond, OK 73034-8262
Ph: (405) 340-5057
E-mail: johnsshack@aol.com

Sherrod, Steve
Sutton Avian Research Center
P.O. Box 2007
Bartlesville, OK 74005
Ph: (918) 336-7778
E-mail: gmsarc@aol.com

Shyry, Darcey
11524 44th Ave.
Edmonton, AB T6J 0Z5
Canada
Ph: (780) 435-2335
E-mail: darceyshyry@hotmail.com

Sidle, John, TES Coordinator
Great Plains National Grasslands
USDA–Forest Service
125 North Main Street
Chadron, NE 69337
Ph: (308) 432-0300
E-mail: jsidle@fs.fed.us

Silcock, Ross
P.O. Box 57
Tabor, IA 51653
E-mail:silcock@rosssilcock.com

Skeel, Margaret, Program Coordinator
Nature Saskatchewan
1860 Lorne St., Room 206
Regina, SK S4P 2L7
Canada
Ph: (306) 780-9273
E-mail: nature.sask@unibase.com

Skiba, Gary
Colorado Division of Wildlife
6060 Broadway
Denver, CO 80216
Ph: (303) 291-7466
E-mail: Gary.skiba@state.co.us

Skoruppa, Mary Kay, Biologist
USGS, Biological Resource Division
6300 Ocean Drive
TAMU-CC Box 339
Corpus Christi, TX 78412
Ph: (361) 985-6266
E-mail: Mary_Kay_Skoruppa@usgs.gov

Snake River Basin Office
1387 S. Vinnell Way, Room 368
Boise, ID 83709
Ph: (208) 378-5243

Steenhof, Karen, Res. Wildlife Biologist
USGS, Snake River Field Station
970 Lusk Street
Boise, ID 83706
Ph: (208) 426-5206 or (208) 331-5206
E-mail: ksteenho@eagle.boisestate.edu

Stepnisky, Dave
Renewable Resources, University of Alberta
18516-84 Avenue
Edmonton, AB T5T 1G5
Canada
E-mail: dstepnisky@excite.com

Svingen, Dan Grassland Biologist
U.S. Forest Service
240 W. Century Avenue
Bismarck, ND 58501
Ph: (701) 50 4463 ext. 107
E-mail: dsvingen@fs.fed.us

Thompson, Bruce
Coop. Fish & Wildlife Research Unit
New Mexico State University
P.O. Box 30003, Department 4901
Las Cruces, NM 88003
Ph: (505) 646-6093
E-mail: Bthompso@nmsu.edu

Trapp, John
US Fish and Wildlife Service
Office of Migratory Bird Management
4401 N. Fairfax Drive, Suite 634
Arlington, VA 22203
Ph: (703) 358-1821
E-mail: John_Trapp@fws.gov

Trefry, Helen
P.O. Box 176, Site 1, R.R. #2
Tofield, AB T0B 4J0
Canada
Ph: (780) 951-8693
E-mail: helen.trefry@ec.gc.ca

Turner, Annette
Hawk Mountain Sanctuary
1700 Hawk Mountain Road
Kempton, PA 19529

Uhmann, Tanys
Natural Resources Institute
University of Manitoba
70 Dysart Road
Winnipeg, MB 3T 2N2
Canada
Ph: (204) 269-2184
E-mail: umuhmann@cc.umanitoba.ca

Van de Hoek, Robert
Bureau of Land Management
4301 Rosedale Highway
Bakersfield, CA 93308

VerCauteren, Tammy
Rocky Mountain Bird Observatory
13401 Piccadilly Road
Brighton, CO 80601
Ph: (303) 659-4348
E-mail: Tammy.vercauteren@rmbo.org

Vermillion, Bill
Louisiana Natural Heritage Program
Department of Wildlife & Fisheries
P.O. Box 98000
Baton Rouge, LA 70898-9000
Ph: (225) 765-2976
E-mail: Vermillion_wg@wlf.state.la.us

Wallace, George
American Bird Conservancy
P.O. Box 249
4249 Loudoun Avenue
The Plains, VA 20198
Ph: (540) 253-5780
E-mail: gwallace@abcbirds.org

Waller, David, Wildlife Biologist
Bureau of Land Management
Glasgow Field Station, Route #1-4775
Glasgow, MT 59230-9796
Phone: (406) 228-3762
E-mail: david_waller@blm.gov.

Walton, Brian, Coordinator
Predatory Bird Research Group
Long Marine Lab, University of California
Santa Cruz, CA 95060
Ph: (831) 459-2466
E-mail: Walton@cats.ucsc.edu

Warnock, Robert, Research Scientist
Nature Saskatchewan
4107 McPhail Avenue
Regina, SK S4S 1G1
Canada
Ph: (306) 586-2492
E-mail: warnock@accesscomm.ca

Wedgwood, Jim
610 Leslie Avenue
Saskatoon, SK 57H 222
Canada

Weir, Colin
P.O. Box 1150
Coaldale, AB T1M 1M9
Canada
Ph: (403) 345-4262
E-mail: Cweir@telusplanet.net

Wellicome, Troy
Environment Canada
Canadian Wildlife Service
4999-98 Avenue, Room 200
Edmonton, AB T6B 2X3
Canada
Ph: (780) 951-8671
E-mail: Troy.wellicome@ec.gc.ca

Williams, Bob, State Supervisor
U.S. Fish and Wildlife Service
1340 Financial Boulevard, Suite 234
Reno, NV 89502-7147
Ph: (775) 861-6331
E-mail: Bob_D_Williams@r1.fws.gov

Williams, Sandy
New Mexico Game and Fish Department
Nongame Wildlife Program
Villagra Building, P.O. Box 25112
Santa Fe, NM 87504
Ph: (505) 827-7911
E-mail: SOWilliams@state.nm.us

Wise, Cathryn, Nongame Birds Biologist
Arizona Game and Fish Department
2221 W. Greenway Rd.
Phoenix, AZ 85023
Ph: (602) 789-3577
E-mail: cwise@gf.state.az.us

Wohl, Kent
Nongame Migratory Bird Coordinator
US Fish and Wildlife Service
1101 East Tudor Road
Anchorage, AL 99503
Ph: (907) 786-3503
E-mail: Kent_Wohl@fws.gov

Woodin, Marc, Wildlife Biologist
6300 Ocean Drive, TAMU-CC Box 339
Corpus Cristi, TX 78412
Ph: (361) 985-6266
E-mail: marc_woodin@usgs.gov

Yamamoto, Julie
California Environmental Protection Agency
OEHHA, 301 Capitol Mall, Room 205
Sacramento, CA 95814
Ph: (916) 323-9538
E-mail: Jyamamot@oehha.ca.gov

Zohrer, Jim
Iowa Dept. of Natural Resources
Wallace State Office Bldg.
Des Moines, IA 50319

Appendix D: Scientific and Common Names of Animals and Plants Mentioned in the Burrowing Owl Status Assessment and Conservation Plan

Table D-1: Scientific and common names of animals mentioned in the "Status Assessment and Conservation Plan for the Western Burrowing Owl in the United States".

Scientific Name	Common Name
Accipiter cooperii	Cooper's Hawk
Athene cunicularia floridana	Florida Burrowing Owl
Athene cunicularia hypugaea	Western Burrowing Owl
Bubo virginianus	Great-horned Owl
Buteo jaimaicensis	Red-tailed Hawk
Buteo regalis	Ferruginous Hawk
Buteo swainsoni	Swainson's Hawk
Canis familiaris	Domestic dog
Canis latrans	Coyote
Circus cyaneus	Northern Harrier
Corvus brachyrhynchos	American Crow
Cynomys ludovicianus	Black-tailed prairie dog
Cynomys gunnisoni	Gunnison's prairie dog
Cynomys leucurus	White-tailed prairie dog
Dasypus novemcinctus	Nine-banded armadillo
Dipodomys ordii	Ord kangaroo rat
Dipodomys spectabilis	Banner-tailed kangaroo rat
Dipodomys spp.	Kangaroo rat
Eremophila alpestris	Horned Lark
Falco columbarius	Merlin
Falco mexicanus	Prairie Falcon
Falco peregrinus	Peregrine Falcon
Falco sparverius	American Kestrel
Felis catus	Domestic cat
Gopherus agassizii	Desert tortoise
Gopherus polyphemus	Gopher tortoise
Haliaeetus leucocephalus	Bald Eagle
Lynx rufus	Bobcat
Marmota flaviventris	Yellow-bellied marmot
Marmota monax	Woodchuck
Mephitis spp.	Skunk
Microtus californicus	Meadow vole
Microtus montanus	Montane vole

Table D-1: Continued

Scientific Name	Common Name
Mustela nigripes	Black-footed ferret
Mustela spp.	Weasel
Peromyscus leucopus	White-footed mouse
Peromyscus maniculatus	Deer mouse
Reithrodontomys megalotis	Western harvest mouse
Solenopsis wagneri	Fire ant
Spermophilus columbianus	Columbian ground squirrel
Spermophilus douglasii	Douglas's ground squirrel
Spermophilus richardsonii	Richardson's ground squirrel
Spermophilus spilosoma	Spotted ground squirrel
Spermophilus tereticaudus	Round-tailed ground squirrel
Spermophilus tridecemlineatus	Thirteen-lined ground squirrel
Spermophilus variegatus	Rock squirrel
Taxidea taxus	Badger
Thomomys spp.	Pocket gophers
Tyto alba	Barn Owl
Vulpes spp., *Urocyon cineroargenteus*	Foxes

Table D-2: Scientific and common names of plants mentioned in the "Status Assessment and Conservation Plan for the Western Burrowing Owl in the United States".

Scientific Name	Common Name
Agropyron spicatum	Bluebunch wheatgrass
Artemisia tridentata	Big sagebrush
Atriplex polycarpa	Saltbush
Bouteloua gracilis	Blue grama
Bromus tectorum	Downy brome, Cheatgrass
Buchloe dactyloides	Buffalograss
Chrysothamnus nauseosus	Rabbit brush
Gutierrezia sarothrae	Snakeweed
Halogeton glomeratus	Halogeton
Larrea divaricata	Creosote bush
Oryzopsis contracta	Indian ricegrass
Pinus edulis	Pinyon pine
Pinus ponderosa	Ponderosa pine
Poa sandbergii	Sandberg bluegrass
Prosopis spp.	Mesquite
Purshia tridentata	Antelope bitterbrush
Sarcobatus vermiculatus	Greasewood
Salsola tragus	Russian thistle
Stipa comata	Needle and thread
Tamarix ramosissima	Tamarisk

U.S. Department of the Interior
U.S. Fish & Wildlife Service
Route 1, Box 166
Sheperdstown, WV 25443

http://www.fws.gov

June 2003